Nude
Nuns
and
Other
Peculiar
People

Charles A. Wells, Jr.

Dear Greg,

Hope you enjoy the
stories. All the best.

Chuck Wells

Nude Nuns and Other Peculiar People
A Collection of Stories from the Heartland
Charles A. Wells, Jr.

COVER PHOTOGRAPH: The auhor, age 3.

Designed by Frank M. Addington

ISBN: 978-1466427396

To Jude, Lucy, and Ben

I've never really thought of myself as an odd person, maybe off-center, but not odd. Those who know me superficially would probably think of me as a pretty normal guy, and I have had no reason to disturb this view. However, it has been my very good fortune to know, like, and associate with a goodly number of goofballs. I am particularly partial to peculiar people. In a perverse sense, I believe my semi-normalcy has contributed to my being a bit of a magnet to eccentrics. This has enabled me to witness, and be a party to, some of their more outrageous adventures. Of course, I can't discount the role of pure dumb luck in providing the opportunity to be a corroborator for some of the stories included herein.

In 1972 I was working as a rookie consultant for a giant firm. I was a tiny cog in a big wheel trying to adapt to the corporate world. At least I wasn't a roofer in Tucson in August, but I wasn't having fun. Then I dreamed up what seemed at the time to be a great idea. I would make my living by enticing a few hundred people to pay me a yearly stipend, and I would go out and have fun. I would send letters and postcards to apprise my sponsors of my adventures. At that stage of life I wasn't particularly good at anything, with one exception: I did fun well. In spite of my best efforts at promoting the benefits of this relationship, this loony proposition did not yield the desired results. In fact, I didn't sign up a single vicarious fun-seeker.

Now, fast-forward 39 years. I have somehow muddled my way through life in a semi-serious fashion, and I have assembled a few vignettes of an ordinary man whose life occasionally intersected with some not-so-ordinary people and events. Most of these stories are distinctly frivolous, but a few are not.

These stories are true to the best of my recollection, although I've changed the names and locations in several instances to protect the

identity of those behaving badly or oddly. When using a pseudonym for a person or place I've followed the convention of marking the name with an asterisk the first time it is used.

On a few occasions I've taken the liberty of poetic license. The nude nun in the Nude Nuns story is really an ex-nun, and only one of the nuns was nude. Hopefully, the reader can appreciate the alliterative awkwardness attendant to precision. I briefly contemplated that Nude Nuns would be a great name for a rock band, but lacking any musical gifts, I never had occasion to put it to use.

My apologies are extended in advance to anyone portrayed herein who is offended or to anyone who feels they should have been included and is offended.

For reference purposes the characters most often mentioned herein are my wife Judy, daughter Lucy, son Ben, brother Bill, and sister Sally.

CONTENTS

PART I **PECULIAR ENCOUNTERS**

CHAPTER 1   Basic Training 13

CHAPTER 2   Mardi Gras 23

CHAPTER 3   Harvard 41

CHAPTER 4   Coast to Coast 59

CHAPTER 5   Drury 71

CHAPTER 6   Pheasant Hunting 95

CHAPTER 7   Prairie Village 103

CHAPTER 8   Iron Men 119

CHAPTER 9   Bowling Green 139

CHAPTER 10   Baseball 151

PART II **ON DUTY**

CHAPTER 11   Riverton Bill 167

CHAPTER 12   Cochise County 175

CHAPTER 13   Albany John 187

CHAPTER 14   Three Funerals 193

PART III **OFF DUTY**

CHAPTER 15   Colorado 14ers 199

CHAPTER 16   China 207

CHAPTER 17   Mt. Huron 225

CHAPTER 18   Lucy's Wedding 231

CHAPTER 19   Fort Waverly 239

CHAPTER 20   Banjo Camp 245

CHAPTER 21   Nude Nuns 249

Epilogue 254

PART I

PECULIAR ENCOUNTERS

CHAPTER 1

Basic Training
1970

The Viet Nam war was still going strong in the winter of 1970. Training centers throughout the United States continued to process new, raw meat for the war. One such camp was Fort Polk located in southwest Louisiana near the bustling towns of DeRidder and Leesville.

It mattered not whether one was a gung ho warrior or weenie reservist, when appearing in public in uniform during Viet Nam era one expected frequent and vigorous displays of contempt, particularly from the Woodstock types, usually female. During the course of my military career, I was spat upon in public on two separate occasions while in uniform, an injustice that rankles me to this day. The garrison cap, more commonly known as the unmentionable "C word" hat, worn during that era was a particular magnet for derision.

The basic deal for enlisted reserves (ERs) was six months active duty and six years of weekends including an annual two-week summer camp. Of all the people I encountered during active duty, few had less skin in the game than I. Months earlier I enlisted as a reservist in the dental detachment of the 325th general hospital brigade. Our unit motto was to later become "All we are saying is give teeth a chance," with apologies to John Lennon. As a fighting dental assistant my potential exposure to real danger was significantly less than most everyone else in the Army, and I was not displeased. I presume military planners prefer their warriors to be alpha males. I was barely an omicron on my best days, but these were the days of the draft, and they weren't too picky.

I arrived at Ft. Polk in January 1970 to start basic training. I was 24 years old, married, and a recent graduate of an Ivy League school with an advanced degree. Each of these attributes set me apart from my fellow trainees. A wise man at the time told me, "If you have an Ivy League education and/or a second home, keep it to yourself." I didn't have a first home, but I took his advice to heart. My gangly stature provided an even more visible distinction. I was 6'2" and weighed 131 lbs. While assessing my options as a prospective draftee, I learned that had I weighed 123 lbs, I would have been ineligible for military service. This would, however, have required the amputation of a major limb.

As I contemplated my new circumstances, I figured, "Hey, basic training is only eight weeks, I'm in good shape, I'll resist the urge to spew my normal flow of witless blather, do what they say, and this will work out." I arrived by air, flying over the pine-covered forests of Louisiana in a WWII generation DC-3, along with a planeload of fellow citizen soldiers. We entered the reception center for two days of orientation. They shaved our hair to the scalp, ran us through a gauntlet of poorly trained medics armed with pneumatic powered vaccinators, made us wait in innumerable lines, handed us our gear, and administered various tests. I was feeling good after being congratulated by an officer for having scored well on a language aptitude test until he suggested, "The U.S. Army is willing to invest in sending you to language school in Monterey, CA to become a Vietnamese translator. Just forsake your enlisted reserve status and sign up for the regular army for three years." I declined. Truly, this was Robert Frost's notion of the road not taken. We were then assigned to basic training companies and platoons.

Basic training units were organized into brigades comprised of five companies, each with five 80-man platoons. Each platoon was housed in a wooden, two-story WWII era barracks crammed full of bunk beds and footlockers. We were loosely assembled in our first formation, and trainee platoon leaders were selected. The drill sergeant searched among those gathered, located the biggest, meanest looking black guy and commanded, "You're the platoon leader until you f___ up." Then our personal effects were confiscated, and the training began.

Like most recent college graduates, I was familiar with Abraham Maslow's 1943 treatise *Theory of Human Motivation* categorizing the hierarchy of human needs ranging from physical, safety, social, to esteem. More simply stated, "breathing trumps self actualization." Basic training brought this theory home with the subtlety of a two by four to the head. In the weeks to come, I thought of Abe often when tired, cold, and hungry. Youthful rebelliousness is readily tamed in this environment.

A typical basic training day consisted of arising at 4 am, taking care of personal needs, and assembling outdoors. Once in formation, we would freeze and wait. It was bone chillingly cold in Louisiana that January. Then we started physical training (PT) featuring pushups, sit-ups, jumping jacks, and a two-mile jog in formation. Around 6 am we ate our chow, then it was back for more PT. We were introduced to weapons, marching, the obstacle course, military organization, and the importance of obeying orders. We went to the rifle and grenade ranges for live fire exercises, to the swamps for orienteering, and the parade grounds where the dominant activity was standing and waiting.

For some mysterious reason the designers of basic training decided we should be exposed to tear gas. I don't know if they thought we might develop a level of immunity by breathing the noxious fumes, or if they just wanted to see body fluids gushing out of our orifices. We were given gas masks, instructed how to put them on, and escorted into a small building the size of a garden shed. They tossed a tear gas grenade in, required us to remove our masks, sit a few minutes, and emerge suitably impressed with the unpleasantness of the experience. Up to this point, I could see a hint of logic in our training.

Sleep was limited and often interrupted with assignments for duty consisting of walking around some part of the fort until relieved, or staying awake in the barracks as a fireguard. Every other week I was assigned to kitchen patrol (KP) duty which required getting up even earlier to work as a dining room orderly (DRO) or cleaning pots and pans.

The threat of being recycled, restarting at day one of basic training, served as the primary sanction to insure compliance. Lesser penalties included extra duty and pushups. "Drop and give me 50 you puke!" All in all, these tools were highly effective. However, one black kid from Alabama had already been recycled once and had no intention of ever completing basic training. He put on a shuck and jive routine so extreme it would have made the 1930's movie character, Stepin Fetchit, look like a Prussian grenadier. Whatever the order he'd do the opposite. He was mildly amusing because he infuriated the brass, but he disappeared after a few weeks.

The physical training was hard on overweight trainees, particularly the long distance runs and the overhead bars. My least favorite event was the low crawl requiring one to crawl under strands of barbed wire for 50 yards. Intermittent bursts of machine gun fire with tracers provided even further inducement to stay low. The physical part was tolerable, and I could feel myself getting stronger.

We were fortunate to have one of the least flagitious drill sergeants in the brigade. A smallish black man, probably in his mid 30s, he was all business and found no pleasure in making things harder than necessary. He was also a highly creative curser, even by military standards. He would insert the f_ bomb in any combination of words or syllables: out f'ing standing, un f'ing believable, in f'ing credible, fat f'ing puke, any f'ing time. I looked forward to hearing a new one each day.

Our platoon was made up primarily of young men from the mid south. Platoon placement was apparently made on geography. Since my home address at the time was Missouri, I was assigned to a platoon populated mostly by lads from Tennessee, Alabama, Georgia, and Mississippi. I was the oldest trainee in the unit, as most were 18 or 19. We were further segmented by our military status: Regular Army (RA) who were mostly draftees, Enlisted Reserves (ER) of which I was one, and National Guard (NG). ER's and NG's were universally despised by the lifers, as we were correctly perceived as poltroons seeking to avoid combat. Five or six of the 80 were college graduates. My social network was limited to two fellows, one from Chicago and another from Boston. How they became part of our "Sons of the Confederacy" platoon, I'll never know.

Noah* was our platoon leader, and in real life he was a running back for the Miami Dolphins undertaking his active duty in the NFL's offseason. He was a bespectacled African American, a graduate of Boston

College, and a good guy. We developed a kinship with our Boston roots. At 6' 3" and 215 lbs, Noah had a body like an anatomical chart. After 3-4 weeks of training we were out in the Louisiana pine forests setting up tents. One of the junior drill sergeants, a chubby white guy, wasn't happy with our progress and yelled at Noah, "Boy! What the f___ do you think you're doing?" Noah charged and grabbed him by the front of his shirt, slammed him up against a tree, and held him dangling with his feet kicking in the air. Two drill sergeants intervened, both black. Noah dropped the guy to the ground and was steaming. On that afternoon he lost his platoon leader stripes but made one thing clear, "Don't f___ with Noah."

One day we piled into cattle trucks to drive to the firing range. We carried full field packs and rifles and wore helmets like ones seen in a WWII movie. They rest on fiberglass liners with webbing designed to fit one's head. Unfortunately, they are heavy, about 5 lbs. No doubt someone got the idea for the bobble head doll by observing a steel pot on my spindly neck. In any event, it was my misfortune to be seated next to a big, redheaded kid from the hills of east Tennessee.

"Red" was one of about ten young men in our platoon who hailed from the hollows of eastern Tennessee. It occurred to me that I had more in common with the average Viet Cong sapper than with these guys. The movie *Deliverance* was still two years in the future, but when I later saw the country folks portrayed therein I thought to myself, "Jesus H. Christ! I served in the army with those people!" I developed a strong distaste for the recently written Tennessee state anthem "Rocky Top," as the hill boys were wont to break into that chant with little provocation. The redheaded kid was the leader of their hillbilly tribe, and, in that truck, I was as close to him as is possible without engaging in intercourse.

Ordinarily a truck ride was a luxury. It meant we weren't running, hiking, or standing. You could set your steel pot in your lap and rest. Sadly, this temporarily, luxuriant state was interrupted as I observed the big redhead spitting chewing tobacco into the steel pot on his lap. I thought, "What the heck is he going to do with this gross reservoir of spittle?" Soon my question was answered. When disembarking from the truck, he placed the half full steel pot back on his helmet liner unleashing a curtain of spit on his shoulders. It was week five of basic training, and thus far I had kept to my vow to basically, "Shut the f___ up." But this scene overwhelmed me, and I was emboldened to say, "That is possibly the most disgusting thing I have ever seen in my entire life."

Whereupon he attacked me! And we started to wrestle. This presented three distinct problems. Red was 6'3" and 250 lbs and could have easily disemboweled me with his bare hands, he was covered with a repulsive mixture of spit and tobacco, and we were armed with M-16 semi-automatic assault rifles and bayonets. Miraculously, other soldiers pulled us apart before harm could be done to me. He glared at me, and I scowled back as best as I could, given my timid persona.

A week later I was assigned to the 3 am shift to guard the Ft. Polk airport. This unwanted duty consisted of walking the perimeter, carrying a baseball bat and an M-16 rifle without bullets, and searching for any Viet Cong miscreants trying to infiltrate this strategically located hub of military activity. Unfortunately, Red was assigned to the same shift and duty. He walked the perimeter clockwise, and I walked counter clockwise. We passed each other twice during our shift, glowered at one another, and I survived. From that point forward I stayed as far away from the Tennessee clique as possible.

Towards the end of basic training, the powers that be allowed a traveling carnival to set up shop on the base the weekend after payday. It was a pretty cheesy troupe that consisted primarily of games of chance and un-amusing rides. I avoided it but was saddened to hear the tale of woe from one of the Tennessee boys who slept in the bunk above mine. He lost his entire monthly paycheck of $124 in an attempt to win a prize worth $1. He was a total naïf and was perfect bait for the carnival's grifters. I could never understand, nor forgive, the Army leaders who allowed this travesty to occur. It was one thing to be transformed from a civilian into something remotely resembling a warrior, but quite another to be robbed blind whilst in the process.

I had mixed feelings about character guidance sessions. On one hand, this part of basic training involved sitting in a warm auditorium with no hard physical labor. On the other hand, it involved listening to an officer, usually a chaplain, explain the Godliness of obeying orders. One freezing, drizzling day the company was sitting in an auditorium for another round of these lectures. This session was devoted once again to the standard topic. For some reason this particular version set my hair on fire. I raised my hand, amazingly was called on to speak to the assembled trainees and trainers, and said something to the effect, "In light of the recent My Lai incident it greatly offends my sense of order for you to suggest that there are no circumstances under which a reasonable person might not question orders."

Instead of politely noting that the U.S. Army field manual cares naught for the sensibilities of a lowly trainee, a large drill sergeant grabbed me by the collar, dragged me to the front of the auditorium, read my name tag, and declared, "Because of trainee Wells here, I want you to know that we are going to leave this warm auditorium, put on our field gear, go out into the sleet, and double time to the rifle range and back."

This is where Noah comes in. Amazingly, I wasn't harmed, though I probably deserved a major ass kicking for disturbing my comrades' serenity. I was later told Noah put out the word, "Anyone who harms him, deals with me." I haven't seen Noah since basic training, but I will be forever indebted to him for this kind act.

I was able to make a minor down payment on this debt to Noah. The last week of basic involved a final PT test. The events included the overhead bars, low crawl, one-mile run, and 150-yard man carry. The last was a timed event where one man carries another over his shoulder in a fireman like fashion. The reward for doing well on the PT test was a weekend pass. Thus my spare frame made me an attractive partner for Noah, although he could just as easily have carried a dump truck. The bad part was I had to stumble through the course with a rock of a man on my back, a small price to pay for my life.

Other than sitting next to spit boy, the events that left the deepest impression were sessions with soldiers recently returned from combat in Viet Nam. These occurred in Tiger-Land, a portion of Ft. Polk designed to replicate Vietnamese villages. The combat veterans addressed the assembled trainees with barely concealed contempt and said, "Listen up, you festering pieces of shit, I'm going to tell you the shit you need to know to keep your sorry asses from coming home in a body bag." This compelling salutation caught my attention. Even though my probability of seeing combat was slight, I did in fact listen up and took to heart the valuable information being conveyed. I was amazed to observe how many of those heading to Nam didn't.

The highlight of every day was mail call. The platoon would be assembled and then a shit knuckle of a junior drill sergeant distributed the mail, usually accompanied by witless commentary such as, "Must be another Dear John letter." Despite this annoyance, nothing lifted my spirits like a letter. I was fortunate to have many correspondents, in part because I wrote letters feverishly in the hope of receiving same. The most memorable were from Rex, a fraternity brother, who was an active grunt in Viet Nam at the time. His letters described being in firefights in the pitch dark firing weapons blindly, contracting malaria, experiencing the abject terror of being on point while on patrol, seeing comrades get wasted, and developing an abiding hatred for his LT who kept assigning him the most dangerous duties. His letters reminded me that my discomforts were rather insignificant.

In week seven the platoon was assembled and the head drill sergeant announced the military occupation specialty (MOS) assigned to each trainee. Since I was an ER, I had little suspense as a 68 E (spoken 68 Echo). By now we knew that the MOS's to fear were the combat specialties: 11B and 11C (11 Bravo and Charlie), infantryman and indirect fire infantry (mortars and radio). Hearts sank when a trainee's name was matched to 11B or 11C, a front row seat in Nam.

I was assigned to KP duty for Easter Sunday, awakened at 3 am, trundled into the kitchen, and awaited my assignment. The company's baker had already arrived and had assembled what I believe were intended to be hot cross buns. Interestingly, the guy was on an LSD trip, and his buns were an indication of his impairment. The mess sergeant arrived, surveyed the situation, called the MP's, and they hauled the offender off.

At graduation, we pooled a few meager dollars from members of the platoon and bought a small radio for our drill sergeant. A man of few words, he said, "Thank you very God damn much." And that was that.

Postscript

Basic training is serious business, particularly in wartime, as young men are taught skills that can truly mean the difference between life and death. The light heartedness of this narrative is not intended to be disrespectful to the real warriors who safeguard our nation.

CHAPTER 2

Mardi Gras

For years a close friend shared tales of merriment at Mardi Gras in NOLA. We were classmates in high school and renewed the friendship in our late 40's. We later added golf and oenophilia to our list of shared passions, and he introduced me to his New Orleans' world where he maintains an apartment in the French Quarter for business purposes.

My earlier visits to the Crescent City had not been pleasing. While in college over spring break, I found myself in a seedy riverfront bar playing a bongo drum chained to the floor when a disturbance resulted in the stabbing death of the man standing next to me. Later, in my semi-adult years, I was working with an attorney in NOLA on a prospective merger when he suggested a blatantly illegal act. I informed him of such, and he waved it off by drawling in his best Foghorn Leghorn voice, "Son, you don't understand. This is New Awlins!"

On several occasions I foolishly rebuffed my friend's gracious invitations to share the Mardi Gras experience, but eventually I wised up.

2005

The apartment is on the second floor of a three-story, 18th century brick building at the intersection of Royal and St. Peter streets, smack dab in the middle of the French Quarter. The dominant feature of the large one-room domicile is an exterior wall comprised of three, floor-to-ceiling, 12 over 12, double-hung, sash windows facing Royal. The middle one opens to a height of six feet and serves as the entryway to a spacious balcony and as an occasional head banger.

The guest list included an engineer from NYC, a dentist from KC, and a long-time, but mysterious, friend. The latter was also a classmate from graduate school, a successful entrepreneur, and we've always thought him to have once been a CIA assassin. He's a bit mum on the subject, but whatever the truth of the matter, we were confident his frightful aura would discourage ruffians from trifling with our antediluvian assemblage.

In preparation for the weekend, our host purchased $1,000 worth of beads. I didn't know such adornments existed, nor could I imagine how we would dispose of this massive assortment of trinkets. We were instructed to bring earplugs for sleeping purposes, as the street noises are pretty extreme, particularly after midnight. The narrow streets of the FQ are lined with three story buildings providing canyon-wall-acoustics for the motorcyclists who find it pleasing to rev their engines late at night. Street musicians start off fairly early in the morning adding to the constant cacophony.

From our balcony, one could easily imagine being in a European setting, until glancing down at the mass of uniquely American humanity. Within a block's distance in either direction, one could see four street statue performers, the most notable being a guy who balances on an ersatz ladder wearing construction garb with a board resting on his shoulder. People seemed to enjoy his act, as they were continually dropping $1 bills in his bucket. Two magicians performed nearby, along with a bluegrass band, and a talented harmonica player. Evangelists were out in large numbers, which only makes sense, given the target-rich population of sinners. A monophonic buzz provided an auditory backdrop as a group of heavily pierced, homely young women paraded wearing tee shirts advocating revolution.

Shortly after my arrival I pondered, "How are we going to pass four days crammed in this little apartment full of beads?" The question was quickly answered. We had vast quantities of beads that were simple and cheap and used as bait. We showered people with the chum while wearing the more ostentatious beads. Occasionally, someone would express an interest in the special beads, and the horse-trading began. Basically it boils down thusly, "Show us your tits, and we will give you a necklace of beads not readily available elsewhere." My host had talked about this for all the years I had known him, but it seemed a bit exaggerated. After all, what reasonable woman is going to bare her breasts on a public street, in broad daylight, for a few crummy beads?

We were the beneficiaries of 100+ flashers in the first two hours and were assured that this was not too bad for starters. Those kind enough to share a viewing of their breasts included women that were attractive, not so attractive, old, young, fat, thin, well endowed, not so well endowed, white, black, Asian, well dressed, poorly dressed, accompanied by men, accompanied by women, unaccompanied, those wearing tons of beads, and those wearing no beads.

The standard exchange goes like this: "Hey Darlin', would you like some beads?" Then chum is thrown. Upon garnering a favorable reaction we'd follow with, "Would you like our special beads?" We'd display the higher quality beads hanging from our necks and attempt to close the deal, "Which would you prefer?" The woman would either flash or not, but, without exception, it would be handled in good humor.

For those few to whom the trade had to be explained, their response would often be, "You're kidding?"

"This is Mardi Gras darling, a little tit for tat, so to speak," we'd explain. Some would ask us to give them the beads first, to which the response would be, "No, that would be tat for tit." Being gentlemen, we were generous with praise.

Surprisingly, those most likely to respond favorably were those accompanied by a husband or boyfriend. The male companion would often become our ally, presumably a gender affinity thing. Only good things were going to happen when a prospect handed her drink to a companion, thus freeing her hands, and approached our balcony. A number of the flashers were such good sports that they showed us their butts as well as their breasts. Those so inclined were rightfully proud of their assets. Occasionally, a pretty lady would show her breasts, and our exclamations of appreciation were such that those who missed the viewing would scurry out to the balcony to request an encore. Our new, anonymous friend would often coquettishly comply.

Several encounters were notable. An elegant couple strolled in our direction on the sidewalk on the opposite side of the street. The woman was uncommonly attractive and expensively attired. She was in power-walking mode, and her body language conveyed, "Don't even think about it." I threw chum in her general direction, which she let fall to the ground with nary a glance. Then to my surprise, while in full stride, she turned in our direction, opened her leather jacket and pulled her tube-top down to give us a full flash of her ample, left breast. She grinned as she walked on.

We engaged a fairly chubby, young woman in conversation. We got past the preliminaries, and she picked out the beads she desired. When it came to the tit for tat thing she said, "I'm a good Christian woman. I couldn't possibly do that." Just at that moment, three guys came walking in front of her, dragging three giant crosses. I suggested that might be a sign from God. She agreed and said, "What the heck" and lifted her shirt.

There are several basic styles of flashing including the lift up, pull down, spread from the middle cleavage, and, my favorite for those with sleeveless garments, the pull in. All were graciously considerate by swinging any beads they might be wearing around to their back, so as not to obstruct our view. It is instructive to observe how thin is the veneer of civilized behavior.

Our dining venues included NOLA's, Arnaud's, Carmella's, and Mr. B's, all excellent establishments and within walking distance from our apartment. Our host frequently entertains clients in NOLA and has mastered the art of concentrated patronage. In return, he and his guests receive exemplary service. While strolling in the evening each of us would wear several sets of premier beads. It was wonderfully commonplace for a woman to notice our beads, request them, and then provide a private viewing in exchange. Our most beauteous encounters occurred in this manner.

A body-painting kiosk operates just around the corner from our apartment enabling meaningful numbers of young women to have their torsos painted and walk about topless to share this artistic effort. One has to admire their willingness to share, if not their judgment.

There is an unseemly part of Mardi Gras fairly well hidden from the revelers. The headline in Saturday morning's paper noted eight murders the preceding day. We didn't personally witness any rowdiness, although the police were out in large numbers. The amount of garbage that is piled up, and strewn about, is not particularly appetizing, but trash trucks and their crews gamely try to keep up with the continually accumulating litter.

After dinner we would stroll to Daphne's* for additional refreshments. Without a guide, one would never find it, as one walks into a nondescript hotel lobby, through a courtyard featuring elaborate gardens and a pool, and then into the bar. It is handsomely decorated, frequented by locals, relatively quiet, and run by the eponymous, but crotchety, Daphne. After being introduced, I told her she had one of the nicest bars I'd patronized. She replied in her clipped New Awlin's accent, "Darlin', you must not get out much."

We strolled down St. Peter to the edge of Bourbon to see the river of humanity. We came upon a group of women interested in our beads. We gave a strand to an attractive young lady, who then gave us a nice torso viewing. This led to an exchange with each of her traveling companions. They were teachers from a small town in Wisconsin. One flasher encouraged her younger sister to show us her tits, and she did. We attracted a crowd and were quickly out of beads.

2006

No friend of New Orleans will forget the morning of August 29, 2005 when Hurricane Katrina devastated the city with winds reaching 175 mph and tidal surges peaking over 16'. The storm left over 1,800 citizens dead in its wake causing the most expensive natural disaster in American history with over $81 billion in damages. By August 31 over 80% of New Orleans was under water, parts to a depth of 15'. Amazingly, the French Quarter was spared from the most horrific consequences of the storm. Eighteenth century Louisianans knew enough to place their dwellings on the highest ground available.

My friend's apartment suffered only minor wind damage, but the surrounding chaos and lack of basic services made the Quarter uninhabitable for months. A few hearty souls attempted to make the best of a very bad situation and somberly celebrated Mardi Gras 2006, but we were not among them.

On Mardi Gras afternoon, the streetscape was covered with people as far as the eye could see. The fun-lovers were dressed in an assortment of goofy, creative, outlandish, expensive, titillating, and/or grotesque costumes. Partying is intense on Lundi Gras (Monday) and the preceding weekend, but nothing compares to the main event.

Life on our balcony replicates the experience of riding on a perpetual parade float with the added advantage of having your own bar and bathroom. Pete Fountain's "half-fast" marching band came by around noon. The musicians ride in a trolley and are accompanied by an assortment of gaudily dressed men throwing beads to the crowd. An abundance of lesser talented and less well-organized bands are also plentiful. As one might expect, all play "When the Saints Go Marching In." Even the bagpipers play their rendition along with the standard, "Scotland the Brave."

Many celebrants form their own unofficial Krewes. My favorite was a group of sleazy looking fellows calling themselves the "Krewe of the Fathers of Anna Nicole's Baby." Another crowd pleaser was an assembly of people dressed as potted plants and crawfish. These were not your basic crawfish outfits but were giant plastic replicas of reddish claws each housing an inebriated human. Couples dressed like Napoleon and Josephine, those mocking politicians and priests, fan dancers, fanciful birds, panthers, superheroes, and inflatable people were in evidence. A disproportionate percentage of the outfits involve colorful feathers. The costumes range in quality from those created by Hollywood professionals to those constructed by unsupervised Brownies. Thousands of fun-seekers comprise the show, but, even so, it is rare to see an outfit duplicated. Some were in such bad taste I wouldn't begin to describe them.

The revelers we most enjoy are the semi-naked women. The best of this year's offerings was a young couple with the man dressed exactly like the 1950's Sunday school depiction of Jesus. The woman's body and hair were painted a sparkly gold. She wore a diaphanous cape, barely covering her shoulders, and clearly revealing her toplessness and remarkable pulchritude. I believe she was dressed as a nude Mary

Magdalene, although it's arguably a misnomer to use that particular participle.

The couple carried a sign saying, "You Jesus freaks are hypocrits (sic), as you too enjoy tits." Presumably the commentary was in response to the numerous groups of evangelists carrying crosses and shouting into microphones condemning sinners and alerting them to their impending trip to hell. Actually they don't really drag crosses but instead shoulder them with a roller skate wheel at the base.

It was fairly warm, facilitating high levels of nudity. One attractive couple wore only thongs. Their bodies were painted with a light blue base with an intricate bird-like theme. I saw them several times during the day, and they were always in the company of a large, appreciative following. Another eye-catching costume featured a heavy, young, unattractive, very black lady. She wore outlandishly loud, orange leather pants and hat and was topless with her ample breasts painted a matching orange. She looked like a day-glo lit lighthouse.

Our own efforts at trading beads for exposure went exceedingly well. Rarely would anyone be offended by the proffered exchange. Some would plead for uncompensated beads, but we'd point out that we are professionals and must maintain certain standards. It is very much like fishing but much more fun and doesn't require cleaning.

Some prospects were almost too easy. They are readily identified by the 50 lbs of beads hanging from their necks. Trading beads with these ladies was like hunting in a baited field. The greatest challenges occur with the well-dressed, attractive young ladies walking with few beads on display. While the probability of a successful encounter drops significantly, the rewards are immeasurably greater.

On Monday morning we were guests of a new friend who invited us for coffee at his elegant FQ home. We entered the nondescript passageway through a large wooden garage door leading into a hidden courtyard featuring manicured gardens, pool, and guesthouse. The main house was a well-appointed, three-story, Georgian style mansion with an intricate, winding staircase and 12 ft ceilings. Our host was an ex-Delta Force sniper and an interesting fellow. From the street the casual observer would think there is no green space in the FQ, but treasures lie behind the gates.

Our host is active in one of the local Krewes, and this year his apartment served as a gathering place for fellow members and for wine storage. Somehow, this connection led to our introduction to Pat*, who kept her luggage in our apartment and was in and out during the weeklong festivities. Pat is 6'1", slender, blond, attractive, and shapely with giant breasts and no apparent Adam's apple. She strode over with alacrity and gave me a hug. At first, and from a short distance, she was alluring. It's not that I have the most highly developed transsexual radar, but something was not quite right. It might have been the Wilford Brimley voice and the baritone greeting, "Chuck! Enchanted to meet you!"

Our tit for tat efforts were mightily undermined when Pat appeared on the balcony in her revealing, red-feathered, stripper outfit as large numbers of young men appeared seeking her favors. It was mildly annoying as she generously dispensed our inventory of beads to her admirers. Once again we never lacked for visual, auditory, gustatory, or olfactory stimulation. One has to admire the spirit of the New Orleanians in the aftermath of Katrina.

2008

Imagine a child's wagon outfitted with a brown, irregular platform shaped and painted to resemble an ashtray, then fill it with two small children costumed to look like cigarette/cigar butts, top it off with two proud parents pulling the ensemble, and you'll grasp a sampling of the tastefulness accompanying Mardi Gras 2008.

Our second story apartment at the corner of Royal and St. Peter continues to be a superb place from which to view a Mardi Gras weekend. Anything worth seeing walks, strolls, or rides past our perch. The weather was perfect with temps in the high 70's every day, greatly enhancing the public displays of nudity.

Fortunately, our host dodged the advances of our transgender acquaintance, Pat, who glommed onto us last year. She/he tried hard to inveigle an invitation, but her/his efforts were effectively thwarted. She made a brief appearance before leaving for more welcoming environs.

This year she/he was dressed in a lady Dracula outfit displaying her ample breasts accented with vampire teeth. The gown was full length, dark purple, with a pronounced collar, and a plunging neckline. Before she/he was an amusing accessory, less so this year.

We started the day with a stroll to Café DuMond for beignets and coffee. The streets were as clean as I've ever seen them. Small, trash sucking Zamboni's, roamed throughout the Quarter. It appears an abundance of post-Katrina money was spent on trash hauling devices.

By mid-morning we were on the balcony observing the street performers setting up, chatting with people on neighboring balconies, and loosening our bead throwing arms. The evangelists blast their message of eternal damnation for sinners. They assemble in groups, some dragging/rolling their crosses, some carrying placards condemning sin and handing out written materials. The signs promise eternal damnation for those listed including abortionists, drunkards, fornicators, masturbators, Muslims, Mormons, Masons, the rich, the poor, P.K.s (preacher's kids?), et al, a group more commonly known as "Everyone".

The most odious among this breed are those with a microphone in hand. One was shouting non-stop through his microphone for all to hear within a two-block radius. Then a heckler appeared, also equipped with a microphone. While the one condemned sin and sinners, the other shouted, "Blah, blah, blah, blah" continuously. It reminded me of a cable news show. The stalemate was broken when the heckler retorted, "God loves me more because He gave me a bigger bullhorn."

The official start of Mardi Gras activities on Royal Street is heralded by the appearance of the Pete Fountain's Half Fast Marching Band. I later learned that this group was originally called Pete Fountain's Half Assed Marching Band, but the city fathers thought this was a little too risqué. One can only marvel at the irony of such an edict in a city where people costumed as genitalia are the norm. Pete rides at the head of a trolley car carrying an accomplished Dixieland band. Several hundred celebrants wearing loose fitting, wide lapelled, colorful suits and Fedoras accompany the trolley, tossing beads to the crowd, and strutting to the Dixieland tunes.

I enjoy the semi-organized groups accompanied by musicians. The marchers sashay pretty much in tune with their music distinguishing their members from other passersby. The musical offerings range from complete Dixieland bands to a guy with drumsticks banging on a plastic pickle barrel. One group was accompanied and inspired by a solo tuba player. My favorite musician is a pretty young lady who plays the washboard beneath our balcony late in the afternoon. This year's blue ribbon for band costuming goes to the Ducks of Dixieland.

I took a brief walk over to Bourbon St, but it was so crowded navigation was difficult, and I returned to the serenity of our balcony. The difference between Bourbon and Royal Streets is pronounced. One block takes you from Mogadishu to Montreal. Royal is more civilized, crowded but not anarchic.

It's amazing how many people bring children to the festivities. One Mom quickly tried to cover the eyes of a little boy when he came face to face to the nose cones of a woman dressed like Madonna. Of all the sights one might encounter in the French Quarter, this was fairly tame, begging the question why this merited the eye shield.

One can't help but notice that there are a lot of men who enjoy dressing as women. One large, hirsute man was wearing a strapless "Gone With the Wind" hoopskirt, and he was meticulous in his efforts to keep the gown situated slightly off his shoulders. Sadly, many of the cross dressers favor costumes acquired at Victoria's Secrets, exceeding even my low standards. One man was dressed as a Morel mushroom, or a glob of vomit, I'm not sure which.

I enjoyed the irreverent musings of an overweight guy in biblical costume carrying a sign saying, "Jesus is Lard," and a young babette with a signboard proclaiming, "The End is Near, Sin Now." An interesting assortment of bicycles was on display including one that looked like a high-heeled shoe and one converted into a spacecraft using aluminum foil.

By 4 pm the stream of humanity thins out and automobiles are allowed back onto Royal. Then when a car passes, the crowds on the balconies pelt the intruding machine with their chum. With few exceptions, this is tolerated, but not always. Late in the afternoon a fairly new Toyota was cruising down the street and received the normal smattering of beads on its roof. A highly agitated, large, young woman stopped the car and got out accompanied by two of her companions. She shouted at the crowd to cease their pummeling, threatened to "kick some ass" and got back in the car. In response, the balcony perched throngs unleashed an avalanche of beads in her direction. She got out again, screamed her threats but, frustratingly, realized how difficult it is to "kick the ass" of those on distant balconies protected by hidden and locked doors. This continued for several more stops providing much merriment to the onlookers, save those of us who thought the ghastly woman might ultimately exercise her constitutional right to bare her arms.

On Mardi Gras evening, we enjoyed dinner at the Rib Room. Shortly after being seated, we noticed Pat accompanied by a man in his early 40's. We cattily wondered how she/he induced this young man to buy her dinner in such a nice restaurant, and how his transgender radar must have been out of order. An hour later we noticed that they stormed out in a huff. The maitre d', a friend of our host, later told us that Pat and her guest left complaining that people were cursing at a neighboring table, offending their sensibilities, and necessitating their untimely departure. More likely, the young man had the disturbing awakening that there may have been too many men on the task he had in mind.

Most of the Mardi Gras veterans noted that this year's event matched or surpassed pre-Katrina times. The tit for tat exchange, the raison d'etre so to speak, went swimmingly. If anything, this year offered optimal conditions for the desired outcome. The mood of the crowd was festive, and the warm temperatures provided an auspicious setting.

On the ride back to the airport, the Middle Eastern cab driver reported that this was a good Mardi Gras for him financially. The weekend started and ended on a good note.

2009

If they no longer held Mardi Gras, thousands of Chinese would be out of work, and Louisiana landfills would go unfilled. While we have our little routine of generously disbursing chum beads as bait for their more extravagant cousins, the people on the balcony adjacent to ours go crazy. Celebrants throw pounds of beads at a time to adults, plastic swords and stuffed animals to kids, and Bacchus insignia beads to everyone. Those riding on parade floats disburse even greater quantities of beads. It's excessive and fun.

The crowds have returned to pre-Katrina levels, people were in great spirits, and the weather cooperated. Multiple parades occur daily leading up to Rex and Zulu on Mardi Gras day. The parades are a really big deal and draw huge crowds who come to view the floats, bands, and marching societies. It would be great fun to be on one of the floats in a major parade, ride around, toss beads to the assembled masses, and arrive at the convention center to continue the festivities. It's less fun to stand on the street straining to see anything, which is why we don't do parades. Our balcony serves as our parade float as people walk to and from the Canal Street activities. For six hours on Mardi Gras day the passing humanity is so dense one could dive into them and not hit the pavement.

Costumes range in quality from those costing thousands of dollars to a guy in blue jeans with a potato sticking out of his zipper and a hand scrawled sign, "Dick-Tater." A clever group of lads decorated a four person bicycle into a Titti Taxi with accompanying signs, "Let Your Boobs Do Your Walking / One peek = One block." We saw them often with different passengers each time. In the gay part of town the costumes tend to favor extravagant, peacock-like feather arrangements and boas.

Two large guys strolled around attired as Muslim women with everything covered except a slit over their eyes. They would periodically shout, "Death to the Zinfandels" and then flash their burkhas revealing unclothed bodices with a patch of hair resembling a ZZ Top beard covering their private parts.

Dorothy and Wizard of Oz characters were in fashion this year, along with dragons, cavaliers, pirates, revolutionary war generals, crawfish, penises, naughty nurses, porn stars, and so on. Most of the costumes aren't readily describable, but are unusually eye-catching. One old guy wore nothing but a Speedo and wingtips with black socks. It appeared he had a squirrel hidden away.

Fortunately, it was warm on Mardi Gras day producing an abundance of painted naked and semi-naked people promenading. It's a delightful phenomenon when a thin layer of paint placed in a few important places can instill the confidence to walk unclothed amongst tens of thousands of people.

The street side evangelists were out in significant numbers informing virtually everyone that they are going to hell. One exchange was noteworthy between the evangelists and a FQ resident. The local guy approached the microphone-emboldened preachers and screamed, "Where do you live? How would you like me to come to your neighborhood and tell you you're going to hell for living in a manner I find offensive? This is my neighborhood, I live here, and I don't appreciate your shouting offensive crap through your microphone. So f___ you!"

Ladder Guy lives in the neighborhood and presumably earns his meager living by standing motionless on a ladder with a piece of lumber on his shoulder, wearing a hard hat adorned like an American flag and a tool belt around his waist. He's done this routine for as long as we've been coming to New Orleans. He stands motionless for a few minutes, and people walk by and put money in his plastic pail. Then he'll take a break, sit on the curb, and drink. As the day goes on he becomes increasingly obstreperous, but notwithstanding can stand as still as a statue. After a few drinks, if someone takes his picture, stops by to stare at him for more than a few seconds, or tries to get a reaction from him AND then walks away without leaving money, he comes out of pose and curses them.

On Mardi Gras morning I took a stroll around the French Quarter to observe the festivities getting underway at ground level. The gay section of the Quarter is particularly lively. Here's a little travel tip for those who don't have a fully developed sense of gaydar. Look for bare-chested guys wearing feathered boas on balconies holding signs, "Show Me Your Dick."

Our transgender acquaintance reappeared on Mardi Gras day. Pat continues to be striking from a distance, but with a voice like Robert Mitchum's in a beef commercial. It was hard to miss her/him sashaying down Royal Street in this year's garish outfit of white leather short shorts with puffs of fake white fur barely concealing her bounteous breasts. She called up at us inquiring, "Remember me? I'll come up later to see you guys."

Having been raised in Prairie Village, KS where the mores basically favor politeness, an encounter such as this puts those values to the test. "Whenever you come, we won't be here," our host semi-audibly replied.

Later in the evening, she reappeared while we were dining at the Rib Room. She was wearing a platinum wig combining the worst of Dolly Madison and Marge Simpson, adding 3' in height to her already statuesque frame. One had to admire her chutzpah as she greeted us with big ole transgender kisses. Once again, she latched on to some unsuspecting schmuck who was taking her/him out on the town. One can only imagine the *Crying Game* consequences of the evening's ensuing events.

This year's ritual tit for tat exchange far exceeded my expectations. For starters, the levels of pulchritude were exceptional providing a target rich environment. Strolling damsels continue to be generous in sharing their favors. We're now more skilled at identifying amenable candidates, partially offsetting the disadvantages attendant to the nonexistent levels of babe magnetism we conveniently ascribe to our accelerating descent into geezer-hood.

A high probability candidate for a successful flashing possesses some of the following characteristics: attractive and 40 years old, a cigarette in one hand and a pink plastic hand grenade containing a drink from Pat O'Brien's in the other, surgically enhanced breasts and an eagerness to display same, wearing a large quantity of beads, and accompanied by one man but no other couples. Women dressed like nuns are also high on the list for reasons I can't fully explain. Women wearing boob-busting bustiers are low on the list, presumably a consequence of the difficulty of an extraction and the requirement of hydraulic powered assistance for the reinsertion. Pursuit of the more unattainable beauties remains a sporting challenge, and we are often pleasantly surprised by the effort. One of the few advantages of growing old is that women of a wider range of age look good to you.

2010

Having your Mom return home from Mardia Gras with bags stuffed full of beads is not necessarily a good thing. It would be difficult to conjure an innocent explanation for this acquisitiveness. While waiting to board my flight home, I overheard a lady in her early 50's bragging on her cell phone, "I had to remove five pounds of beads from my luggage, because I exceeded their limits." Once again, we facilitated the efforts of those inclined to behave badly.

A week earlier, the New Orleans Saints treated their loyal and long-suffering fans to their first Super Bowl victory. Legions of fans lined the parade route on Canal Street to celebrate. People were just plain happy, and NOLA experienced the largest, most festive, least troublesome Mardi Gras in the last 25 years. A radio commentator noted that pick-pocketing was down, although he didn't mention how he garnered that little tidbit. The success of the Saints contributed to an uber-festive environment.

On Mardi Gras, morning dozens of horse carriages start lining up underneath our balcony signaling the initial gathering of the Bacchus parade. The celebrants gather with their cocktails and bags laden with trinkets and beads they will shower on their admiring onlookers. On a pre-arranged signal, a Dixieland band starts playing and the fully loaded carriages clip clop away.

Shortly afterwards, we were entertained by a motley parade led by two lovely ladies dressed in Gone With the Wind gowns and holding a sign with large letters "KOE". As they approached it was quickly apparent that we were now being entertained by the Krewe of Elvis with several hundred men, women, and children all dressed like the King and accompanied by their lively Dixieland band playing an up tempo version of "Love Me Tender." The Elvises were so densely assembled that one could have fallen amidst the revelers only to be cushioned by massive side burns.

I took a brief stroll to get a view of the festivities from ground level. I was dressed in my customary old white guy costume consisting of khaki's, loafers, and a purple sweater. In my normal habitat this attire renders me invisible. Amongst people dressed as crawfish, space aliens, Elvis, and naked people painted to barely conceal their gender specific mysteries, I stand out like a fat foot in a small shoe. People would actually stare at me. You know it's going to be a great day when a guy dressed like cold cuts mocks your attire.

There is always a large gathering of young, counterculture people featuring dreadlocks, unkempt brown and gray clothing, piercings, and mildly offensive body odor. They're usually occupied as street performers or beggars. The conformity of their appearance would suggest that they had been extruded from the same mold, the irony of which is most likely lost on them.

Our most useful acquisition this year was an upgraded confetti cannon. It operates much like an M72, shoulder fired, light anti-tank weapon system. Cartridges of confetti and streamers are loaded into the device in a color-coordinated manner and crammed down with a plunger. Compressed air cartridges provide the propellant. When launched, the purple, gold, and green concoction showers everyone and everything within a 50 square yard area. Passersby would plead for a repeat performance.

Late Tuesday afternoon, we were approached by one of the prettiest young ladies on the planet. Envision a Sports Illustrated swimsuit cover girl. She was dressed fashionably, as was her male companion. She was wearing a single strand of beads over her full-length woolen Pea coat buttoned to the throat. She strolled directly up to our balcony and, pointing to our display, commanded, "I want those beads." She fully understood the nature of the trade, unbuttoned her coat, lifted her blouse, shared a lengthy view of her stunning bodice, smiled graciously, and collected her beads. Heck, we would have given her our TV!

We usually shoo away males seeking beads, adhering to a mission-central focus. Guys are an unwanted distraction. One college-aged man/boy was particularly insistent. He bounced around under our balcony like a Mexican jumping bean in a cartoon, and we politely waved him away, tried to ignore his pleas, and then basically told him to go away. He had short hair and was wearing jeans and a crew neck sweater, and he wouldn't heed our admonitions. We'd shout, "We don't give beads to males over age ten."

He then illustrated our error by shouting, "I'm a girl!" lifting her sweater revealing an impressive pair of un-male like boobs. We relented and gave her the beads of her choosing.

The main character in Mark Twain's book, *Pudd'nhead Wilson*, was a young lawyer who just moved to the fictional Mississippi River town of Dawson's Landing. He was publicly branded a nitwit, or pudd'nhead, by the locals upon learning of his hobby of collecting fingerprints and his efforts to persuade others of their importance as a unique identifier for every human being. After several years of attending Mardi Gras and carefully observing several thousand boobs and their owners, I'm venturing into similar territory. I believe it is possible that the female breast is as nonpareil a distinction as a set of fingerprints. At the very least, this merits further study.

Our statuesque transgender acquaintance was back again this year. I presume most everyone has known someone during his/her childhood who was a pest. That's Pat. She once used our apartment as a staging area for her various costumes and subsequently glommed on to us like a wet booger on a baby. She has all the appeal of a case of shingles. Being mature men, we avoid her attempts at renewed familiarity by hiding. I saw her earlier in the weekend, during one of my walks, but she didn't see me. Once again, she had some poor slob in tow walking into a bar.

On Mardi Gras afternoon, I saw her walk past our balcony. She was wearing an elegant black pantsuit with a white blouse and a wide brimmed, black fedora chicly tilted on her lengthy mane. She had just walked past our perch, when I whispered to my host, "There goes Pat." She must have ears like a dingo, as she turned around and looked up. She then returned and said she would stop by when she gets into her costume. During my ground level stroll, I again saw her sashaying down Royal Street. This year's costume was reminiscent of the evil queen in Snow White. It had a high collar like an Elvis Las Vegas outfit but with the front cut in a "V" down to his/her pubic region. The skin of her soccer ball sized boobs looked perilously close to exploding from implant tension. Up close her skin is the color of baby aspirin and might frighten lesser men. Later in the afternoon, she approached our balcony, but, fortunately, we espied her before being seen and faded inside. She called to one of the other guests and inquired of our whereabouts. The messenger loudly inquired, "Pat wants to know if you are here?"

She couldn't have helped but hear the muffled retort, "Tell her we're not here!"

We wrapped up the Mardi Gras celebration with our typical feast at the Rib Room followed by cocktails at Touches. After promenading and ridding ourselves of our remaining beads, we retreated to our apartment at 11:55 pm. A few minutes later one could hear the witching hour admonitions broadcast via bullhorns, "Mardi Gras is over, you must be off the streets." At midnight a brigade of New Orleans' finest ride shoulder to shoulder on horseback down the streets of the Quarter starting on Bourbon St. They are followed by dozens of paddy wagons, and they clean the streets of all humanity. Behavior that was acceptable at 11:59 is a go-to-jail offense at 12:01. We observed the annual denouement from the safety of our balcony.

One might think we would outgrow this, but I certainly hope not.

CHAPTER 3

Harvard

1967 – 1969

I emerged from the subway station in Harvard Square on a warm sunny day and encountered the first of many surprises. I anticipated rolling lawns gracing a spacious country setting, I had somehow assumed was the norm for an Ivy League university. Instead, I beheld a distinctly urban view. Predictably, the Harvard Square subway station disgorges its passengers at the main entrance of the Harvard College campus. An elegant brick entryway with iron gates leads to a grassy area and to a statue of John Harvard, the young English clergyman who, in 1638, donated 400 books to a school in a faraway land and, in so doing, gained everlasting fame.

The campus buildings form a perimeter around the college separating it from the nearby urban clutter like the walls of a fort. Harvard Square is not really a square, but instead a cluster of irregular blocks of commercial activity located at the intersection of several major thoroughfares. Cambridge is situated on the north shore of the Charles River just west of Boston. Massachusetts Avenue (aka Mass Ave) is the major thoroughfare through Cambridge, and is renamed Harvard St. for that portion bordering the University. At Harvard Square it intersects with Brattle, Mt Auburn, and JFK each running off in different directions like a starburst on a map.

Prior to my arrival at Logan airport that day, I had never been to the east coast, or west coast for that matter. So like the rube I was, I arrived with a duffel bag containing all of my worldly possessions, only one of which required electricity, an alarm clock. My technology consisted of a manual Smith-Corona typewriter and a slide rule, items that can now be viewed as curiosities in museums. I navigated the subway system from

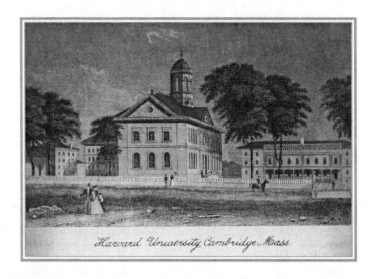

Harvard University, Cambridge, Mass.

the airport to Harvard Square station, emerged, and asked directions to the business school. I walked the half-mile past Eliot House and the University boathouse and crossed the Larz Anderson Bridge to my new home for the next two years.

Ten months earlier, I had applied for admission to the Harvard Graduate School of Business, aka HBS, more arrogantly known as "The" Business School. I was a reasonably capable student, intended to get an MBA, did well on my graduate admission tests, and thought I might as well aim high. The application process was fairly arduous, requiring lengthy essays, a task that surely weeded out the less serious candidates. Amazingly, I was admitted. I later concluded they must have mistakenly thought I was the offspring of Native American missionaries from the plains, as my mailing address was Tomahawk Road, in Prairie Village, KS, and I was a graduate of schools named Prairie, Indian Hills, and Shawnee Mission. Whatever the reason, I was pleased to be there and thought it would be prudent to put in the effort necessary to prevent them from discovering the ruse.

The business school occupies a separate campus and is located on the south shore of the Charles River in Boston. It is much newer than the College, built in the early 1900's, but no less elegant. The stately Baker

Library commands the dominant position on campus with a large dome and a manicured lawn facing the main Harvard campus across the river. A busy thoroughfare, Storrow Drive, separates the campus from the river, but it's more like an uncovered tunnel and doesn't obstruct views of the grassy, park-like banks of the Charles.

I was assigned a suite on the third floor of McCulloch Hall, all the living quarters being cleverly named after former secretaries of the treasury. The hall fulfilled every expectation of what one might expect at an Ivy League university, featuring elegant Georgian style architecture, a slate roof, and, fittingly, ivy covered. I walked up the three flights of stairs to my two-man suite of rooms and was amazed to find a distinct living room with a fireplace, high ceilings, and wainscoting. Our windows looked to the east offering a view of the Charles and the Boston skyline. My roommate, fittingly named Charles, and I shared a spacious bathroom with three other suites.

Maid service was one of the many luxuries we encountered. Irish ladies came in a couple of times a week to clean up, change the sheets and towels, and keep things in order. Presumably, their language resembled English in some remote fashion, but I could barely understand a word they would say. "Time for ye boys to be off now, so we can tidy up a bit," was about all I could discern. Whatever the language barriers, it was grand to have someone tending to these matters.

Class work

Most of the people I met during the first few days of orientation were from prestigious schools, with a heavy concentration from the Ivy League, MIT, Stanford, and the military academies. The vast majority came with several years of work experience on Wall Street, in the military, or with major U.S. corporations. About 20% were international students. The class included a smattering of returning veterans, JDs, MDs, and CPAs, distinctions that made a favorable impression on me at the time. I was one of the 1/6 of the class admitted directly from an undergraduate school and was one of the few from a less eminent school in the Midwest. As such, I was more than a bit intimidated as classes began.

Our class of 700 was segmented into 7 sections of 100 students each. We spent the first year of instruction exclusively with our section, D in my case. We had 3-4 classes per day, each lasting 1 hour and 20 minutes. "They" recommended spending 2 hours of preparation for each hour of class. "They" were right, especially for those of us motivated to not appear doltish to our peers. All classes were taught using the case method. A case consisted of a 20-40 page brief written by someone on the HBS staff about a real business situation. We were frequently reminded that at this stage of life, one wouldn't have to live with the consequences of one's business decisions, and, as Conway Twitty once put so well, "It's only make believe."

Most first year courses were held in Aldrich Hall, and each classroom was a multi-level amphitheatre with rows of semi-circle seating surrounding the professor's stage. Each student brought his/her own nameplate to place in front of them, so the professor could readily identify individuals. The apogee of intensity occurred when the professor started the session, recounting the key elements of the case, paced about theatrically, and then thrust his arm at a student to start the discussion. Juergen Ladendorff, a flamboyant marketing professor, was one of the most memorable and intimidating. He spoke with a heavy German accent, and he could send an electric jolt up your spine when he turned and shouted, "Vell, Mr. Vells, the Anchor Steam Brewery CEO is in a bit of a pickle, vat would you do if you were in his shoes?"

The first time I was called on to start a case discussion, I was barely able to form words. I squeaked a response, but somehow muddled my way through. After a few months, one learned to stare at the professor in as bold a manner as possible emitting pheromones suggesting, "I've got this one down cold, and I'm begging you to call on me," which would assuredly insure that you were not. This was much easier said than done.

Part of the learning experience was to give students more work to do than they could reasonably accomplish, thus requiring prioritization and teamwork. Accordingly, most everyone formed study groups to share the load. The typical daily routine for the first year consisted of classes from 8 am – 3:30 pm, intramural sports and play until 5 pm, dinner at 6 pm, solitary study until 10 pm, and study group from 10 pm – midnight. My crew consisted of an Englishman with a degree from Oxford, a Boston Brahmin Harvard College graduate, a Colgate football player who came to HBS by way of Wall Street, and a street smart Chicagoan with a Cal Tech degree. Each would focus on one of our cases and summarize the key issues for the others. Everyone was pretty good about fulfilling their duties, and we did reasonably well relying on others' analyses when called upon in class.

The professors were almost all superstars. They were entertaining, theatrical, smart, and dedicated to their craft. It was a rare 1 1/3 hour class when one wasn't intensely engaged, either out of fear of being called at random and not having a cogent response, or simply that the topic was interesting.

The Monday through Friday routine was intense, but, in order to insure that weekends weren't wasted on recreation, we were assigned a WAC's (written analysis of case) due at 6 pm on Saturday evening. Most everyone delayed work on the arduous task until the Friday evening before it was due. Smith and Wellesley English majors would later savage the written work with their red pens pointing out misuses of the language. Then the professors would take their turn at critiquing these missives.

Almost every afternoon before dinner, a guest lecturer was available to students followed by a sherry reception. I never developed a taste for sherry, but the speakers were always famous and usually interesting, featuring the likes of Art Linkletter, U Thant (then secretary general of the UN), Jimmy Ling (founder of LTV the second largest steel and aerospace company in the US), and other such dignitaries. One afternoon I went to hear U.S. Senator Henry Cabot Lodge speak to a small gathering. His lineage read like a Who's Who of American History. He was a tall Yankee, silver-haired, handsome, and aristocratic. I was fully prepared to be totally impressed when he started talking about "bananer" republics in South America. Up to this point I had timidly accepted the approbations of the northeasterners who hinted that my mild southern accent placed me amongst the lower forms of human life. Just as I was about to buy into the proposition that I was dictionally deficient, I heard a Boston Brahmin butchering the word banana. I subsequently felt more comfortable embracing my own linguistic legacy.

Financial aid was granted at HBS in the form of business concessions operating on campus. Students delivered the Wall Street Journal and the New York Times, maintained vending machines, provided transportation, resume typing, and copying services. Mine came in the form of running the Gallow's Grill, a late night food operation located in the basement of one of the residence halls. I had the concession for most weekends, which involved setting the menu, buying the food and beverages from the University food service operation, hiring classmates to spread the workload, and manning the operation. I served burgers, steak sandwiches, grilled cheese, BLTs, milkshakes, pop, and beer. I became a pretty competent short order cook, stayed busy, had a chance to visit with fellow classmates, customers, and their dates, and made a little money. It was an eye opening experience.

Amadu*

One of the first people I met was my suite mate, Amadu*, from Sierra Leone* by way of a private school education in England and UCLA. For a lad fresh from Prairie Village, KS an African suite mate was about as exotic as I could imagine. Amadu was short, stocky, and as black as any person I had ever seen. He had a broad nose that spread from ear to ear, and an even broader smile. He spoke with a crisp British accent, was enthusiastic about everything, loved being in America, and would brighten a room by his presence.

Shortly after getting acquainted, we learned that we both played Ping Pong and arranged to meet after class one day to play. I fancied myself a fairly good player, having once won the intramural tournament while in college, along with the singles badminton championship, although sadly these athletic achievements added little luster to my chick magnetism levels. A spider web of tunnels and underground rooms connected the buildings at HBS, an accommodation to the severity of Boston winters, and one of these subterranean warrens housed a Ping Pong table. We wore coat and tie to class, so I showed up to meet Amadu in my classroom attire, loosened my tie in preparation for the contest, and picked up a sand paper paddle lying around the room. Amadu arrived in gym shorts and shoes with his personal paddle carried in its own zippered case. He not only bested me in costuming but also in the games that followed.

The late 60's were the time of flower power, hippies, and a sexual revolution aided by the relatively recent ubiquity of birth control pills. Boston also had the greatest concentration of college students anywhere in North America. Within a few miles of Harvard, one found Radcliffe, Massachusetts Institute of Technology, Boston College, Northeastern, Wellesley, Babson, Holy Cross, and many other schools. One of the interesting anthropological characteristics of many progressive/liberal northeastern American females of the era was a right of passage involving copulation with a black man. Amadu was the fortunate beneficiary of this fad. One would be hard pressed to call him handsome, but he was charming, and we learned to expect a constant parade of gorgeous, scantily clad girls sharing our bathroom. Early on, we'd ponder, "Whose guest was that?" but later we'd know it was someone "visiting" Amadu.

I was fascinated by the fact that Amadu's father had multiple wives. I would inquire, "Now exactly how does that work?"

He would respond with a wry, mischievous smile, "It works well for all. Competition is a very good thing."

Harvard Yale Game

My first fall in Boston I received a call from a college fraternity brother attending Yale Divinity School. He was coming to Cambridge for the Harvard – Yale game that weekend and wanted to get together. We met on a chilly Saturday morning at Charlie's Kitchen, a popular hangout on Harvard Square. Like all bars and restaurants in Boston at the time, it functioned more as a shrine to JFK, serving food and drink merely as an afterthought. I met my friend and a couple of his Yale buddies around 10 am, and we drank beer and chatted until noon when one of the guys said, "I've got to go suit up." It turned out he was the starting tight end for the Yale eleven. I reminded myself, "We're not in Nebraska now." The guy wasn't remotely huge, but he was smart, witty, carefree, and now full of beer. We left an hour later to join him at the game.

The Harvard football stadium is located on the Boston side of the Charles River, just across the street from the business school campus. It's a horseshoe shaped bowl open at the north end. The stadium is appropriately covered with ivy and, with the fall colors, offers a traditional setting one might envision in a Hollywood script. One of the many fine things about Ivy League schools was that they really did have student athletes. The quality of the football didn't measure up to that of the big conferences, but when playing with schools following similar rules, it was competitive and fun to watch.

In 1967 the stadium was one of contrasts with alumni and parents dressed in a manner suitable for a polo match in the Hamptons, and students attired like Jimi Hendrix preparing to set his guitar on fire. The best part of the games were half times, when the bands would consistently push the envelope of good taste. The most memorable occasion being when the Princeton band formed the shape of a penis and balls, with the woodwinds dressed like sperm and ejaculating out of the band-member-formed shaft all to the sounds of Rimsky-Korsakov's "The Flight of the Bumblebees."

Recreation

While the first year of school did not lend itself to abundant time for recreation, it wasn't for lack of options. The Harvard University boathouse was located on the opposite shore of the Charles from the business school. One needed only to show up, present your student ID, and demonstrate that you had passed a swimming test at the school natatorium, and they'd set you up in a shell or a sailboat. One could then row or sail downstream towards MIT, downtown, and Boston Harbor, or upriver past Soldiers Field towards Watertown, Concord, and Lexington. The river was always a buzz of activity, even though the water was roughly the texture and color of Dr. Pepper.

Sections formed intramural teams for rugby, basketball, and softball. My favorite was razzle-dazzle football, a game played with six on a side, all players were eligible receivers, and passes could be thrown at any time from any place on the field. It basically consisted of running around for an hour and was a great diversion from the day's studies. Interesting speakers were available every evening at some part of the campus. One evening the Mahareshi, spiritual adviser to the Beatles, would be lecturing, the next it would be Timothy Leary, John Updike, John Kenneth Galbraith, Norman Mailer, or some other notable from the world of arts and letters. Harvard University is fairly compact geographically, so one could easily walk to the offerings available from the College, the law school, Radcliffe, or other graduate schools. The University provided an overwhelming array of choices of how to spend one's time.

Simon*

One of my classmates hailed from Johannesburg, South Africa. He spoke glowingly of all things American, and it was interesting to view commonplace items from his perspective. For starters, SA had no television at the time, a function of political control not technology. Simon* was a big, fun loving guy who mildly resembled the Disney cartoon character Goofy. He would marvel at the highways and infrastructure that we took for granted. After listening to one of his glowing descriptions of America, I asked him if he thought he would try to stay here after he graduated. He replied, "Well, I don't mean to be an unkind guest to your country, but it would never occur to me to stay here. The life style afforded to those of relatively modest means in SA is superior to that available here to all but the very rich."

New York City

One of my section mates and friends was from NYC, had graduated from Columbia, and managed his family's money while in school. He spent virtually every non-class moment when the stock market was open, trading securities using the phone in my room. He was significantly more sophisticated than I in virtually every aspect of our lives, but somehow we formed a friendship.

He invited me to spend the weekend at his home in NYC, so off we went in his newly acquired Land Rover. We arrived Friday evening at his upper eastside apartment in time for dinner. I had never been to NYC before, so I was pretty much astounded. I had no knowledge of the comparative wealth of neighborhoods in the city, but, upon being greeted at the front door by a liveried butler, I cleverly deduced that this was an upscale part of town. He took our coats and my meager luggage, and a female servant asked me if I would like a drink. We arrived in the midst of a cocktail party with about eight well-dressed older people mingling, so I put on my most sophisticated air and ordered a bourbon and water. The servant then brought me a shot glass with bourbon and a highball glass containing water with no ice. She brought similar drinks to others on her tray. I then poured the bourbon into the water and started to sip while everyone else downed their shot glass and walked into the dining room and sat down for dinner. They looked me over as though I were a night soil toiler in a Bangladeshi refugee camp. Up to this point I thought I was fairly adaptable in most social settings. I was wrong.

My host rescued me and later showed me around his hometown. I enjoyed the weekend but was not totally smitten. A trash strike was underway in the city, dog crap littered the sidewalks, and I was surprised how the richest people on the planet earth lived in these majestic dwellings only to emerge from their fancy lobbies into piles of filth. Sunday morning as we were preparing to return to Boston my friend informed me, "It is customary for a guest to leave a tip for the servants." I didn't know of such a custom and was a bit puzzled but inquired as to the proper amount and did as instructed.

Thanksgiving 1967

My college sweetie, the lovely Judy Cadle, flew to Boston to spend the weekend with me for Thanksgiving. I awaited her arrival at Logan airport and showed off my newfound urbanity by successfully navigating the subway system back to Harvard Square. She surprised me by a new look, with her haircut extremely short, closely resembling Tinkerbell. She wanted to attend a class, so she sat in the back of the amphitheatre during a Human Behavior in Organization (HBO) case, taking in my new environs. Afterwards, some classmates inquired about my visiting little brother.

HBO

The professor who taught Human Behavior in Organizations would invite groups of students to his house for dinner to get better acquainted. He was a gracious host, and it was pleasant to get away from the routine of Kresge Hall meals, even though the university food was uncommonly tasty and plentiful. In the course of casual conversation, he mentioned that he was on the admissions committee that reviewed applications. He said it was a difficult process as over a dozen candidates had applied for each opening. He remembered my application and told me that what stood out were my essays on the importance of fraternity life to my personal growth. He said it caught his eye because the conventional wisdom of the era in more prestigious universities was that fraternities were passé and boorish and here's this provincial kid extolling their virtues. Go figure.

One of the exercises in his class was to simulate nuclear disarmament negotiations. Each team of five students was given five slips of paper each representing a nuclear warhead. The teams then met with their opponent to discuss reducing the number of nuclear weapons they would retain in their arsenal. At the outset we were informed that the best outcome for each pair of teams would be if both reduced their arms to zero. The worst outcome for a team was disarming and being attacked by an opponent that didn't disarm. The second worst outcome was attacking an opponent thinking they had disarmed but finding they were equal or superior in arms. Five negotiating sessions were held, and a team was limited to reducing one weapon per session. The teams would meet, and say, "We'll eliminate one weapon if you will." The opposing team would predictably say, "Okay, sounds reasonable." Then the teams would reconvene in a private setting and decide a) whether to eliminate the weapon or not, b) assess what the other team would do, and c) decide whether to attack the opponent or not. The decision was then reported to a monitor who determined if another round was necessary. In our section ten contests were undertaken. None of the pairs mutually disarmed.

Hitchhiking

We had a three-day weekend in early February 1968 so I decided I would go to Springfield, MO to see Judy, still attending Drury College, my alma mater. One of my suite mates lived in Oyster Bay, NY, owned a single engine Cessna, and was flying home for the weekend. He agreed to drop me off at LaGuardia, which was quite an adventure in itself being jostled by the jet wash of the giant commercial aircraft. In retrospect, I might have inquired about my host's piloting experience before flying through the most crowded airspace in the nation, but it didn't occur to me. He dropped me off at the general aviation terminal where I inquired if anyone was flying to St. Louis. I was dressed in preppy garb with a cheap corduroy sport coat and tie and was quickly able to hitch a flight on a corporate jet and arrived in St. Louis around 9 pm on Friday night. It was bitter cold as I stood outside Lambert field holding a sign saying "Springfield, MO". I didn't arrive at my destination until the next morning after 13 different rides. I was stranded in a gas station on the interstate near Rolla, MO at 1 am trying to warm up when Billy Joe Strothkamp, a fraternity brother from Drury, appeared. He put me up for the evening, brought me back to the interstate the next morning, stayed until I got a ride, and said farewell. I ended up flying back to Boston on a standby commercial flight. The hitchhiking was too arduous.

1968

On January 30, 1968 the North Vietnamese and Vietcong began the Tet Offensive that might arguably be called the turning point of the U.S. involvement in Viet Nam. Most historians agree that the offensive was a military disaster for the Vietcong, but it dramatically reshaped the American public's perceptions of the war. Up to that point the war was not center stage in the public's consciousness. President Lyndon Baines Johnson's response was to ramp up the number of American soldiers from 200,000 to the peak reached of 542,000 by 1969.

Until the events of early 1968, I had been largely apolitical, but now I viewed LBJ as a direct threat to my wellbeing and that of my contemporaries. I subsequently attended my first political rally held in Fenway Park for Eugene McCarthy, the senator from Minnesota who was challenging LBJ in the Democratic presidential primary as the anti-war candidate vehemently expressing dismay at his own party's continued escalation of the war. Interestingly, Bobby Kennedy had earlier been recruited to be the anti-war candidate to challenge LBJ, but he declined.

I was one of the thousands of college age kids who joined the "Get Clean with Gene" campaign in the March 12, 1968 New Hampshire primary. I took a few days off from the school routine to canvas door to door on behalf of the Minnesota senator in Manchester. McCarthy won 42% of the vote to LBJ's 49%, but the outcome sent shockwaves among the political establishment showing the deep divide in the country over the war. My 15 nanoseconds of fame occurred when a portion of my face was visible in a crowd scene surrounding the Senator on the cover of Time Magazine.

Bobby Kennedy entered the race against LBJ four days after McCarthy's "victory." LBJ surprisingly dropped out of contention on March 31, but he continued his efforts to expand the war with the resulting need for a massive infusion of cannon fodder. The graduate school draft deferment was eliminated, and I was one of about 100 HBS students affected by this pronouncement. Harvard acted quickly and provided several options. They would hold a place in a future class for anyone drafted or who enlisted once they returned from their military service. They also created an accelerated program to enable our sub-group to graduate in December 1968 instead of May 1969 by creating a summer program that would replicate a semester's work. I chose the latter hoping to get my MBA before my draft number was called.

I alerted Judy of the change in plans. She was finishing her junior year at Drury, but had been taking heavy loads each semester and planned to graduate in December. I was able to obtain a summer job for her working as a secretary for one of the professors at the business school. Through a notice on a school bulletin board, I arranged for Judy to share an apartment in Cambridge with two other girls. We were all set, except I had unwittingly placed Judy in a setting with two hirsute students from New Jersey. I later learned that they used a yard rake to clean the hair from their bathtub. They were just slightly more foreign than had I arranged for her to live with Martians.

Judy and Chuck - Cape Cod - 1968

Summer

I made arrangements to share an apartment in nearby Watertown, MA with two other classmates, Ken and Jack, both great guys. I bought a 1962 Corvair for $225 and was now mobile. As an English major and well-read person, Judy concluded my vocabulary was deficient, and gave me "30 days to a more powerful vocabulary" lessons each afternoon on our drive from school. The daily routine started with a full load of classes, then Judy would come over to the apartment to cook dinner for us. I would then drive Judy back to her apartment and return for the evening's studies.

On weekends we would explore the northeast. Being Midwesterners and accustomed to driving significant distances, we were delighted to discover how close everything was. Our weekend trips took us to Montreal, Maine, New York City, Philadelphia, Washington DC, Cape Cod, and Martha's Vineyard. We once rented a sailboat, puttered around Marblehead harbor, and returned safely thus escaping disaster, a noteworthy feat considering I had never before set foot on a sailboat.

On one distinctly memorable weekend trip to Cape Cod, we were motoring along the Mid Cape Highway heading to Provincetown. I commented inanely on the pink paint coloring the overpasses, and Judy began to cry. I inquired as to the source of her lamentation, and she whimpered, "Aren't you ever going to marry me?" I stumbled for a coherent response and don't really remember being able to form words, but we became engaged and were later married on December 28, 1968. It wasn't until 40 years later that I began to fully appreciate the insignificance of my role in this sequence of events. Judy dated a guy at Drury who later found fame, if not fortune, as the lead singer for the rock band, The Ozark Mountain Daredevils. Apparently, she thought my mundane prospects were better, and thus we became Chuck and Jude the Obscure.

Football Riot

Like many sports lovers with limited talent, I turned to sports officiating while in college. During my second year at HBS, I became certified to referee junior varsity high school football games. I assembled a crew with three other classmates, one of whom formerly played fullback for Yale, and we journeyed around the Boston area every Saturday afternoon. On this particular day, we were one guy short and started the game with three officials. I was the referee. On the opening kick off, a player was injured away from the ball. None of the three of us saw the cause of the injury, and no flag was thrown. The coach of the injured boy came on to the field shouting and cursing at me "Jesus, why the f__ didn't you throw a flag, didn't you see what they did to my player."

"Coach, we didn't see it, let's get the game going," I replied. The coach wouldn't leave the field and continued to curse and inflame his fans. "Coach, give it a rest, you're going to have to get off the field or I'm going to have to throw a flag for unsportsmanlike conduct."

The coach was getting increasingly belligerent, the crowd was getting uglier by the minute, and my Yale fullback colleague closed in for support. I threw the flag and made the signal for unsportsmanlike conduct. The coach then went berserk and started appealing to the mob in the stands and again turned his wrath on me.

I finally said, "Coach, if you don't get off the field, I'm going to call this game a forfeit." He said something along the lines of, "F___ you!"

and I called the game one play into the contest. I immediately went over to the coach of the home team who was responsible for paying us, received our check, and the three of us got into my 1962 two door Corvair. As we were inching our way out of the parking area, we were surrounded by a mob that started rocking the car. We eventually found our way to open road, and breathed a huge sigh of relief. There was later an inquiry by the league, and our crew was exonerated and retained on the officiating roster, but regretfully no sanctions were taken against the flagitious coach. We were taking courses on human behavior in organizations, but nothing matched the lessons of that afternoon.

Roxbury Alliance*

Martin Luther King was assassinated on April 4, 1968 sparking destructive riots throughout numerous cities in the country. Boston's version of these riots occurred in the predominantly black community of Roxbury, just south of downtown. Two months later on June 5, Bobby Kennedy, having recently co-opted Eugene McCarthy's anti-war platform in his run for the presidency, was assassinated by Sirhan Sirhan in Los Angeles. The racial and anti-war tensions of the time were palpable and felt by almost all thinking people.

Knowing we would be staying in Boston for the HBS summer session, Pete, a classmate, and I learned of an opportunity offered by the consulting firm of Arthur D. Little to hire two HBS students to help develop a business in Roxbury that would provide substantive employment for young African-American males. We were young and idealistic and were hired. ADL received a Ford Foundation grant precisely for this purpose and provided $50,000 to a group in Roxbury called the Roxbury Alliance* with the proviso that they would use Pete and me to help them develop and execute a business plan.

We concocted an enterprise to distribute advertising circulars door to door. We obtained contracts from several grocery chains and consumer electronic stores, purchased vans, designed routes, established quality control procedures, and opened for business. By August we had 100 teenagers employed at $3.50 / hour, more than double the $1.60 minimum wage at the time. The Roxbury Alliance leaders, young men in the vanguard of a calling later to be known as community organizers, set up an office on the main street in Roxbury, and held court. With an abundance of idealistic college students in the area we would often get visitors walking in to the offices offering assistance. The Roxbury Alliance folks would be universally dismissive of these drop-ins and would later tell amusing tales mocking the white chicks who paraded through the offices. Presumably, they told similarly derisive ditties about Pete and me in our absence.

We continued to work with the project through December 1968 when we graduated. Unfortunately, the RA did not handle success well. They spent the money they were earning on fancy office furnishings and cars, and we later learned that the business failed.

Peace Corps

The norm for a second year HBS student for the era was to participate in campus job interviews and then fly off to various locales for more intense interchanges. I took trips to NYC, LA, Atlanta, Orlando, and Chicago to visit various companies and received a number of reasonable offers. Unfortunately, I had a military obligation looming so I also looked at various draft avoidance strategies, most notably the Peace Corps. Judy and I discussed this, applied and were accepted. We were assigned to go to Addis Ababa, Ethiopia after completing language training in Monterey, CA. I was assigned to work in the ministry of television, and Judy would teach English.

This plan, however, was interrupted when I received my draft notice. I contacted the draft board and requested an audience where I could explain my situation. I traveled to Olathe, KS for the hearing and standing before six overweight, middle-aged, gentlemen, I attempted to make the case why my service in the Peace Corps was worthy of a draft deferment. One of the board members caustically said, "Son, spare us the crap about saving the world, you're just trying to save your sorry ass." My request for deferment was denied. Sadly, the guy had nailed it. Fortunately, I had 30 days before reporting for duty, and during that interval I enlisted in a U.S. Army reserve unit in New York City, beginning the harsh transition from Ivy League to olive drab.

Ben atop St. Sunday's Crag

Coast to Coast
2003

When Ben graduated from college, I proposed that we take a father/son trip before he escaped into the responsibilities of adulthood. Accordingly, we walked across the northern portion of England following the 200 mile Wainwright Coast to Coast (C2C) footpath that takes the hiker from west to east through three contrasting national parks: the Lake District, the Yorkshire Dales, and the North York Moors, arguably the prettiest parts of Great Britain. If you envision the British Isle as a body, with England as the legless, misshapen torso and Scotland the head, then we hiked across the throat.

Alfred Wainwright designed the trail to be broken into 14 day hikes each ending in a charming English country village. We adhered to the tradition requiring walkers to dip their boots at the starting point in the Irish Sea at St. Bee's and then immerse their bare feet in the North Sea at Robin's Hood Bay at the end of the journey.

We flew to Manchester, caught a cab to the railway station, and, after three train changes, reached our starting point in St. Bees, a small hamlet overlooking the Irish Sea. We were graciously welcomed by our B&B hostess and were presented with the maps that would guide our journey. We hiked around town, threw stones in the Irish Sea and were eager to begin our trek. We encountered a few computer cafes along the way, and I sent the following missives home to chronicle our journey.

Patterdale, England – June 1, 2003

Ben and I have completed our fourth day of walking through the Lake District in the northwest corner of England. It would more accurately be described as the mountain district. The term English mountain may sound oxymoronic, but, for each of the last four days, we've made ascents and descents of 3,000'. The namesake of the coast-to-coast track, Alfred Wainwright, favors walks along ridges rather than through valleys, affording more pleasing vistas. The walk is designed to offer the most spectacular and varied views of the English countryside while avoiding commercial thoroughfares save an occasional crossing. We have yet to walk on any roads other than when we arrive at our evening destinations. We have seen no transmission lines, cell towers, roads, or any other signs of commercialization.

We have, however, seen thousands of sheep and have encountered every imaginable design of stile and gate, by which we cross over or through stone and wooden fences. Some of the stiles are miniature mazes designed to confuse livestock and dull-witted humans, some are elaborately crafted stone staircases, and others are simple wooden ladders. The number of differing, yet creative, solutions to the problem of getting over or through a stone fence is remarkable. We've not seen a single strand of barbed wire nor any form of metal fencing. Almost everyone we've met has been helpful and uncommonly prescient in discerning that we are Americans.

The paths are not always well marked, so we've relied heavily on our map reading abilities. The competent use of the compass is critical. At the highest elevations the trails are barely discernible, and cairns, small piles of rock constructed to be obviously manmade, often mark trails other than the direction we are going. We've been advised by more experienced hikers to be wary of the cairns as children love to stack rocks wherever they go, so their random ubiquity diminishes their usefulness. We took a wrong turn on Day 1, and an elderly lady came out of her charming, storybook cottage to point out our error. She then filled our water bottles and showed us a shortcut to return to the track.

We went through an area called Nanny Catch, a narrow valley with a beautiful brook running through it. The surrounding hills rise up steeply like walls but they are covered with lush grass. I've never seen terrain like it elsewhere. I presume this is a function of living in a climate with gentle rains, as distinct from thunderstorms. If this were in the U.S. the near perpendicular rise would preclude the growth of anything other than scrub brush, or trees. We've seen more variation of sheep than I knew existed.

Centuries of use turned a cart path into a trench through which we hiked for about ½ mile. It was so deep that we could not see out to the surrounding farm fields. Ben observed a tiny lamb entrapped in a briar patch running along the edge of the trench. He extracted the little critter, and it scampered off bleating its appreciative baahs. This act of kindness was tempered somewhat by our subsequent, frequent dining on lamb.

On Day 2 we walked along a boulder-strewn path along the five-mile shoreline of Ennerdale Lake, then came to an extremely steep climb over the first of five major ridges comprising the Lake District. Our reward was a view from the mountaintop overlooking Borrowdale Valley. The panorama featured a distant clear stream surrounded by a patchwork of green fields bordered with stonewalls, leading to a village reminiscent of dwellings in a fairytale. The stonewalls, many built in the 1300's, are truly works of art, and they can be found in extremely mountainous terrain as well as in the valleys. We walked through a little village, Seatoller, on our way down to our lodging in Rosthwaite.

On day 3 we hiked through Borrowdale valley, which is the rainiest place in England, and, miraculously, no rain. We've now had four dry and partially sunny days. The temperatures have been perfect with highs in the 70's in low lands and 50's at the higher elevations. Locals told us that we are quite fortunate in that the norm is driving rain when crossing the various ranges.

Our last mountain crossing started with an ascent of 3,400' leading to Kidsty Pike, the highest point on the trail and the last of the peaks before entering the Yorkshire Dales. A mountain is also a fell. We've encountered a few fell runners, remarkable athletes who race up and down the mountains. A dale is a valley. A thwaite is also a valley but in an area first settled by Norwegians. We have often found ourselves in shoe-sucking bogs, the worst of which were encountered at the highest elevations.

We've chanced upon numerous water crossings. Ben bounds over them. I slog through with the same pace as though I were on dry ground. I relented and purchased a pair of hiking poles that help enormously on the downhill part of our hikes. I have also abandoned my hiking boots in favor of my Echo street shoes.

After the first day, I doubted my ability to make it the entire 14 days and 200 miles. But today, I am refreshed and, with the aid of Vioxx, anticipate being able to complete our journey. Better living through chemistry and all. The guidebooks accurately note that the first five days are the most spectacular in terms of views but also the most toilsome.

We're on the same schedule as two gentlemen, Peter and J.R. (age 76 and 60), from Norfolk, England. They've been delightful dinner companions and are a wealth of useful information. Both have made the C2C journey before. Peter is a giant of a man and was a former marine serving the Empire in the Far East in the waning stages of WWII. Afterwards, he worked as a tool and die maker for General Motors. J.R. is a quiet, cerebral librarian. Both are members of the Ramblers Club, an English hiking society with one million members, and they wear the uniform consisting of stylish hiking shorts, calf-high woolen socks, and rugged boots, an outfit that prominently displays Peter's tree trunk sized legs. According to our new friends, the abundance of hiking trails throughout the British Isles are a legacy of the preceding centuries when only the very wealthy owned horses. The remnants still provide an abundant variety of hiking venues for the citizens.

We met a group of Canadian women who started out the same day and stayed in the same first night lodgings in the lovely hamlet of Ennerdale. Unfortunately, one of their companions broke her leg falling on loose shale into Ennerdale Lake. The English health care system fixed her up at no charge, and a rescue team of ten lads came into the wild to carry her back to a road on a stretcher. Unfortunately for the Canadians, their journey has now been cut short while they tend to their injured comrade. We ran into them later, and they reported that they were most impressed by the emergency care received, but less so with the follow-up, as each treatment required waiting an entire day in the clinic.

This evening's B&B, the Ullswater View Guest House, has been the best so far. Our bedroom and bath are surprisingly modern and spacious, the surrounding gardens and grounds are immaculate, and the hostess has been welcoming and gracious. Each of our lodgings have provided a "standard" English breakfast consisting of cereal, juice, bacon, sausage, eggs, mushrooms, stewed tomatoes, toast, and coffee. I tried the black pudding (aka blood sausage or fried pig's blood) but wouldn't recommend it.

We had an interesting conversation with George Peat, a fellow guest who is a sheep farmer from Scotland. He said I sound like a character out of an American western movie, and I can barely understand a word he emits, unless he consciously speaks very slowly. I asked him if he refers to someone who raises sheep as a farmer or a rancher? He responded quickly and with great animation in his strong Scottish accent, "Aye laddy, I'm a farmer. Ranchers are nothing but lazy farmers."

We had dinner with our fellow travelers tonight in the White Lion pub and were joined by a new hiker, Nick, an unemployed electrician from Darbyshire, who's hiking with his dog Tess, a handsome black and white border collie. This is a very dog friendly place, and canine companions are commonly found on trains and in pubs.

Each B&B hostess sends us off with a packed lunch for the day's journey. The first day I informed our hostess of my picky eating habits and requested a sandwich with no mayo or butter. When it was lunchtime I was a wee bit surprised to find grape jelly on my turkey sandwich. It didn't occur to me to ask her to hold the grape jelly. The next day Ben ordered our lunch with the instruction, "No condiments."

Tomorrow we have a 17-mile day and the following day is our first 20+-mile day, so my burst of energy from today may be short lived. We scaled St. Sunday's Crag before arriving tonight. I typically walk slower than Ben, particularly on the steep ascents. The lad graciously carried my pack a few times over the most difficult parts, and I didn't protest. There have been two or three lengthy stretches where the hike involves bona fide hands-on-the-ground-in-front-of-you-and-over-your-head climbing.

Our friends from Norfolk told us that the key to this trip is that the first week you rely on physical preparedness, and the second you depend on inspiration. My preparation consisted of carrying my bag for a few rounds of golf, so I may need to rely heavily on inspiration.

Richmond – June 5, 2003

We are now at the public library in Richmond, a medium sized community, with a prominent castle (c. 1100) overlooking the River Swale and a thriving town center that reminds me of Bath, England. As we entered the town after our 18-mile hike journey, we walked by a road sign that read, "Caution, Old People Crossing" with an accompanying caricature of a stooped shouldered old man in a walking pose. Ben insisted that I be photographed alongside it.

The English are quite rigid when it comes to the use of the word town, which Ben and I formerly used to describe every community irrespective of size. We have now been advised that the proper terms are: hamlet, a tiny gathering of dwellings; village, a step above a hamlet usually featuring a pub and a post office; and market town such as Richmond that has a population of at least 10,000 with cricket fields, hospital, et al.

We've now traveled 120 miles in eight days. We are hiking machines and getting stronger. We crossed the Pennines yesterday, the English continental divide featuring a grouping of stone structures called the Nine Standards. It was a pleasant surprise to reach the summit after an arduous climb and encounter the nine giant obelisks similar in scale and appearance to Stonehenge, yet placed on one of the highest points in England. Their origins remain a mystery.

Day 5 was the 50th anniversary of the Queen's coronation, quite a big deal to our friend Peter. After a tough 16-mile day we arrived at Shap (rhymes with crap), home of an abandoned 13th century Abby. We stayed at a guesthouse built in 1608, adorned with suits of armor in the downstairs hall. It was lovely to look at but not particularly comfortable. The top of the door to our room came to the bottom of my nose, and both Ben and I were longer than our beds. At breakfast our hostess, Jean, a short, cheerful, round woman about my age, chatted amiably and asked where we lived. When I told her Kansas City, she broke into song, in a pleasing voice, with her version of "Everything's Up to Date in Kansas City." She told us that, at age 10, her parents hired her out to a neighboring farmer as a laborer. She acquired the record album from the musical *Oklahoma* and learned the words to every song. She pretended that she was a cowgirl in America as she worked with the horses and cows. We also had a nice breakfast chat with a couple from Norway who assured us their homeland is the place to go for mountain hiking.

We caught up with Peter and J.R. and the two healthy Canadian women and walked with them for a few miles before motoring on. We've seen a large number of pheasants today walking along our path before arriving in the market town of Kirkby Stephen. Interestingly, as we trudged into town we noticed 5 or 6 colorful, large peacocks flying over us. We were later told that there are 40 of them who have made their home here.

We were tired, cold, and haggard as we arrived at our lodgings, a handsome townhome in the center of town. Our cheerful hostess told us to wash up, and she would prepare some tea. We entered the sitting room where Chris had built a fire in the fireplace, served us tea from an elegant silver service, and offered us an assortment of delectable scones and pastries prepared by her husband. She then said, "Well, now that you're refreshed, let's have a chat." So far, I would rate our lodgings as excellent.

We joined Peter, J.R., Nick and Tess for a farewell drink and dinner at the King's Arms. They are going to spend a day resting in Kirkby Stephen as we march on. We had particularly heartfelt leavings, and Peter shook hands with Ben and bade us farewell in his sonorous baritone, "There is hope for the future of mankind with fine young men like you."

Inglesby Arncliffe – June 6, 2003

The journey from Richmond to Inglesby Arncliffe of 23 miles was the least fun we've had thus far. After eight miles we arrived in Bolton on Swale, a small hamlet where my feet required major first aid. I've tried a number of foot-care strategies throughout the trip. The first was to wear one pair of thin, tight fitting socks inside a looser pair of thicker woolen socks. This did not produce the desired result, and I developed blisters. On the advice of Peter and J.R, I applied a generous dose of Vaseline underneath one thin pair of socks. This worked in reducing further damage, but didn't help the healing process from earlier missteps. One needs to re-apply the Vaseline at least once mid-day, as the greasy concoction quickly evaporates.

The fellow that provides the Sherpa service transporting our luggage drove by as we were resting, asked if we were doing okay, and inquired if we wanted to bag it for the day and take a lift. I was sorely tempted but concluded such a capitulation would compromise the integrity of the adventure.

Today's hike took us through the only section of the journey that isn't in National Trust land. The Vale of Mowbrey offers an enchanting name but a comparatively uninteresting hike. The only noteworthy portion of the day's journey was being chased by a flock of chickens in a farm field. Jimmy Carter reported once being pursued by an imaginary rabbit, but for me it was chickens. I'm not sure how bad it could have been had they caught us. Others shared experiences being chased by bulls, but we merited only a paltry poultry pursuit. As we entered the village of Inglesby Arncliffe we crossed a major motorway for the first time. It required a taxing, short sprint after the long day. We had a quiet dinner at the only pub in the town, The Blue Bell, and played gin.

Property here is amazingly expensive. We saw a shabby town home on one acre of land in this tiny hamlet that had a public auction sign on it. I asked a lady about it, she said it just sold for 225,000 £.

We've now walked over every imaginable surface: shale, loose gravel, dirt, peat, bogs, grass, wheat fields, and over ridges, through forests, fields, streams, vales, becks, and huffs. We have crossed fences using innumerable stiles and gates, and a wide variety of bridges over rivulets, brooks, creeks, and streams. Since our footing is of such importance, we've learned that we much prefer walking through a sheep pasture than those inhabited by cows. Not only are the cow droppings larger and malodorous but their hooves make the terrain more difficult for walking. Sheep level out a pasture made uneven by cows merely by grazing. The sheep in this part of England are radically different from those in the Lake District.

To pass the time as we walk, Ben and I play Botticelli and twenty questions. Map reading and landmark finding duties also keep us busy. On relatively flat ground we average 2 ½ miles per hour including stops for map checks, water, and lunch. We can easily attain sustained speeds of 3 mph. Tomorrow we enter the North York Moors, the last of the three national parks (actually a national trust which is similar to our historic districts where nothing can be built or added without meeting strict requirements). In four days, Lord willing, we will arrive at Robin's Hood Bay on the North Sea.

Ben and I are usually in bed by 10 pm, and we are not having any difficulty sleeping. We are also burning calories at a high rate, requiring a trencherman's appetite to keep pace. Tomorrow is supposed to be quite scenic, the payback for another day of climbing. Ben is going strong physically, but my feet are extremely tender.

One's perspective of time and distance changes when walking is your only mode of transportation. It is a refreshing contrast.

Grosmont - June 9, 2003

We left the Vale of Mowbrey and entered the North York Moors, a tract of high, peaty wasteland typically covered with heath, featuring poor drainage and cumbersome footing. The good part was the change in scenery. The bad part was the 2,700' ascent. We only hiked 14 miles, but it was quite arduous. We gained our first glimpse of the North Sea from a ridgeline. We spent the night in a small hamlet, Urra.

There was no pub so dinner was served at our lodgings. We shared the dinner table with two English mountaineers and a young American couple from Asheville, NC, Elly and Glen. The Englishmen impressed us with their hiking experiences in Ghana, Kenya, Tanzania, Switzerland and their climb of Kilimanjaro. We also had an interesting discussion about the newly proposed European constitution and the prospect of England abandoning the pound in favor of the Euro. They definitely thought that would be a bad idea and the end of English sovereignty. Dinner started at 6 pm, and we didn't bid adieu until after 11:00 pm after many pints of ale and bottles of wine.

Elly told us an interesting story. As a teenager, she hiked the Coast to Coast walk with her dad, Joe Jack. Joe Jack also walked the length of the Appalachian Trail with his son. At Joe Jack's 60-year high school reunion in Rutherfordton, NC, everyone was asked to say something memorable that they had done in their lifetime. "I walked across England with my daughter, and I walked across America with my son," Joe Jack shared.

Some goober then queried, in his pronounced country accent, "What's the matter Joe Jack, don't you have a car?"

Our days usually consist of walking 7 to 9 hours. Mostly, we are lost in our own thoughts, watching our footing, and taking in the surrounding beauty, but periodically Ben opens up and shares his observations much to my delight and enlightenment. While ambling through the North York Moors Ben shared his perspectives about philosophy. Normally taciturn to an extreme, he was refreshingly expansive, and I enjoyed listening to him discuss the views of Nietsche, Kant, Locke, Schopenhauer, and Descartes. He was able to explain these difficult topics in a comprehensible manner to someone as dim as I.

A portion of the day's journey took us down an old railway path, offering the best walking conditions of the trip. It was one of the few occasions when the wind was at our back, and, with the slight downhill grade, our cruising speeds approached 5 mph.

We arrived in Glaisedale, the loveliest village we had yet seen. We crossed a picturesque stone bridge over a gently flowing brook in a glen shaded by giant oak trees. One could imagine Robin Hood and his merry band enjoying the environs. We stopped to enjoy the view and noted a plaque that told the story of the bridge. It was built in the late 17th century and named in honor of a young woman who lived nearby. The story told of a poor lad infatuated by a girl from a wealthy family. Her father would not allow her to marry a boy of no standing, so he went off to sea, subsequently made a fortune, and returned to his hometown and funded the construction of the bridge in honor of his lost love that had married another. Even Ben thought this was sweet.

After a 19-mile chilly hike in the mist over a moor reminiscent of scenes out of *The Hound of the Baskervilles*, mostly into a headwind, we checked into our B&B just in time to miss a torrential rain with large hailstones. Instead of walking in it, we enjoyed drinking our tea, eating scones with jam whilst being warmed by a roaring fire. Ben was particularly taken by Glaisedale and took particular note of a small cottage that was for sale. We had another quiet dinner followed by a darts game before retiring.

We're now in Grosmont where a nice cafe owner is letting us use his personal computer. Tomorrow we'll enjoy a leisurely five-mile stroll along the headlands of the North Sea before arriving at Robin's Hood Bay. We've now traveled over 200 miles and are still functioning. We've left the moors and have returned to normal countryside consisting of small farms and villages. Absent some grave misfortune, we should arrive safely early tomorrow.

England's beauty compares quite favorably to that of America, but our ugliness can be said to clearly outmatch theirs. In northern England, there are no billboards, no trash, no unkempt properties, few unkempt people, no overhead wires, et al. The farms here are so picturesque, it's like walking through the movie set of *Babe*.

Manchester - June 11, 2003

We arrived in the small seaside village of Robin's Hood Bay yesterday afternoon to complete our 220-mile hike, if you count our missteps and side-trips to our lodgings and pubs, roughly the distance from Kansas City to St. Louis. We took a brief barefoot walk in the surf and threw our Irish Sea stones into the North Sea. Afterwards, we registered at the Bay Hotel having successfully completed the Wainwright Coast to Coast hike. We ran into our new friends Glen and Elly and joined them for a farewell dinner. This morning we caught a bus to Scarborough and then a train to Manchester, with brief stops in York and Leeds along the way. Ben took me to the Chinatown in Manchester for a tasty dinner that provided a pleasant change from the pub food of the past few weeks.

The trip has delivered all that was promised, taking us through beautiful countryside and shielding us from the realities of the world for 14 days. We've encountered many well-traveled people, and most everyone has Italy and New Zealand high on their list of favorite places. Yesterday afternoon in the seaside pub in Robin's Hood Bay, we overheard some elderly ladies talking about their recent hiking trip to New Guinea.

On our last morning in Robin's Hood Bay, Ben pointed out the lettering on our Kellogg's Cornflakes cereal box saying "Ludicrously Tasty." I guess that about sums up my feelings about the trip. My weight is now a shade under 12 stones and Ben's is about 10 ½ stones. It's been nice to eat large quantities of food every day, knowing it's needed to fuel the day's exertions. We are both anxious to eat something a little spicy, even if we have to tone down the quantities.

Postscript

After we'd been home a few weeks, I noticed a postcard Ben had sent to Judy from England and couldn't help reading it. In it he wrote, "….it has been a good trip, really pretty, and being with Dad for two weeks has only been slightly suffocating." Judy assured me that this was high praise.

CHAPTER 5

Drury College
1963 – 1967

I was 5'2" and weighed 95 lbs starting my senior year in high school. I had the distinction of being the smallest boy in a class of 700 students. One good thing about being uncommonly diminutive was that people expected so little of you. "Look! He can grasp a fork! Amazing!" At graduation most students were contemplating their futures, I was merely grateful I finally reached puberty. It occurred three year's worth of gym class too late, but better then than never.

Once a friend's Mom drove us to a movie and rudely asked, "Why are you so short and skinny?"

I considered responding with a query about her plethora of deficiencies but instead fabricated, "Oh, it's just a pituitary problem. Thanks for your concern." I never understood why people got a free pass when mocking skinny people when a modicum of social convention protected virtually every other form of abnormality. But "c'est la vie," as we were wont to say in Prairie Village.

When I was middle aged I was with my Mom when she ran into a woman she knew. They exchanged pleasantries, politely tittered about a shared memory, and we walked on. I asked what transpired, and she hesitatingly told me the following story:

"Mothers talk to one another about their children's activities, and some are more meddlesome than others. When you were a senior, a group of busybodies were working to obtain prom escorts for girls without dates. One of their unsolved cases was Sarah,* the smallest girl in the class, and they called me to encourage you to ask her to the prom."

Thankfully, Mom nipped this intrusive effort in the bud, never said a

Drury College

word about this entreaty, sparing me the knowledge that a bunch of old women even knew of my existence, much less that they had suggested, "Hey, Helen why don't you have your miniature son ask his female counterpart to the prom?"

During high school, I muddled along living in my brother's shadow. He was tall, 6' 3", and a varsity athlete with a wide circle of friends. He included me in most of his activities, ensured that I got to play in the various pickup games that dominated our world, and generally treated me well. He had fairly large ears and was endowed with a nickname that evolved from Dilly Dally, one of the puppet characters in the *Howdy Doody* TV show, to Dilford J. Dally, to just plain Dilford. It used to annoy me greatly that anyone would mock my big brother, but he took it with good humor, relieving me of the burden of retribution. Bill matriculated to Coe College, a liberal arts school in Cedar Rapids, IA. I liked the idea of a smaller school, but concluded it was time to break away from my sibling dependency. So I picked Drury College in Springfield, MO.

Getting Started

My parents dropped me off at the New Men's Dormitory. The dorm certainly wasn't new, as it was built in the 1920's, and the male occupants were not yet men, but it was once new and the name stuck. My first roommate was a farm boy from somewhere in southwest Missouri. He got up with the chickens, went to bed at dusk, had George Washington hair, and would respond to my attempts to converse with his idea of clever repartee, "I don't chew my cabbage twice." We were not meant for each other, and I was fortunate to have connected with another fellow freshman equally dissatisfied with his first roomie.

Scott was from a small town near Springfield, and he was fun, funny, handsome, athletic, tough, and popular with the ladies. Most importantly, we shared many values and interests, primarily our frequent, wistful, and mostly fruitless, in my case, carnal contemplations.

Our first bonding experience occurred early. Each floor of the freshmen dorm had an upper classman living at the end of the hall. Wing-dings allegedly provided some supervision for the newbies. Ours provided more torment than assistance, but he had a car and would occasionally take us to Griff's Burger Bar for a late night snack for a fee. One Friday afternoon, in a display of unexpected generosity, he bought us two six packs of Primo beer (one for him, one for us) with our money and drove us to one of the many river respites surrounding Springfield. We were standing on a gravel bar near the water line drinking beer, skipping rocks, and enjoying the warm fall afternoon. Our escort kept his distance and started throwing rocks in the water near us. He was a big, intimidating guy, and the rocks were getting closer and closer. Scott yelled, "Hey f__face, stop the bombardment."

"What's the matter, you dweebs afraid of a little water? " he replied.

The debate escalated and the rocks kept coming. Scott reached the limit of his patience, picked up a rock about the size of a lemon, and fired it at our tormenter. From our vantage point it appeared to hit him right in the jewels, and he dropped like the wet sack of shit he was. He didn't make a move or sound. Scott said, "I think he's playing possum, so we'd better keep our distance, or he'll kill us." I agreed. After a few minutes it appeared he might actually be hurt, so we stealthily approached, certain he would arise and beat us to pulp. We approached with an escape route in mind, intending to sprint away should danger arise.

He was balled up in the fetal position, holding his dearest parts and moaning. We tapped him gently on the shoulder in a manner one might use with a poisonous frog, but all he did was groan softly. By now it was apparent he was really hurt, so we carried him back to his 1957 four door Ford, put him in the back seat, retrieved the car keys out of his pocket gingerly, so as not to disturb his injured unit, and drove him to Cox Hospital. We dragged him into the emergency room, got the attention of someone, and walked back to school. He never said a word about that afternoon, nor did he retaliate. I later learned that he became a Missouri Highway Patrolman, although it's unknown whether he ever sired any offspring.

Scott and I both pledged Lambda Chi Alpha fraternity. I was a shy lad, and the fraternity culture played a defining role in my becoming less shy. Pledges were required to have a date at all social functions. Asking a girl out was a pretty daunting task given the high probability of rejection and due to the primitive telecom offerings of the era. Each floor in the freshmen dorm had one phone, and one could count on a fairly large audience when calling a girl for a date. The background noise and accompanying hoots of derision greatly compounded the unpleasantness of rejection. My situation was made more extreme given my proclivity for dating girls whose first name was "The," as in, "Could I speak to The Kahuna, please?"

Springfield, MO was, and still is, a Bible-belt town. It was commonplace to be approached by complete strangers asking if you've been "saved" and offering you salvation if you'd commit your life to the Lord Jesus Christ and join them at their church. They'd even send a bus. The town hosts the world headquarters of the Disciples of Christ church and is generally a pretty tame community. However, there was a seedier side to which we quickly gravitated.

Springfield hosted a comprehensive array of sinful diversions. We were dependent on upper classmen for transportation, and they would take us to an establishment on West Chestnut featuring a late night bar, continuous live music, slot machines, gaming tables, ladies of the evening, dirty movies, and underage drinking. At 18 I could have passed for 13, and no sane person would have remotely mistaken me for 21, but no problem. The sin of your choosing was readily available, and I was eager to learn.

Sadly, Mickey Owen was elected sheriff of Greene County two years after my arrival, and he closed our newfound haunts. Mickey, as you may recall, was famous for dropping a called third strike in the seventh game of the 1941 World Series that ultimately led to the defeat of his Brooklyn Dodgers by the New York Yankees, undoubtedly contributing to his being perpetually pissed off at fun lovers.

A roadhouse called Bebops was tucked away on a country lane in the southwest corner of Dallas County, north of Springfield on the way to Buffalo, MO. A rumor gained traction that the 1960's rock n' roll band Buffalo Springfield was so named because the group saw the eponymous sign while traveling to California on Route 66 with Buffalo to the north and Springfield to the south. Bebops featured a lively rock n' roll band and a tolerant view of underage alcohol consumption.

On fall weekends, after everyone had returned their dates to their dorms or homes, we would travel to a river setting, build a bonfire on a gravel bar, set up a keg, sing fraternity songs, and contemplate matters of great urgency. The older guys knew the words to every imaginable limerick of the genre, "There was a man from Nantucket." It was great fun until interrupted by Buff Lamb, sheriff of Christian County.

Buff closely resembled his counterpart Jackie Gleason in the movie *Smokey and the Bandit*, although only a few of us got an up close and personal look at the man. He came with a bullhorn and a couple of deputies and descended on the partying Lambda Chi's. Most of the boys present were not in compliance with local liquor laws, and three were caught. I was one of those fortunate to have escaped the highly skilled lawmen and hitched a ride back to campus. The three unfortunates spent the night in the Christian County jail and, after thoughtful negotiations, were released on their promise to never again set foot in Christian County. Such were the days of, "Boys will be boys, wink, wink."

On Friday afternoon November 22, 1963 at 12:30 pm central time, President John F. Kennedy was assassinated. Most everyone born before 1955 remembers exactly where he/she was when hearing this news. At 1:00 pm that afternoon, I entered Dean Watling's freshmen English composition class. Instant communications weren't the order of the day, but troubling rumors were emerging, and the class time was spent seeking an update. By the time class was over, we were greeted with confirmation that President Kennedy was dead. We felt a sense of shock in a macro sense, but also a pathetic concern for the more immediate. Will the Ma Walker party be cancelled? Yes. Everything was cancelled for the weekend, and even immature minds understood this was a seminal event.

Batman

Scott and I moved into Belle Hall, a 12-room dormitory located above the commons, the dining hall that served the entire student body. There we met one of the more bizarre individuals I'd yet encountered. For starters, he kept a monkey in his room. It swung from the exposed heating pipes, screeched at all hours night and day, and left foul droppings. Fortunately, even he tired of being showered with monkey shit, and it disappeared to some home for unwanted primates.

The television show *Batman* was one of the more popular shows at the time, and our unique dorm mate had taken to living his life as Springfield's version of Bruce Wayne. He fashioned a costume closely resembling the real thing, enlisted another student to serve as Robin, and drove around town in his Pontiac convertible looking for wrongs to right, or maybe it was the other way around. I forget.

Our room was at the end of the hall, and, fortunately, his room was as far away from us as possible. One evening we were awakened from our study induced slumber by the crashing sound of broken glass. Batman was bowling with a real bowling ball into a pyramid of coke bottles, with Robin retrieving the ball, sweeping away the broken glass, and setting up new bottles.

When a vacancy opened up, I jumped at it and left Belle Hall for the fraternity house.

Fraternity Life

The Lambda Chi house was a three-story home built in the 1920's with about 2,500 square feet of living space and was home to 22 boys. Gaining one of the spots in the House was highly coveted, even though living conditions were Spartan and crowded. The décor was inventive although hardly stylish. We shared one bathroom on the second floor with a communal shower and two toilets. A plaque in the bathroom had been dedicated to William P. Enoch, an upperclassman noted for his legendarily odiferous emissions, surely one of the initial causes of global warming. Privacy was nonexistent. Our housemother, a nice older lady, provided a modicum of adult supervision, but mostly hid in her apartment to escape the 24/7 chaos. And we had a housedog, Duchess, a German shepherd who enjoyed an abundance of attention.

Before classes started in the fall, freshmen interested in joining a fraternity participated in rush week. This involved attending rush parties at each of the fraternity houses. The house would be cleaned, the brothers would don their navy blue blazers with the fraternity coat of arms, and we would line up to greet the candidates. The "face men" would form the front of the line. Those of us whose many fine qualities were less visibly discernible would be relegated to the back. After a few such parties, the fraternities and sororities presented their new pledges in front of the school library. It was a great time for the upper classmen to scout out the freshmen girls, where I first espied the lovely Judy Cadle and later asked her out.

Hazing was relatively benign in the Lambda Chi house. The pledge class assembled each Saturday morning to clean the house, were required to have dates for social functions, and maintain a minimum grade point average. If grades fell to a certain level, the pledge was required to attend monitored study sessions. Actives were available to tutor those struggling with a subject. It was pretty logical and grownup.

Pledge fathers were selected with the intent of helping the newcomers. It didn't always work out. One evening I was double dating with my new pal, he apparently liked my date better than his, and, unbeknownst to me, made the switch. Screwing people over turned out to be good training as he later became a litigator, validating the axiom that 95% of the lawyers give the other 5% a bad name.

Pledge training consisted of learning fraternity and chapter history, the Greek alphabet, and the names of everyone. Hell week was a little more intense, but not much. One learned to stay away from some of the upperclassmen, but most of the older guys were pretty mellow and protected us from the more zealous, newly initiated actives.

If one encountered an active during the hell week, he could request that you recite the following Epitome creed and/or request the time:

"I am the epitome of the mungiest crud, a lower form of animal life than that of the amoeba. I take great pride in living off the waste material of all animals, especially that of the chicken, a creature infinitely more noble than I."

Active: *"Pledge, what time is it?"*

Pledge: *"Sir! The inner workings and hidden mechanisms of my chronometer are not in accord with the great celestial movement by which all time is commonly reckoned. However, without fear of being too far amiss, I estimate the correct time to be approximately… may I gaze, sir?"*

Active: *"Yes."*

Pledge: (looks at watch) *"5:03 p.m., sir."*

I am told such silliness is no longer allowed, and hell week has been renamed inspiration week, sparing subsequent generations from lessons in humility.

At the end of our pledge period, we decorated a fraternity paddle as a gift to our pledge father. This involved obtaining the signatures of every member of the fraternity, the Crescent Girl (fraternity sweetheart), and five signatures of girls from each of the five sororities and tracing same onto the paddle along with the coat of arms. At a party dedicated to this purpose, the pledge presented the paddle to his pledge father who would bend over, grab big Jim and the twins, and await the blow to his behind. The pledge then had the option of choosing to merely hand the paddle over or give a candy assed swat, either out of heartfelt compassion or in the hope of gaining reciprocity. Alternatively, he could inflict a painful blow to assert his manhood and damn the consequences. My decision was relatively easy, as I hadn't forgotten the bird-doggin' I'd received earlier from my pledge father. Even though I had grown nearly 10" my freshman year, I was still a rather gangly lad with barely a thin layer of skin protecting my bony ass, but I blasted him with all my might and suffered the same in return.

Dead Man

Some guys had nicknames that came easily and became permanent fixtures. The Dead Man, aka Death, could pass for 45 when he was 19. He had a heavy beard, thinning hair, and a distinguished look of maturity. Accordingly, he was mocked for looking old, being close to death, and thus the Dead Man. One of Death's great talents was that he could insert a tennis ball into his mouth and close his lips. He could do the same with five golf balls. This pleased us greatly. He was from Kansas City, and I saw a lot of him while home for summer and holidays, and he was often at my parent's house. My Dad always recognized him but never remembered his real name and would say, "Hey, Death, how're they hanging?"

Physical distinctions can't be well hidden when 22 boys share a single shower facility. Accordingly, an uncircumcised lad lastingly became Skinner. Buddha, TZ (Twilight Zone), Butter, Blow, Spodeyer, H Cubed, the Reverend, and the Junkman quickly replaced parentally given names. We tried to pin Craven Morehead and Heywood Jablome on some unwary brother, but without success. I was too bland to warrant a legitimate nickname.

Party Weekends

In 1963 the Rolla School of Mines was a predominantly male engineering school. They took a break from their challenging studies twice a school year, homecoming in the fall and St. Patrick's Day in the spring, at which time they were ready to let off some steam. Each fall the Drury Lambda Chi's would travel the 111 miles northeast to Rolla to challenge our fraternal counterparts to a flag football game. The real reason for the trek was the arrival of busloads of girls. They came from nearby all girls' schools, apparently eager for male companionship. We stood in line with the Miners as the girls got off the bus, and various pairings occurred. My date for the weekend hailed from Lindenwood in St. Charles.

A fraternity brother lived in Rolla and graciously volunteered his parent's house for our weekend lodging. We arrived after midnight with our dates, knocked, and no one answered. We opened the front door, entered the living room, and encountered a naked boy lying on top of a naked girl on the couch. Both sound asleep. Our arrival awakened our host's mother who inquired who we were and what we were doing in her house. As we began to explain, she noticed her rather chubby, younger son's compromised situation, shrieked, slapped him on the back, and suggested he disengage. To us she emitted an exasperated sigh, "Sleep wherever you want, but please be gone by the time I wake up."

Signs of the Times

My brother was also a Lambda Chi, but at Coe College. He was president of his chapter his senior year and was party to a mildly revolutionary event. In 1965 they pledged a black member, the first in the fraternity's history. The national office's response was swift and cravenly. They pulled the Coe charter. Bill, along with others from his chapter, was instrumental in getting it reinstated and allowing the black member to remain in the fraternity, and the "times were a'changing."

Because Drury was a liberal arts college, students were required to take courses one would have preferred to avoid. In my case it was public speaking. I would have rather stuck thumbtacks into my eyeballs than make a speech in front of others. With the help of a terrific professor, Bill Kelsay, I got through the class, and with his urging and encouragement, I entered a speech contest. The topic was "What I Would Do if I Were President," and the audience was the student body. Mine was a civil rights speech advocating equal rights and denouncing the Bull Connor days of the time. I won the competition and the $300 prize and was feeling pretty darn good about it, as tuition and fees for a semester cost $375.

The weekend after this micro-triumph, a large, drunk student came up to me at a party and spat, "What are you, some kind of nigger lover?" He hit me hard in the stomach and walked off. A year later when I was running for student office, I was approached by one of the few black students then at Drury, and he graciously volunteered to make a nominating speech on my behalf, aiding my election.

The Junkman

Rex* was the most charismatic person I had ever encountered. He stood out in every way. He was the life of the party, quarterback of the fraternity football team, captain of the college swim team, best voice in the Greek sing, class president, good student, smart, and witty. Most impressively, he had a way with the ladies. Pretty girls liked Rex, Rex liked pretty girls, and he oft enjoyed the favors of the local damselry. He had eclectic tastes, attracted more to Rabelaisian shapes than one might expect for a slender, athletic guy. He wasn't handsome in the classical sense, but resembled John Denver had he had red hair. His sexual escapades would have made Wilt Chamberlain look like Don Knotts, but what most set him apart, was his "joie de vivre."

Rex shared the only basement room in the fraternity house. A window at ground level provided unconventional access from the driveway for those so inclined. In the 1960's Drury was affiliated with the Congregationalist Church and held forth proudly with their motto "Forty Acres of Christianity." This proclamation was accompanied with many well-intentioned rules, among them prohibitions on cohabitation and drinking. These rules were mostly obeyed in the fraternity house, Rex's room being the noticeable exception. A local girl, affectionately known to all but Rex as Lumpy, was regularly observed squeezing in and out of the basement window at all hours.

One fall Rex brought a 1949 Desoto four door sedan to school. It was roughly the size of a four-lane bowling alley, had suicide doors, four rows of seats, and was the perfect car for quadruple dating. For reasons presumably having to do with his lack of pickiness in female companions, he became known as the Junkman, his car the Junkmobile, and its arrival was a sure sign that adventure and fun would soon follow.

One spring day a party was organized to celebrate the birthdays of Rex and a popular Sigma Nu. In spite of the intense rivalry between the two fraternities, we got along well, and everyone enjoyed any occasion for a party. The setting was a farm near Strafford, MO through which a clear river ran. Boys and dates arrived mid Friday afternoon, a keg was set up, and good feelings were the order of the day. At dusk a bonfire was built, couples coupled, and some goober would drag out his guitar and sing, "If I Had a Hammer" before being pummeled with beer cans.

As the evening wore on, a commotion drew everyone's attention to Rex. He placed a beer can on his head and dared a pistol packing fraternity brother to shoot it off, ala William Tell. Most fraternity members were familiar with firearms, and they were not uncommon when at the river. The presence of a gun wasn't shocking, but the idea of shooting a beer can off someone's head was. Everyone pleaded with Rex to forsake this dangerous game and enjoy the party. He was undeterred and repeated the challenge to his collaborator, who promptly drew his pistol and shot the can off his head.

I left the party shortly afterwards, took my date home, and returned to the fraternity house. I was one of the few actives in the house when the common phone rang at midnight. I answered, and it was Rex. "Hey, could you come and pick us up? I just rolled my car, and we're in the middle of the interstate near Safford." I drove to the vicinity of the accident and noted the wreckage of the Corvair convertible that had turned turtle. Miraculously, Rex and his date were unharmed and sitting in the grass.

I picked them up, drove his date to her house, and then returned to the fraternity house. Rex was in good spirits, considering all that had befallen him. He was staggering, so I helped him as we walked up the stairs. We eventually reached the second floor landing when Rex threw his hands in the air, lost his balance, and launched us backwards finally coming to rest on the first floor. Astonishingly, neither of us was hurt, but I wasn't happy.

Kaw River

One summer the Junkman, two other friends, and I decided it would be fun to canoe down the Kaw (aka Kansas) River from Lawrence to Bonner Springs just west of Kansas City. Estimating the river was flowing two mph, we planned to start early, float the 25 miles, and reach our destination by dark.

The four of us set out early one Saturday morning in August in the Junkmobile. We parked the old clunker in a field on a promontory overlooking the Kaw just west of Bonner Springs, thinking that this location would be visible from the river when we returned. We then loaded our two canoes on the top of Roger's* 1957 Chevy and drove to Lawrence.

Roger was a year older than the rest of us and commanded some respect as the senior member of the group. His strong suit was that he was game for anything. His weakness was his recklessness. In his company in the preceding six months I had witnessed a stabbing in a riverfront bar in New Orleans, seen him quick draw and shoot a beer can off of Rex's head, and water skied by the moonlight at midnight.

Roger was an avid hunter and kept our fraternity house stocked with venison and other delicacies. One spring evening he killed a badger and set its carcass in the fraternity house toilet with the head barely sticking out above the seat. I was the first to encounter the creature by unwittingly sitting on it, giving me a fright as its rough fur and gnarly teeth brushed my delicate bum. This did, however, provide much merriment to the concealed onlookers. Another victim snuggled into his bed-sheets one evening only to discover he was sharing it with a freshly caught, live, large mouth bass.

The Kaw is dammed in Lawrence, so we put in below the dam and headed downstream. We embarked with several cases of beer, coolers full of ice, a few sandwiches, and a bag of Cheetos. Roger wore his pistol and holster.

The river was flowing well as we embarked. We had visions of merely sitting back, steering our canoes using the back paddle as a rudder, letting Mother Nature's gravity provide the power, and savoring the summer day in a pastoral setting. Unfortunately the temporarily abundant water flow was a consequence of the discharge from the dam. After several miles the flowing water ceased to exist, and the barely discernible current was confined to the edges of the riverbed. It was August, it hadn't rained in weeks, and the temperature reached 100 degrees that day. We alternately dragged our canoes and floated the remainder of the journey. The river bottom was like quicksand making dragging slow and arduous. But we were young, stupid, and had plenty of cold beer.

By nightfall we were sunburned, tired, and still stupid but now out of beer and food with no idea how far we had gone or where we were. Around 11 pm we came to a bridge indicating a nearby town. We stashed the canoes on a bank and climbed up the treacherously steep slope to a highway leading to Desoto. We walked into town and found a drive-in burger joint open. We were starved and thirsty and ordered our food. Roger's pistol apparently motivated an observant and concerned citizen to call the police. Before we could get our food, we were whisked into custody and placed in the Desoto jail. The police were reasonably nice, but they apparently frowned on bedraggled people walking about carrying firearms. They needed to check the ownership of the gun and its owner. No other occupants shared the jail, so we each had a cot. We were roused by the police a few hours later, told that the gun checked out, and we were free to go. We protested and asked if we could spend the night and leave in the morning but were told, "Get the f__ out of here, this isn't a f__ ing hotel."

It was 3 am, and we were back on the streets of Desoto. Miraculously, we attracted a groupie in the form of a 13-year old boy who stood outside the jail awaiting our release. He said, "You guys want to stay at my house? My parents are gone, and they won't mind." Given the lack of better offers, we followed the kid to his house, which turned out to be indescribably disgusting. He invited us in and said we could sleep on the kitchen floor, which was littered with dog crap. We were tired and in no position to be choosy, so we stayed and lay down amidst the filth.

Shortly after sun up a large man and a woman arrived. "Who the f___ are you, what the f___ are you doing in my house?" After noticing Roger's pistol he added, "You better f__ ing know how to use that gun." The 13-year old kid was long gone. We fled in haste.

We trekked back to the river. Possibly the only semi-reasonable decision we made during the entire trip was sending our fourth companion, Steve, ahead on a rescue mission. Steve's assignment was to hitchhike back to KC, get the Junkmobile, and drive to a spot where he could pick us up. Once Steve was on his way, we headed back to the river and continued our journey. We foolishly departed without acquiring food or water.

Steve was Rex's friend from high school. He was a delightful companion and a skilled hitchhiker. As he later explained, he used the old crutch and sling trick, tearing his tee shirt to make a sling and fashioning a crutch out of a large stick, thus appearing more sympathetic to passersby. This seemed a bit excessive, but he claimed it worked.

By midday Sunday, we were dangerously thirsty. The heat, the diuretic effects of the previous day's beer, and the lack of other options had us contemplating drinking the muddy waters of the Kaw. Then we came upon two fishermen in a johnboat. They had a big water cooler, and we pleaded with them to share. At first they refused, then, perhaps noticing Roger's pistol, reconsidered. This was a life-saver as the temperatures again soared over 100.

By mid afternoon we reached the promontory where we left the Junkmobile. Apparently the landowner did not appreciate having an old car parked in his fields, and he plowed a moat around the unwanted guest, making it impossible to retrieve.

Steve hadn't been idle. He and my Dad appeared in our family station wagon. Steve contacted Dad and told him of our plight. Dad interrupted a party he was hosting for business associates at our home and came to the rescue. He negotiated a settlement with the pissed off farmer to liberate Rex's car, drove Roger back to Lawrence to get his car, brought me home, introduced me to his friends, and got me food and water. Amazingly, during the drive he didn't utter a hint of opprobrium. Thank God for great dads.

Later that summer Rex sang in Roger's wedding in Chicago. We were not terribly enamored with his choice in brides and viewed the weekend as an occasion for fraternal mourning. Predictably, Rex showed up in an alcohol altered state, sat next to the church lady organist who bristled at his unkempt appearance, and then nailed the best presentation of the worst, and most inappropriate, song ever, "The Perfect Love".

Junkman – Part II

Rex served as a grunt in Viet Nam and saw extensive combat. A few years after the war, he moved to a small town south of Kansas City. His charismatic personality still radiated, and before long he had an eclectic following that included his former college friends who were mostly young professionals and his new friends who were mostly young country toughs, druggies, and thugs. The only common denominator was everyone loved Rex. One summer Saturday afternoon at a party of Rex's old and new friends, Rex came up to me and said, "Chuck, I don't know what happened between you and so and so, but he told me he intends to kill you."

"You're kidding?" I replied.

He said, "No, I'm not. I think I have persuaded him to spare your life for now. I hope you don't think it rude of me to suggest that you and Judy might want to leave." And we did, although I never learned what I had done to antagonize my prospective assailant. Over time, mightily offending some people was a gift I would develop to a near art form.

Uvulas

I was always one of those earnest, serious lads the alluring ladies preferred to befriend, saving their more earthy favors for reprobates, like my friend Benny. He came from a well-to-do family, was handsome, blond, athletic, funny, and lived totally in the moment. Upon entering any room he instantly became the center of attention. He had a contagious laugh and was game for anything. Among his many fine qualities was the ability to tell a compelling story. He had a way of capturing your attention, knowing laughter was imminent. Some say his outrageousness accelerated when, in eighth grade, his Mom forced him to enter a church talent contest, and his accordion act placed him in a tie for first with a dwarf playing a harp.

One Saturday night Benny was feeling poorly, suffering from some affliction. The other Lambda Chi's were heading out to a party, leaving Benny to languish alone. He concluded, "Hey, if I'm going to feel crappy, I might as well go out and party and be with friends. It can't be any worse than staying in bed." And so he did. Yet after several hours of drinking, he found himself with a swelling uvula that was interfering with his breathing. He went to a water fountain, bent over to take a drink, and his enlarged uvula erupted out of his mouth like a red carpet being unrolled for a corporate jet owner. Maybe it's just me, but I've always found it disconcerting when an interior body part emerges unexpectedly. Benny would go up to other partygoers, open his mouth, point towards his now viewable, swollen uvula, and shout, "Aaargh!" as he could no longer talk. People thought, "Isn't that Benny a barrel of laughs?" Eventually, a concerned and coherent soul suggested Benny seek medical treatment.

Benny presented himself at the emergency room of a nearby hospital. By now he was breathing with difficulty and was suitably frightened. He went to the triage nurse, pointed to the uvula protruding from his mouth, and said, "Aaargh!"

She said, "Have a seat, and someone will be with you in a few minutes."

Benny then mustered up all his pain tolerance to actually emit words, "You don't understand, I can't breathe, I desperately need help."

"Breath through your nose," she suggested, and he did. A little later an emergency room doc examined him, snipped several inches of uvula out of his throat and suggested he go home and rest.

Benny recovered and continued to bring great joy to several generations of Lambda Chi's, as he matched John Belushi's character in *Animal House* with a seven-year, mirth-filled college career.

Keepers of Student Chastity and Discipline

Dr. Watling was the dean of men. I had no idea what it meant to be a dean, but it seemed like the college equivalent of assistant principal in high school. He was wound tightly but seemed like a pretty good guy even though his duties as Dean made him the enforcer of school rules. His female counterpart was Dr. Mildred Schrotberger. Even the writers of the 1982 movie *Porky's*, couldn't have concocted a better moniker, nor could they have scripted a more perfect character as the keeper of student chastity c. 1963. Mildred was a severe spinster. The less kindly among us speculated that her personal knowledge of carnal activities might have been limited. Each year the new class of freshmen would reliably include girls named Faith, Hope, and Charity, a pool from which Mildred would find her favorites.

The rules that Deans Watling and Schrotberger enforced covered the relatively minor requirements of wearing coat and tie to dinner and conducting oneself in a reasonably adult like manner at Sunday night vespers. Curfew violations and drinking were the big-ticket items under their purview. Drinking was forbidden for Drury students any time any place, and girls were to be in their dorms by midnight on Friday and Saturday night and by 10:00 pm the rest of the week. Both sets of rules were uniformly disregarded, and the ongoing game of cat and mouse between the rule breakers and rule enforcers only served to heighten the excitement.

Stone Chapel was the oldest building on campus, built in 1873. It featured a steeple, bell tower, and clock. It had beautiful stained glass windows and creaky, wooden floors. When I was a freshman, a group of seniors decided it would be amusing to lead a milk cow into the belfry of the chapel. Later in adulthood, I encountered the instigator of this stunt, and he told me what happened:

"We broke into the church late one weeknight and led a 'borrowed' cow up the winding, narrow stairs. One of our co-conspirators grew up on a farm, and he led the cow, and two of us city boys pushed from the rear. We were quickly covered in cow shit but soldiered on. We eventually got the cow as far as we could go, placed a bell around her neck for good

measure, went back to the fraternity house, cleaned up, and waited. We weren't certain what happened next, but presumably upon opening up the chapel the next day, someone must have heard and smelled a distressed situation. The first person they called was Dean Watling, and the first thing on his mind was finding the perpetrators, which he never did. They found a nearby dairyman to help coax the cow down from its perch and somehow returned the cow to its proper owner."

Dean Watling did not return to school for my senior year. I don't know if the accumulation of the many battles lost finally took their toll, or if his departure resulted from something more mundane.

Cars

Shortly after I left for college, my Mom purchased a new 1963 Chevy Impala with a 283 cubic inch engine. It was lemon yellow with black interior and bucket seats. Mom was a high school English teacher, wore glasses that made her look a bit prim, but always drove a car that was the envy of most high school boys. One evening over the Christmas holiday, I borrowed her new Chevy and took my date to the Red Dog Saloon in Lawrence. We danced, drank beer, and had a good time. On the drive home my date unfortunately got sick and spewed forth a massive quantity of bile all over the passenger seat and dashboard. The cherished "new car smell" was to never again return. I was quite perturbed as I took my date home.

It was bitter cold, but I was able to find an all night car wash that was open. I scrubbed the big pieces and hosed the floor mats and the inside of the car, but everything froze as soon as it got wet. After hours of futility trying to restore Mom's car to some presentable form, I went home, parked the car in the driveway, and went to sleep.

Mom was not what you would call a harsh disciplinarian. As Lucy would later say about her Grandmother, "If you were to confess to her that you were an ax murderer, she would say, 'Well, isn't that nice dear.'" It wasn't that she was ditzy or uncaring, just extremely non-judgmental. While I was sleeping off the night from hell, I heard Mom pull out of the driveway early in the morning. She never expressed a hint of displeasure and just rolled with the punches that came her way, courtesy of her wayward son.

The summer after my freshman year, I worked at the Coca Cola bottling plant in Kansas City. The job entailed standing at the end of a conveyor system carrying freshly bottled cartons of Coke and stacking them. The job was boring, physically hard, and generally unpleasant. I was paid $1.73 per hour and, gallingly, had to pay $35/month in union dues for the privilege of receiving this meager wage. Bottles of pop came out of the filling machines cold, slotted into wooden cartons, and shuttled along the line to laborers who stacked the cases eight high on a pallet sitting in a two sided metal bin. The first couple of days the foreman watched me like a hawk, but after a week I was able to keep pace. Workers were permitted to drink all the Coke they wanted by just grabbing a bottle off the line, and I drank about 20 a day resulting in a well-quenched thirst, and a face full of volcanic pimples.

On the plus side, I got stronger, and I worked with an interesting, short Italian guy. He had forearms that would have made Popeye's look like Olive Oyl's. He could lift and throw a carton of 12 oz. Cokes with one arm by squeezing two bottles together in the center of the wooden case. His knowledge of the English language was limited to a few curse words and unmentionable colloquialisms referring to female genitalia that he used often and with great enthusiasm.

More importantly, I earned enough money to buy my first car, a 1959 Volvo PV 544. It had a five-speed transmission with a stick shift on the floor and bucket seats. At the time of my purchase it was colored varying shades of sun-faded orange. When I went to see the man selling the car, he gave me the keys and said, "Go take it for a spin." Unfortunately, it was parallel parked on a hill between two other cars. It was a stick shift, and up until then I had only driven a stick shift car once. I finally got the car out of its parking spot, fell in love with it, paid the man $600, and became the proud owner of my first car.

My old roomie, Scott, acquired a 1963 Corvette convertible his sophomore year. I was able to move the dial pretty far from the nadir of the dorkometer when driving around in the Vette, even with the Kahuna riding shotgun.

Turning 21

When I turned 21, my parents gave me $1,000. I was headed to graduate school and could have used that money to reduce the debt I was soon to incur. I could have purchased Berkshire Hathaway stock and would by now be one of the richest men on earth, but instead I bought a 1961 Austin Healy Mark II convertible. It was red and had six, one-barrel carburetors that required a PhD in air/fuel mixture to keep the machine running. It was both a piece of art and crap, proving the adage that the only thing British-built that doesn't leak oil is a screwdriver. But I loved it. It went vroom, vroom, and it stood out in the Ozarks. I kept the car a year, spent a lot of time trying to keep it running, and, fortuitously, sold it for $800 eleven months later.

I was responsible for organizing a party in a farm field outside of Springfield for the fraternity. It happened to be my 21st birthday, but that was incidental to the party. I had a date with the lovely Judy Cadle and wanted to impress her with my capable handling of the affair. As people were starting to arrive, I drove a tractor down a hill and over a rise to the bonfire site I had selected. I sprinkled a gallon of gasoline on the assembled logs, lit a match, and blew myself up. I was thrown 15' into the field, and the hair on my arms and eyebrows had been burnt off. As I stumbled to my feet and inventoried my body parts, a crowd of people came running over the rise to survey the cause of the explosion and the resulting ball of fire. Once everyone realized that I was alive, their concern turned to mockery, particularly painful coming in the presence of the lovely Judy.

Later in the evening, after dates were returned to their homes and dorms, several of the brothers took me out on the town to further celebrate the arrival of my majority. Among the local bars we patronized were the Frisco Tap Room, Gene's, and Dottie's Lounge, all fine establishments, but it was the Twilight Inn that we considered home base and thus the place to celebrate one's coming of age. We arrived at midnight, the place was full of regulars, and the juke-box was blaring with George Jones' version of "The Race is On." We ordered cold beers, French fries, and pickled hard-boiled eggs and nestled into our booth. The owner came over to visit, and one of my companions told him we were celebrating my 21st birthday. He promptly threw us out, apparently failing to appreciate the pre-21 patronage.

The River

The terrain in the Ozarks region is basically rocky. The only things that grow require little in the way of soil or nutrients. The primary consequence has been that people in this region, including my ancestors, have been much poorer than those who wisely inhabited more fertile environs. The good news is that the spring fed streams, creeks, and rivers are crystal clear. The banks are lined with oaks, hickory, and willows, and the surrounding meadows display an abundance of wild flowers in springtime. One could leave the campus and travel in any direction out of Springfield and find a delightful setting within 10 miles. At least a dozen known river spots were easily accessible, featuring grassy banks, a rope swing from an overhanging tree, a deep pool for swimming, and complete privacy. With most of the activities of interest to your average college student forbidden on campus, river settings served as our year round respite.

The James River flows into Lake Springfield, the water source for the city, located south of town. A few miles on a dirt road takes one to a secluded gravel bar on the river surrounded by alluring meadows. One Sunday afternoon, the spring of my senior year, Scott and I took our dates, both later to become spouses, to this setting for a picnic and a swim. It was a warm, sunny afternoon, and we quaffed a few malt beverages, shared a picnic lunch, swam, and enjoyed the day.

Unbeknownst to us, we were being observed by a game warden hiding behind a tree for God knows how long awaiting either a misdeed on our part or a voyeuristic gander. Scott and I were skipping rocks on the river when we saw a beer bottle floating in the river. Scott and I made a bet to see who could get closest to the bottle some 30 yards away. The likelihood of my hitting that tiny container, only a third of which showed above the water line, was about the same as a goat with a typewriter coming up with *War and Peace*. But alas, I nailed it on the first try, whereupon the vigilant enforcer of the law jumped out from behind a tree, arrested me, and took me to the Greene County jail. Prior to this brush with the law, I spent my college years without so much as a parking ticket, and now I was being hauled to jail. Scott, Cathy, and Judy waved their not very forlorn farewells, as the cretin from behind the tree took me away. I hid my head in shame for breaking a bottle in one of the formerly pristine Ozark riverbeds. I was fined $35, released, and chastened.

My maternal grandparents, Jesse and Mayme Welsh, lived in Springfield during my college years, one of the factors influencing my decision to attend Drury, and they went out of their way to help me. My grandmother would invite me and friends over for home cooked dinners featuring the best fried chicken, green beans, home made rolls, and apple pie imaginable. She washed and ironed my shirts and politely listened to my inane, self-absorbed tales. She was generous, kind, and loving. One couldn't ask for a better grandmother. She also read the police report in the Springfield newspaper and had a well-developed sense of humor. So, I was more than a bit mortified when she called the next morning and said, "Chuck, I saw your name in the paper this morning in the police report." This was not my finest moment. Who wants to disappoint their grandmother?

Postscript

The summer after I graduated from Drury and a few weeks before I was to leave for Harvard, I was sitting in my parent's family room, and my Dad reminisced, "Looking back, I'd have to say that my college years were the best time of my life." My Mom's reaction was instant and chilly, causing my Dad to rapidly back pedal into, "Hmm, well you know, of course, not as good as being married to your Mother and having kids and all."

"Dad, that's kind of depressing to think that I've just now wrapped up the acme of my existence." But the truth had been uttered. The stage of life with complete freedom and few responsibilities had come to an end.

Coy is not pictured

CHAPTER 6

Pheasant Hunting

$\mathbf{M}$y first hunting trip occurred courtesy of my friend Gerard. He loaned me a 12- gauge shotgun, gave me a Miller High Life, orange, day-glo hat and vest, accompanied me to Wal-Mart to get a hunting license, a few boxes of shells, and off we went in search of pheasants in north central Kansas.

After dining sumptuously at the all-you-can-eat-high-sugar-and-salt-crappy-food Sirloin Stockade buffet in Junction City, we arrived at our appointed destination south of Belleville, KS. Our lodgings were in a relatively new and spacious farmhouse with bunks in the basement designed specifically to accommodate pheasant hunters. Four others comprised our hunting party: two lawyers, a railroad executive, and Coy*. Gerard had hunted with this group several times before.

Upon first glimpsing Coy I beheld a giant of a man standing 6'7" and weighing 250 lbs. He was sporting a necklace made from animal claws and fangs with a Bowie knife strapped to his belt. I later learned he was a housepainter from a small town south of Kansas City. With my keen observational powers, I quickly noted that Coy was unique. It appeared a time machine had picked him up from his accustomed 18th century, Jeremiah Johnson environs and plopped him into our midst in 1998. We were sitting around our host's kitchen table, and I politely asked, "Hey, Coy what's the deal with the necklace?"

He enthusiastically identified each bear, mountain lion, wolf, and bobcat claw and tooth as though it were a charm bracelet. Then in a preternaturally calm manner he said, "These are from animals I've killed over the years. I honor their spirit by wearing this necklace. It makes me one with each of them." He paused for effect, stared at me with a piercing gaze, and continued, "I live for blood sports!"

I timidly replied, "Cool."

With five, reasonably well off, citified professionals and nary a single labor-induced callous among us, I was thinking, "How the heck does this guy fit in with this group?" Coy was the guest of a mild mannered lawyer with one of the prestigious downtown firms. We later surmised that they must have met at an AA meeting, since the only attribute the two shared was an aversion to spirits.

As I was to learn over subsequent years of pheasant hunting, there are several options available. One can hunt on public lands available to all comers, private land with the permission of the landowner, leased fields where you pay a fee by the day or season, and baited fields where pen-raised pheasants are placed for the convenience of the hunter. The latter could not remotely be called sport, somewhat akin to going to the meat counter, buying a pork chop, and telling the wife and kiddies you went boar hunting. Ideal pheasant hunting land has chest high prairie grass adjacent to recently harvested grain fields and a water source. Thus the pheasant can find shelter in the dense grass but have ready access to food and water in neighboring fields.

First Morning's Hunt

After a lumberjack breakfast served by our lovely hostess, we met our guides for the weekend, Casey and George. We were going the poor man's route and planned to hunt on public lands and occasionally seek the permission of local farmers to hunt on their land. That is where Casey and George came in. It was early November, the first week of Kansas' pheasant season, so the more knowledgeable among us figured that we might have some success in the fields accessible to the public. Casey was hired to assist in gaining access to private land.

Casey was a big, kindhearted, good ole boy. He was about 60-years old, drove a big, older Cadillac, shared many entertaining stories, and was a delightful companion. We never determined the precise nature of their relationship, but George, about 50, was a large, simple man, reminiscent of Lenny in Steinbeck's *Of Mice and Men*. Casey looked after him and did so with kindness. I never saw George without Casey nearby.

Throughout our weekend's travels we observed that everyone was especially kind to George.

Gerard prepared me for my first hunt in terms of safety, laws, and etiquette. Experienced hunters are rightfully wary of shotgun carrying neophytes. He told me how to identify roosters from hens, as the penalties for shooting hens are severe. Roosters have brightly colored feathers. Hens do not. For those not familiar with game management, remember these basics: if you want to sustain the population, kill the males, if you want to decrease the population, kill the females.

Shortly after daybreak we were walking in a field of golden prairie grass, six abreast, spread out over a ¼ mile, with two hunting dogs pacing in front of us. I was the fifth down the line from the leftmost hunter with Coy on my right. As instructed, I had my safety on and was excited in anticipation of my first hunt. Before walking through one third of the field, a pheasant flew up in front of us traveling from left to right. I heard the guys on my left shout in order, "Hen! Hen! Hen! Hen!" So I held my fire. Then Coy blew it out of the sky, presumably so he could be one in spirit with the freshly vanquished bird. Coy then retrieved the hen and said to me, "Here, hold this in your vest." I declined. The other hunters chastised Coy for this errant deed, at least to the extent one chastens a heavily armed, psychopathic, mountain man. This pretty well set the tone for the next two days.

There are at least three important ingredients to a successful pheasant hunt: there must be birds in the fields, you need a good dog to flush them out in front of you but not too far, and you need to be able to shoot with accuracy at the fast moving target(s). One of the best parts of the hunting experience is to observe a good hunting dog in action. They are eager to get into the field, bound through the deep grass, point and flush out the game, retrieve the birds after they fall, and receive approval from their owner. If a man walks 8-10 miles during the course of a day's hunt, then a good hunting dog travels 100 miles. When a bird has been shot and falls into the dense grass, either dead or wounded and running, it would be virtually impossible to find it without a good dog. The tricky devils can run hundreds of yards after being shot.

Our group had one dog that was a good hunter, one that was totally dysfunctional, and one a pleasing companion. The railroad man had the great hunter, Easy. She was trained to zigzag about 10-25 yards in front of her owner, go on point when she identified a bird, resulting in the bird being flushed out in the hunter's killing zone. Gerard's dog, Sundance, an aging but beautiful golden retriever, was the companion dog. He walked at pace with Gerard just enjoying the day. Shane*, the dog owned by Denny*, one of the lawyers in the group, would zigzag over the field 50-150 yards in front of the hunters, flushing the birds skyward way out of range, insuring the field would be devoid of targets for the remainder of the day. Denny also blew a whistle incessantly in an annoying attempt to rein in his wayward dog. Neither Denny nor Shane contributed much to the enjoyment of the trip.

About midday we arrived at a new field and planned our approach. Coy and I, being dogless, were instructed to go to the end of an 80 acre rectangular field to block, while the other four walked towards us with their dogs from the opposite end of the field. In theory, pheasants run in the grass away from the approaching dogs and hunters, then get to the blockers at the end of the field and presumably fly up and get killed. This theory fails to account for the fact that fields have sides as well as ends, and the birds can run like the wind through the grass.

Before Coy and I started off to our assigned blocking duties, a fight broke out with Shane attacking Sundance. They were quickly separated. As Coy and I strode off down the country lane to our posting position, Coy said, "If Shane attacked my dog like that, I'd a killed him." He paused to let this sink in and continued, "Most likely, I'd a killed Denny too!"

He did not say this in jest, so I meekly replied, "Hey, how about those Chiefs!" I was really warming up to this guy. We were starting to bond.

The ditch between the road and farm field was heavily wooded, and we walked the ½ mile to our assigned blocking station. Before reentering the field, I turned to see Coy running back down the road, aiming his gun, and shooting at a covey of quail that we disturbed. He fired five times at a dead run and killed three quail. I was told that you're only allowed to have three shells in your gun. Coy was either unfamiliar with or disdainful of the hunting laws. In any event, it was pretty darn good marksmanship.

Quail fly fast and at the level of a man's head. Pheasants fly much higher making for safer hunting.

Just before sundown, we headed to a scenic bluff where we planned to ambush a flock of prairie chickens as they returned to their nests to roost for the evening. They send out a lone sentinel who determines if the coast is clear, then he flies back to guide the rest. We set up our position, prone on the lee side of a ridge under a line of thick cedars with the sun setting at our backs, and waited. After hiking the entire day, it was a nice respite to lie in the sun-warmed grass. Someone signaled the arrival of the sentinel. We readied our guns. Then, sure enough, the flock of prairie chickens flew high over us, we blasted away, and all escaped unharmed. They are powerfully speedy critters. It was more like a blur of birds.

One of the best parts of pheasant hunting is that it offers an excuse to hike outdoors in this lovely part of the planet and take in the breathtaking vistas. The whole of the view exceeds the sum of the parts: the patchwork of greening fields of winter wheat, yellowing heads of un-harvested milo, waves of reddish gold prairie grass, remnants of 19th century farm houses and barns, distant buttes, crystal clear air, cottonwood lined creeks, cattle grazing on distant rolling hills, hawks soaring, and the pink and blue streaked skies in the late afternoon.

The settlers in these parts were particularly inventive when it came to fence posts. Given the scarcity of trees they quarried sections of limestone by hand drilling a row of 1" diameter holes 8-12" apart and 5-6' deep in a block of limestone. They filled them with water and awaited a hard freeze for the 350-pound blocks to break off creating a fencepost. Then the hardy souls carted them off using a sledge, dug an 18" hole, and tipped the heavier end down, and with another 319 such posts they had a mile's worth of fence structures that would serve present and future landowners for the next few millenia.

When one is charged with the weighty task of blocking pheasants, there is ample time to reflect on one's surroundings and admire the toughness and resourcefulness of the inhabitants.

We had a decent day's hunt on for our first day. We returned with 15 birds among the six of us. None was brought to its demise by my efforts.

Our trip organizer, the railroad guy, ended up bagging eight of the birds, largely a function of his having a good dog in front of him, being a good shot, and being willing to shoot at birds in front of his fellow hunters. He would always say afterwards, "If you were quicker I wouldn't have had to shoot your bird."

After dark we returned to our farmhouse lodgings to a filling and tasty dinner, some cards, and a few drinks. Our host and hostess invited us to watch a videotape of cop car chases and wrecks, a special treat provided at no extra charge.

Second Day

We were up and fed before daybreak and were sitting around the kitchen drinking coffee, planning the day with Casey and George. Casey said, "Since we didn't have much luck on the public land, today I'll try to get you on some private land." So off we went.

Fortunately, Gerard, Sundance, and I ended up riding with Casey and George in his old Cadillac as we drove from field to field and had a better chance to listen in on their conversations. Casey lives with a lady named Ila Fern, and they run a dry cleaning business together in a town near Belleville. The most memorable part of our travels occurred when we got separated from the other hunters and were trying to rendezvous. Casey pulled up to the intersection of two indistinct country farm roads in a wooded area and said, "George, which way should we turn?"

George slowly drawled, "Well, Casey, that depends on where you want to go."

While driving up to a farm owned by an elderly bachelor, Casey told us that the old gentleman was once his grade school teacher, so he'd known him all his life. He said, "Now you boys stay here in the car, because Mr. ___ doesn't like strangers. I don't think he's ever been laid, so he's a little cranky." This news cracked George up, and he blushed.

Somehow Coy and I got separated from the others and were hunting near a heavily wooded creek. If we flushed a bird we wouldn't have to compete with quick draw for the shot, but we were without the aid of a dog, and I was alone with Coy. I was walking about 30 yards to Coy's left, when a covey of quail flew between us heading right over my head. Coy started firing, and I hit the deck. I shouted to Coy to cease firing. He laughed and assured me I was in no danger because he was too good a shot. The shower of spent shotgun pellets falling on me said otherwise. I had cause to wonder, "Which of my body parts might next appear on his necklace?"

We continued on down another wooded draw, this time with Coy leading, since not getting shot by Coy now took precedence over lesser concerns. Coy made the universal hand signal for halt, touched his finger to his lips, turned to look at me and whispered, "I think I smell a buck." We walked on and, seconds later, a giant doe appeared 25 yards in the distance. He took aim with his shotgun, pulled an imaginary trigger, and softly said, "Bang!" The doe ambled off unaware of this theatrical display and her near brush with death. I'm thinking to myself, "That's some pretty impressive sniffing. Buck? Doe? Close enough." With his shotgun still in his right hand, Coy started beating his chest like a Comanche warrior in a cowboy movie and loudly chanted in some make believe Indian dialect. I was definitely warming up to Coy.

We later rendezvoused with the other hunters, walked a few more fields, and called it a day. I finally got my first bird. Back at the farmhouse, it was time to clean our catch. Coy adopted me as his pet by this time and was eager to educate me on the art of pheasant cleaning. He took way too much relish in disemboweling the vanquished creatures, but his instructions were thorough, and I learned a new skill.

The group split up the birds, so I was able to take home a few. That Thanksgiving we marinated and smoked the pheasant breasts making for an exceedingly tasty appetizer, made even more pleasant by the memorable new experience. I've not seen Coy since.

Prairie Village

CHAPTER 7

Prairie Village
1953 – 1963

One day Dad announced that we were moving to Kansas City. I had no idea where Kansas City was, but as long as I wasn't being left behind I was confident it would be fine. Dad accepted an offer to become a band instrument salesman for McLean's Music Company.

We showed up at the doorstep of our new home on Tomahawk Road in Prairie Village, KS in October 1953. Our new town featured remnants of the Santa Fe Trail, adding even more luster. It was a brand new middle class suburb of Kansas City with churches and schools being built to accommodate the arrival of WWII veterans and their newly sired offspring. The Village Shopping Center featured a gas station, drug store, bank, ice cream parlor, etc. The homes came in one of five basic plans. Ours was a single story, single car garage, three-bedroom, one bath dwelling with a basement. Dad later sold that house in 1966, and he proudly recounted, "Boys, you know your Mom and I paid $19,000 for that house in 1953 and sold it for the same price. Now that's a pretty good deal isn't it?"

A moving van's arrival portended the potential of new playmates, and kids would magically appear to inquire, "Are there any children moving in? How old? Boys or girls?" Within days we met virtually every kid within a three-block radius and found many boys who shared our passion for sports.

Every non-school waking moment was devoted to sports in our corner of the Village. Bill and Scott, both a year older, were the best athletes in the neighborhood, but what I lacked in talent I made up for by being earnest and available. Baseball took center stage, but basketball was a close second. We would roam a several block radius from our homes on our bikes in search of the best driveway basketball court. It wasn't necessary to know the homeowner. Six to eight boys would show up in some unknown family's driveway with our ball, made shiny by hours of play on asphalt, and start our game. Later the grade school across the street added an outdoor court, relieving our need to trespass. Kids would show up after school for regular games, sides would be picked, and I quickly adjusted to the stigma of being chosen last. We were undeterred by cold or rain and played until dark when everyone scattered home for dinner.

Television

Dad brought home our first television in 1955. We had seen TV at other people's homes, but this was a big deal. Programming was only available a few hours each day consisting of *Howdy Doody*, wrestling, boxing, and *The Milton Berle Show*. In between, the broadcasters would display a stationary test pattern, at which we would stare. Newton Minnow in his "Vast Wasteland" speech, may well have been correct in predicting that television's entry into our homes would lead to the downfall of society. Years later, I told my son that I was ten when we bought our first television. He was ten at the time and totally unimpressed by this tale of hardship. One of his friends overheard this exchange and paused a bit before inquiring, "What did you use to play your DVDs?"

Mom's Oldsmobile

Dad traveled often for business and had a company car for that purpose. He acquired a green and white 1955 Oldsmobile Rocket 88 for my Mom. I loved that car. I would sit in it while parked in the driveway, move the seat up as close as possible to the steering wheel, and pretend I was driving. The hood ornament featured a rocket with three fuselages connected by a wing. Inside the cockpit of this amazing machine were two rocket-like nose cones, surely the inspiration for Madonna's bras, protruding out of the dashboard. With the use of seat belts still years in the future, this feature was presumably designed to insure that passengers would die a quick and ghastly death in the event of a head-on collision. To prevent such an occurrence, Mom would allow her three kids to stand in the front seat alongside her. When we would come to a stop sign she would extend her right arm to insure we stayed safely in place. Had automotive engineers observed this thoughtful tactic, I'm sure there would have been no need for the costly safety devices that followed.

Alcohol

From my vantage point it appeared that "The Greatest Generation" enjoyed hard liquor. My parents were particularly fond of Jim Beam whiskey on the rocks, and their friends drank varying concoctions involving similarly potent spirits. Often times Dad and Mom would return from an evening out on the town with their friends from the music business, and a jam session would ensue. Dad and his fellow musicians would be feeling no pain from the evening's libations, but it didn't impair their musical offerings as they unpacked their instruments and played.

As observant children, we thought this worthy of emulation. When Bill and I were old enough to babysit ourselves and Sally, we would drink Coca Cola and 7Up out of Dad's shot glasses, mimic our cowboy heroes who also appeared to enjoy whiskey, dramatically swipe our hands across our moistened lips, and yell to our sister, "Hey woman, rustle us up some grub." The phrase, "Bite me you maggot" had not yet been invented, so she would merely ignore us.

Sally

Even though Sally was three years younger, we were close, particularly after we moved to Prairie Village, and I became aware of her presence. We owned a record player, and rock n' roll was the rage of the age. Sally and I weren't exactly candidates for *American Bandstand*, but we danced ourselves silly in our basement. For a big Saturday night, we would walk to the Velvet Freeze, purchase a cardboard pint container of ice cream, return home to watch The Lawrence Welk Show, and dance with Mom and Dad. Pretty corny, but what did we rubes in the hinterlands know?

Sally was a sprite of a girl and was appropriately adored by everyone with whom she came in contact. She was cute, smart, and abundantly spunky. She had Mom and Dad wrapped around her little finger. Bill and

I were fairly self-contained and showed up to eat and sleep, while Sally ruled the homestead through guile and cunning.

On her twelfth birthday, Dad took Sally and several of her friends to Fairyland Park, an amusement park in Kansas City featuring a classic wooden roller coaster and an assortment of other wonderful rides. Sally and three of her friends boarded a horrifying ride featuring a bullet shaped, 4-passenger cabin attached on both ends of a Ferris wheel sized rotating arm. The rider experienced two distinct, simultaneous, hurl-inducing forms of centrifugal force.

Bill, in an uncharacteristic display of orneriness, bribed the carnie operator to extend the ride while Sally was aboard, and he did. We listened as Sally and her comrades screamed for the ride to end. Early on they were playful shrieks, but that quickly turned to fury. When the ride finally ended, Sally strode up to the operator and slapped him across the face with all the force she could muster. The carnie was a tall, lanky, young man dressed in a dirty tee shirt and jeans, with an abundance of what must have been prison tattoos, and was totally surprised by the ferocity of the attack and the unlikely source. Later, when Sally learned the true author of the errant deed, she rightly turned her wrath on Bill with an intensity that would make a gypsy's curse feel like a butterfly kiss. These events foretold Sally's future as a successful family law attorney.

Folly Theatre

One summer day, a neighborhood friend drove into our driveway in his mother's car. Doug had just turned 16 and invited us to go driving around town. I was 13 and had never been the passenger in a car driven by a contemporary. Our grand adventure began with a trip to a nearby burger joint, Wolfburger's, known more for the quality of their pinball machine than their food. After dining and pinballing we headed down the street to play a round of miniature golf. Our horizons were endless. After a competitive contest of putting through the clown's mouth and windmill blades, Doug suggested we go downtown to the Burlesque.

The Folly Theatre at the time was the same one featured in Rogers & Hamerstein's classic tune in *Oklahoma*, "Everything's Up to Date in Kansas City." The building dated back to Kansas City's origins as a true cowtown and was still operating in 1958. At 13 I could have easily passed for nine, but this was of little concern to the middle-aged woman selling tickets. The theatre was similar to most movie venues of the era, excepting the dinginess and the large stage. Had Luminol and black lights been available and applied to the seating, the place would have glowed like a nuclear test site. The theatre was fairly crowded, and most of the attendees were older men, many wearing raincoats. We sat in the balcony, in order to be less conspicuous. I somehow harbored the idea that the police might raid the place and haul us off to jail.

The performance began with an old guy in a loose fitting suit telling dirty jokes. Most of them were over my head, but people seemed to think it was funny. Then came the strippers. They were quite well rounded as I recall. If you saw the movie *Auntie Mame*, you have an idea of the basic stripper moves of the era. They would start out with feathered boas, dance around a bit, and eventually end up with a g-string and pasties. It wasn't particularly titillating, as, lamentably, I was still years away from puberty, but it was still pretty darn cool. I contemplated that this was about the randiest thing I'd ever yet imagined.

When I was well into middle age, a group of philanthropists restored the Folly to its allegedly original grandeur. It subsequently became home to events most commonly frequented by NPR types. While attending a cocktail reception fundraiser for the restoration effort, I conversed with an elegantly dressed matron, who would have served as a perfect foil in a Groucho Marx movie, as she droned on about the Folly and how important it was to retain its historical value. All I could think of was the stark contrast between the evening's black tie affair and the afternoon thirty years earlier when chubby women danced naked on the stage for the amusement of creepy old men and one wide-eyed 13-year old boy.

Junior High

My three years spent at Indian Hills Junior High were eminently forgettable. I would ride my bike the two miles to school, do the required work, and let my mind wander. In gym class we would run the 1-mile perimeter around the school, so my spindly legs enabled me to become familiar with the small creek that was part of the scene. One day in art class, we were assigned to sit along the creek-bank and draw anything that captured our eye. Jonathan Hoffmeister decided to get up close and personal with a rabid squirrel that bit him, giving the rest of us a much-needed dose of excitement.

Occasionally Bill and I would walk a block to catch the school bus to junior high. A girl in my class lived across the street from the bus stop. I knew her by name, but we weren't friends or even friendly, as she seemed distant and struck me as someone who might someday kill her parents with arsenic-laced grape juice. One morning she hopped on the bus, like any other day, and was later called home from school midday. That morning she had, as I had foreseen, laced her parents' grape juice with arsenic, caught the bus, and continued her normal routine, as her parents died an agonizing death writhing on the kitchen floor of their modest Cape Cod home. Prairie Village was not immune to the full range of human tragedies.

Hog was the nickname of a boy who lived on the street behind our house. I never knew the origins of this moniker, as he possessed no physical traits that would link him to the porcine appellation. He was a decent boy, but was never treated quite well by the other kids in the neighborhood. It appeared his only offense was to reside in a house in which the previous owner had hanged himself in the basement. Kids, being kids, decided the only child of the new occupants of the accursed house must somehow be deficient, and he was assigned to the periphery of neighborhood activities.

The Company Car

Dad's job involved traveling to small towns in Missouri. In the fall of each year, he would arrive with a car load of band instruments at the rural high schools and kids would show up with their parents to sign rental agreements for the Selmer saxophone, clarinet, trombone, or tuba of their choosing. When not traveling he would work at the store located in downtown Kansas City to wait on customers, many of whom were professional musicians. The most impressive part of the operation was the shop where skilled craftsmen repaired the complex brass and woodwind instruments with a dizzying array of tools. The Good Times News Stand was located next to Dad's store and sold newspapers from all corners of the globe along with every imaginable comic book and girly magazine, providing a titillating incentive to visit often.

Shortly after Bill began driving, Dad unwisely let him use his station wagon for the evening. Every cubic foot of space behind the front seat was loaded with thousands of dollars of musical instruments. Presumably inspired by the 1962 Oscar award winning movie, *The Music Man*, and in possession of pretty darn near 76 trombones, Bill led a cavalcade of classmates down the main drag of Prairie Village each blowing one of Mr. McLean's new instruments. Amazingly, all were returned in reasonably good order, save some spit, and Bill escaped detection for this mischievous deed.

Bill had even less musical aptitude than I, surely a disappointment to our talented Dad, but he compensated by developing a love for Broadway musicals. He could recite the words to every song in The *Sound of Music, West Side Story*, or *Bye Bye Birdie*, an unusual feat for a boy who later did not turn out to be gay.

One snowy eve, Bill once again had possession of Dad's instrument-filled station wagon. This time he and his companions decided it would serve well as a ski lift. Bill drove while several of his friends held onto the back bumper and skied along the snowy pavement in their street shoes, until something distracted Bill, and he crashed into a parked car. Miraculously, no one was injured, excepting Dad's company car. We were always trying to help Dad along in his career.

Bill and I were riding in the front seat of Dad's 1961 Ford station wagon returning from an errand, and we were talking when one of us used the word "queer" in a context meaning "odd" or "out of place."

"Boys, don't use that word."

"Why?" we queried.

"Just don't," he intoned in a fatherly way. We looked at each other, shrugged our shoulders, and moved on to another topic. Only later did we realize that we just completed the full extent of our father/sons sex education chat.

Junior Businessman

My first introduction to the world of work occurred when I signed up to deliver the "Kansas City Kansan" newspaper to 75 homes in the neighborhood. Early on, this seemed like a good idea, but, after two winters of getting up at the crack of dawn, it grew tiresome. Most dispiriting was the collection part of the business. Once a month I would dismount my trusty Schwinn, knock on the door of my customers, ask for payment, and then deal with the handful of reprobates who would say in a high pitched, Monty Python voice, "You'll have to come back when my husband is home. He takes care of the bill paying." I was too timid to respond as I wished by carrying a ball-peen hammer to bean the miscreants into submission. My meager delivery boy earnings were greatly diminished by this behavior, and I moved on.

One summer Dad thought it would be a good idea for Bill and me to paint our house. To suggest that Bill was a tad unhandy would be akin to propounding Liberace might be gay. This chore was not one of his strong suits, leaving me with the heavy lifting. We scraped, primed, and painted the one story house an ugly, dark brown. We managed the daylight reasonably well to insure we worked in the shade and listened to the radio that continually played the second worst song ever, Wayne Newton's "Danke Shoen." Upon completing the job in a moderately competent manner, one of Dad's friends asked me to bid on painting his two-story house. I asked Bill to join me in the venture, but he said, "You're on your own. I'm never going to hold a paintbrush again as long as I live." I estimated the job, was hired, bought an extension ladder, paint, brushes, and other assorted equipment, paint, and thus embarked on my first real business endeavor.

By the time I was a senior, I had several people working for me and had a few house-painting jobs going, although not smoothly. I was hired to paint the house of a classmate's mother in Leawood, a fancier address than Prairie Village. The house was on a large corner lot in an upscale neighborhood, and I sought to do a good job. Unfortunately, two of my classmate co-workers weren't much in the mood for their task, and they took to painting the bottoms of one another's feet while they were up on the ladder. Taunts would then lead to a chase leaving white footprints on the formerly immaculate lawn, reminding the homeowner of the folly of her decision to hire high school boys.

Carl and the Cuban Missile Crisis

In September 1962, the fall of my senior year in high school, the Soviet Union started placing intermediate range ballistic nuclear missiles in Cuba. Soviet premier Nikita Khrushchev apparently decided to test the young American president's mettle. Two years earlier, during his campaign for president, JFK rode in a motorcade down Mission Road, the main street in our town. Then, as president, he was called upon to respond to the presence of Soviet weapons 90 miles off the coast of Florida leading to the Cuban Missile Crisis. With the possible exception of the Berlin Blockade, this was to be the closest the two nations ever came to escalating the Cold War into outright nuclear conflict.

It was deadly serious business but made less so unintentionally by Carl, then the principal of Shawnee Mission East High School. Carl was not a handsome man. He was tall and gangly, and his face combined the worst features of Abraham Lincoln and Ichabod Crane. He was most notorious for his inane morning announcements lauding the pep club for their decorations of the non-sectarian winter bush, still known to many as a Christmas tree. Carl was ahead of his time in political correctness.

Now that something truly momentous was occurring, Carl showed his true strength of character. I was sitting in Mr. Cartwright's Spanish class when Carl's familiar voice came on the public address system. He told us of the showdown between the U.S. and the Soviets and the potential for devastating consequences. "In case of nuclear attack, get under your desks and cover your head with your hands," he instructed. I wasn't the strongest student in Mr. Kahler's physics class, but I had a sufficient grasp of the power of nuclear weaponry to conclude that Carl's advice was not helpful. I'm not sure if he thought this up all by himself, or if he learned such silliness from a comedy skit. Perhaps he was smarter than we thought, in reducing a seriously frightening geopolitical event into an exercise in self-mockery. The ability of a ½ inch wooden desktop, supported by a hollow metal frame, to protect a child from a nuclear blast remains untested.

Chauncey and Ted

My favorite class in high school was drafting, and I took some variation of that subject for three years. Our teacher was an old, gray-haired man named Chauncey Gorsage. One would expect someone so named to be mocked by adolescent boys, but not so. He was a good guy and particularly kind to me because I was the right-sized boy for Soapbox Derby, and he was one of the very few to think I might turn out okay or to even acknowledge my existence.

I met Ted in drafting class, the start of a lifelong friendship. He was a gentle giant, a great basketball player, and a kind soul. We became a Mutt and Jeff duo throughout high school. We later added luster to our negligible coolness quotient by dubbing our intramural basketball team the Scitsaps, spastics spelled backwards.

By my junior year, our principal activity in Chauncey's class was to plan the location of a movable fire hydrant one of our classmates had stolen. He kept the two hundred pound, yellow iron casting in the trunk of his car, but needed help moving it. We moved the fire hydrant once a week for the entire school year before tiring of the prank.

Rod

Like virtually every school in America in the 1960's, Shawnee Mission East had its share of hoods. They were readily identified by greasy hair combed into a ducktail, leather jacket, and engineer boots with a chain across the top of the foot. Presumably this attire was influenced by the cultural icon James Dean's portrayal of Jim Stark in the 1955 classic movie *Rebel Without a Cause*. They passed as the "dangerous" boys of the era though their misdeeds would pale in contrast to later generations of rebels. I had little contact with greasers, as I was invisible to anyone remotely cool. When I entered my teen years, my aunt bought me the book *Twixt Twelve and Twenty* written by the conspicuously, un-cool crooner Pat Boone. I was so far down on the nerd scale that I actually read it, although I can't recall any of Pat's advice being particularly useful other than avoidance of self-abuse.

One hood took an interest in me for reasons other than torment. Rod lived down the street from Ted, which brought us into contact on fairly neutral turf, as distinct from at school where his stature could have been compromised by too public an association with a dork such as I. Rod was a big guy, walked with a swagger reminiscent of John Wayne, had the obligatory ducktail and leather attire, and owned a sweet hotrod automobile crafted from a 1937 Chevy.

I once told Rod about being bullied by a kid who came up behind me, pushed my books out of my arm, then hit me in the stomach after I turned around in protest. He said, "You need to stand up for yourself. No one else is going to do it for you." He pondered a moment and continued, "A skinny little shit like you needs to learn how to box." In Kansas at the time one could obtain a learner's permit to drive upon reaching the age of 14. I've kept my first driver's license to document my once diminutive stature. I was 4' 10" and weighed 85 pounds, roughly the size of a normal fifth grader.

Rod proceeded to give me boxing lessons. He would insist I use the lighter gloves, and he wore the heavier ones, saying the bigger ones were softer and wouldn't hurt as much when he hit me. My head felt like Jello in a blender after Rod's pugilistic practice sessions. In later life I reflected on Rod's efforts to make me a tiny bit tougher. He failed to emphasize the obvious. To be a competent fighter, one must be intrepid, brave, and capable of withstanding pain. All qualities I lacked. Throughout my life I was unfortunately involved in three fistfights, and, in spite of Rod's instructions, each was an unpleasant, losing proposition.

One spring evening in our junior year, Ted and I were shooting baskets in his driveway when Joe drove up in a 1961 Chevrolet two-door coupe with a stick shift on the floor and bucket seats. Rod was riding shotgun and said, "Hey you boys want to go for a ride in the country?"

"Sure," we replied.

Once out in the nearby gravel country farm roads, Joe asked me, "Have you ever driven a stick shift?"

"No, but I'd like to."

Joe stopped the car, got out of the driver's seat and invited me to take his place. He provided some elementary instructions about getting a feel for the clutch engaging, giving it a little gas, and off we went. It was a forgiving clutch and after a few tries I started to get the hang of it. He had me stop on a hill and start up, let me downshift a few times while going relatively fast, and was generally a pretty competent instructor. After a bit I was getting more comfortable and asked Joe, "Is this your Mom's car?"

He then sheepishly confessed, "Not exactly. Earlier this evening I noticed it sitting on the street with the keys in the ignition, and I just sort of drove off with it."

I hit the brakes, pulled over, and got out along with Ted. "Thanks for the lesson. See you back in town."

Squirrel Hunting

On a bitter January day in 1962, Ted, Tom, and I decided to go squirrel hunting on an island in the Kansas River (aka Kaw) just west of Kansas City. Ted and I brought single shot bolt-action .22 caliber rifles we borrowed from our Dads. Tom was equipped with a .22 caliber pistol, belt, and holster he had borrowed from a large friend. The belt was too large to fit around his waist due to the friend's girth, so Tom wore it over his shoulder like a bandolier. We hopped into Ted's Mom's car, and off we went to Zarah, KS.

Ted's Mom's powder blue 1955 Pontiac sedan served as our primary source of transportation throughout our high school years. Ted and I cleverly stabbed holes in the muffler with an ice pick enabling the car to emit quasi-manly sounds to compensate for its unmanly color. We learned one could turn the ignition off while coasting downhill, wait a few seconds, turn it back on, and generate a loud backfire with flames shooting out of the tailpipe. We were moving the needle to a near breaking point on the dorkometer.

Our destination was a large, unnamed island 75 yards from the southern bank of the Kaw near Zarah. We parked the car along side the river bank, crossed four heavily trafficked railroad tracks, descended a steep wooded slope, and traversed the ostensibly, frozen river to reach our intended hunting grounds.

For 16-year old boys, we came well prepared. In addition to weaponry and ammo, we brought several quarts of Mugs Up root beer in waxed cardboard containers resembling a megaphone. We also acquired Swisher Sweet cigars with rum soaked tips. To celebrate our success in safely reaching the island we lit our cigars and downed our tasty root beer. Given the cold we didn't tarry and embarked upon our search for the elusive game.

We quickly discovered there aren't any squirrels on a heavily forested island in the middle of a frozen river in January in Kansas. After an hour of futility traipsing through the woods, carrying increasingly heavy rifles, shooting at random targets, and freezing, we decided to pack it in sans squirrels.

Midway in the channel between the island and the bank, Ted fell through the ice. At that stage of life, Ted was 6'3" and 175 lbs, I was 5'0" and 90 lbs. This disparity could have had tragic consequences, but, fortunately, Ted didn't fall all the way through and caught himself with his elbows on the unbroken, ragged edge. Tom and I were able to assist Ted in crawling out of the freezing water onto more solid footing. But while engaged in this effort, Tom accidentally hit the trigger of his pistol and shot himself in the calf. He started shrieking and jumping around grasping at his injured leg, a bad idea given we were on an ice flow, but understandable under the circumstances. Ted was drenched from the waist down with water rapidly turning to ice. Tom had a hole in his calf, was bleeding and in pain. In this condition, the three of us emerged from the river to climb the steep, snowy slope towards the car.

Gun shot wounds and hypothermia are difficult to hide from parental scrutiny. Tom was fortunate to have had the proverbial "flesh" wound that entered and exited his calf without damaging either bone or arteries, although his leaping abilities were forever impaired. Ted warmed up quickly once we were in the car. For some mysterious reason we were spared from the potentially harsher consequences of this poorly conceived misadventure.

Sexy Six Go South in '62

In the spring of 1962 six boys piled into a 1961 Ford Falcon station wagon for a six day trip to Pensacola, FL. Four of the six were high school seniors, so we decorated the car with a sheet painted "Sexy Six, in '66", referring to the seniors' anticipated college graduation date. I can't imagine any less sexy boys than we, but there were six of us. Dave, whose parents owned the car, drove the entire distance. Bill, Jim, and Fred filled out the senior portion of the group, and John and I were the juniors.

This was clearly an era pre-dating over zealous parenting. Six teenage boys had a terrific time without alcohol, drugs, cigarettes, or girls. I don't believe any of the six of us even uttered a single curse word. We were a pretty wholesome lot, which I presume was fairly typical for the era, but I don't believe this produced any lasting ill effects.

We drove to Springfield, MO after school on the Wednesday preceding our Easter break where my grandparents hosted us for the evening. They were gracious and welcoming, as one would expect from high-performing grandparents. From Springfield we drove to Little Rock, AR. Five years earlier President Eisenhower dispatched 1,200 army troops to quell the disturbance that occurred when nine brave Negro children dared to challenge the norms of the era and were denied admission to Central High School. We wanted to see firsthand the site of this landmark event but were mildly disappointed, as it looked like a nicer version of the high school that we attended.

Driving on, we were introduced to our first glimpses of cotton fields, Spanish moss, a chain gang, and other signature views of the Deep South. We stopped in McComb, MS to dine at a restaurant called the Dinner Bell and were served family style at a large round table featuring a lazy Susan. We arrived near closing time, but the proprietress graciously extended her hours to accommodate us. She sat down to dine with us and bragged how Fulgencio Batista, the recently deposed dictator of Cuba, once dined at her restaurant. She laughed heartily when I picked up what looked like an oatmeal cookie and took a bite only to be surprised that I was munching on fried eggplant. We also noticed that the wait staff of young black women did not take kindly to our presence, and we later learned that our appetites had consumed the leftovers that would ordinarily have been given to them. From McComb we traveled to Hattiesburg, MS where we encountered a raucous group of Mississippi State football players who used foul language to which we were quite unaccustomed. They offered us beer, and we declined.

We arrived at Pensacola after midnight, pitched our tents amidst the sand dunes, hopped in our sleeping bags, and went to sleep. This base camp served as home for the next few days as we played in the sand and surf, went into town to play miniature golf, attend drive-in movies, and rent a ski boat. It's hard to imagine anyone willing to rent a ski-boat to 16-17 year old boys, but they did. None of us had ever skied or driven a boat before, but no problem. We didn't have a credit card, nor do I think such a thing existed in 1962, but somehow we entered into the transaction, skied for the first time in our lives, loved it, and returned the equipment in good shape. The days passed quickly as we played like small children amidst the sand dunes and frolicked in the surf.

We left Pensacola early on Easter Sunday. Part of the bond the six of us shared was that we attended the Village Presbyterian Church, were members of the Fellowship of Christian Athletes, and were pretty straight-laced kids. We spent five unsupervised days, yet didn't engage in any activity that would have embarrassed our Moms.

We weren't total choirboys. A few months earlier three of our number relocated 200+ driveway reflectors to the front yard of a girl we knew, in a juvenile, but felonious, display of affection. It amused us greatly to drive by her house and admire the bright glare of our wayward handiwork. We hadn't yet been introduced to more incorrigible behavior.

Around 9 am we drove through a small hamlet, Citronelle, AL and heard church bells in the distance. We collectively thought, "Hey, it's Easter morning, let's attend church services." And we did. We entered the small Presbyterian Church looking a bit bedraggled having spent four evenings slumbering in sandy sleeping bags, but the congregants received us warmly. The preacher mentioned us in his sermon and made us feel welcome. Afterwards, people surrounded us being curious to learn who we were, where we were from, and how we came to arrive on their doorstep. One elderly gentleman, Mr. Byrd a retired postman, was most gracious and invited us to Sunday dinner saying, "My wife and I have four boys, all grown and gone, so you lads are going to be my sons today." He then treated us to a fried chicken dinner at the town's only café. We bade our farewells and continued our journey back to Prairie Village.

Boob

Webster's dictionary defines a boob as 1) a stupid awkward person, a simpleton 2) a boor, a philistine. Synonyms include dunce, fathead, fool, goof, goon, imbecile, jerk, nitwit. The dictionary fails to mention the most common colloquial use referring to a woman's breast.

None of these options are pleasing in a name, and I'm not sure how I got stuck with it, but to several of my brother's female friends that was how I was known. The most charitable explanation would have Bill telling friends of our Folly excursion years earlier, and my subsequent affinity for the aforementioned body part. More likely, the originators just thought I was a doltish clod. I would have preferred to be called Bronc or Hondo, but it was my fate to be called Boob, later shortened to Boo by girls too delicate to include the more titillating, trailing b. Fortunately, when Bill's class graduated this unwanted moniker faded, but this nickname may have been more prescient than anyone knew at the time.

CHAPTER 8

The Iron Men

Bruce, Cliff, Alan, and I first started going to Cliff's family's cabin at Beaver Lake in northwest Arkansas in the mid 1970's. We would water ski, fish, play poker, swim, drink, and spin yarns. Later, golf was added at a course affectionately known as Prairie Dog Dunes, featuring rock-hard fairways that facilitated longish drives accompanied by rooster tails of dust. We had worked together early in our careers at Arthur Andersen, formed a lasting friendship, and looked forward to our occasional respites.

On our first trip we met an old man living in a trailer next to Cliff's cabin who entertained us with tales one rainy day. If his stories were to be believed, he came in second place in a sprint to Jim Thorpe in the 1936 Berlin Olympics and later saved Jim from an airplane fire in Alamogordo, NM while working as a fireman. He was mightily entertaining, and we listened to his tales with appreciative enthusiasm.

Cliff's place was located on a spacious, tree-covered peninsula. The cabin was modest and un-air-conditioned, but the screened in porches with fans provided a pleasant setting for poker and summer time slumber. We spent most of the day in and around the dock and boat, and occasionally we would water ski or fish. Alan would bring his ratty life preserver, float around with a beer in his hand, and share his views on the world. It was pretty darn pleasant.

Our signature activity was gambling. Whenever we incurred a tab for groceries, a few six packs, or a gourmet meal, we'd flip coins until one of the four had the outlier, identifying the guy to foot the bill. This had the unintended consequence of replicating the American healthcare system and inflating the cost of every meal. We rapidly concluded, "Hey,

From left: Cliff, Bruce, Alan, author

I've only got a one in four chance of picking up the tab, I can count on my comrades ordering excessively, and so shall I." As one might expect, over a 35-year period, it all evened out, save the cost of dispensing with my customarily thrifty attentiveness to the right side of the menu.

In addition to restaurant gambling, poker was our primary game of chance. One rainy day at the Lake of the Ozarks we played nonstop for 24 hours with a hand constantly in play. Bathroom breaks, pizza arrival, and other non-essentials were handled by anyone who had folded. After one such marathon, we started to think of ourselves as pretty manly, given our ability to multi-task with drinking, eating, card playing, and even a few endeavors requiring physical activity, and decided that one needed to be an iron man to play with such vigor. And so it was that we mockingly anointed ourselves as the "Iron Men," and our bellies grew, and our brains became more addled.

Bruce

Bruce was the catalyst for the Iron Men events. A handsome man, his profile closely resembles that found on a Roman coin excepting the wreath. He grew up in Marceline, MO, most well known for being the hometown of Walt Disney, and would speak often and glowingly of his idyllic childhood. During high school he played starting halfback, safety, and punt returner on the football team, at halftime switched into his band uniform to play cornet in the marching band, and during timeouts sold hot dogs at the concession stand and led cheers. The boy was versatile.

His Dad was a railroad man, as Marceline was then a major hub on the Atchison, Topeka, and Santa Fe rail system. Bruce had fairly high paying summer jobs working on the railroad providing him the means to acquire a 1965 Mustang Cobra, making a cool guy even cooler. But rather than follow his Dad's footsteps, Bruce took his newly minted Culver-Stockton math degree and went to work for the consulting division of Arthur Andersen (soon to become Andersen Consulting and later Accenture), where we met in late 1969.

We were thrown together in a unique culture and were taught to believe that we (AA & Co people) were the smartest people in the room. The organization promoted working long hours, sacrificing personal and family needs, and playing hard. It was an "us vs. the world" mentality that was deeply imbedded in many thousands of young people of the era with lasting effect, some good and some bad. Early on, Bruce was particularly skilled at the "playing hard" part of the equation.

We were both living temporarily in Tulsa, OK but working on separate client engagements. Our typical day consisted of working from 8 am – 8 pm, then we'd head out on the town, party hard until the wee hours, and start over again. We became frequent patrons at humble and fancy dining spots ranging from the Cramalot Inn, a truly cheesy diner fashioned out of a retired streetcar, to Nabil's Steakhouse and the Tulsa Petroleum Club. We'd wrap up most evenings with a stop at the Nooner, a strip joint featuring the clever and talented Kansas City Cowgirl. She would tantalizingly tuck her ample breasts into a 10-gallon hat, which, once removed, would delight the crowd. Such were our bonding moments.

Back in Kansas City the play part of our evenings morphed to the seedy bars near downtown. One night at a bell ringing party celebrating the departure of one of our colleagues, our group walked into a strip club at 31st and Main. A modest crowd had formed, but the seats adjacent to the table high stage were empty. "Great" thought we as we propped our elbows on the stage to gaze admiringly at the performer preparing for her show. A footlocker sat on the stage within an arm's length of our table with what appeared to be a light bulb shining within. Any lingering mystery was quickly resolved when the stripper pulled a massive boa constrictor out of its temporary home and shook its pumpkin-sized head in our direction. I've never been known for my quickness, but somehow I was at the back of that room without knowing how I got there. We left a litter of overturned tables and chairs in our wake, and the crowd in the back hooted derisively at our unmanly retreat. Only then did I notice Bruce, sitting unperturbed like P.G. Wodehouse's character, Jeeves, with his legs crossed delicately at the knee, lighting a cigarette, and motioning slight nods of appreciation to the snake-draped stripper. The man had style.

Alan

Alan came to AA & Co and, in due course, to the Iron Men by way of Osborn, KS; Benedictine College in Atchison, KS; the U.S. Navy; and University of Michigan MBA program. Alan is one of the smartest people I've ever known. He is relatively quiet and reflective, is a keen observer of people and events, shows a spiritual side on occasion, and possesses a low tolerance for fools. His finest attribute is his infectious laugh, one of the most pleasing sounds one can experience. If Alan is laughing, everyone is laughing.

Alan was the third of eight kids and grew up under hardscrabble circumstances on a grain and livestock farm. He's one of those rare folks possessing both book smarts and practical knowledge. After college he enlisted in the navy and was assigned as the junior intelligence officer on a destroyer operating out of Pearl Harbor.

He shared a haunting story about his first night at sea. His destroyer was leaving Pearl Harbor just as the sun was setting. Alan put on his freshly starched, dress whites in preparation for his first meal in the officer's mess. He wasn't familiar with the ship, so he embarked for dinner using an outdoor walkway. While strolling near a railing, a rogue wave hit the ship, knocked him down, and sent him sliding overboard. He saved himself from certain doom only by catching the lip of the deck. It was dark, and they were 100 miles from Pearl. No one saw the mishap, so if he lost his grip, he would drown, and no one would ever know what happened to the Kansas farm boy who was supposed to have been on duty. He eventually pulled himself back onboard, went back to his room, cleaned up, composed himself, went to dinner, and, after experiencing a near miss few can match, never went outside again.

Alan told another story from that same cruise. They were somewhere in the middle of the Pacific when a typhoon hit. The crashing seas were taller than the ship, and the destroyer would shudder violently as the bow would crest over one set of waves and nose into the following trough, leaving the suspended propellers spinning in the void. Alan was with a group of terrified young officers and seamen standing near the Captain of the ship, an old salt in his young 30's, on the bridge. Alan described the captain sitting in his chair calmly pouring a cup of coffee and lighting his pipe as though he was sitting in front of his fireplace at home. Alan recalled, "I learned more about leadership at that moment than at any other time in my life."

Cliff

About midway in our Iron Man relationship, Cliff became rich and famous, so sadly that makes him off limits for storytelling. It's not that he's not an interesting chap, just that it would be bad form to intrude on the privacy of a semi-public man.

Meyers Chuck

Meyers Chuck, Alaska is a village consisting of 34 dwellings situated on the mainland coast about 50 miles north of Ketchikan. A chuck is a saltwater harbor protected by an island and is open to the sea at both ends at high tide. Meyers Chuck is further sheltered from the Pacific Ocean by the Prince of Wales Island that lies across the Clarence Strait. This 11-mile wide channel serves as the principal highway for a steady stream of the cruise ships sailing to/from Glacier Bay. The village has no vehicles, and it is a six-week walk to the nearest road. All commerce is done by boat and seaplane.

The few inhabitants journey across the strait to the larger village of Thorne Bay, 20 miles distant, for their food and fuel. Water comes from a gravity fed system of pipes leading from a mountain lake. Sewage flows directly into the Chuck and is regularly flushed by the twice-daily tides rising and falling over 20 feet. Electricity comes from diesel-powered generators owned by each resident. Heating comes courtesy of firewood that can be found washed up on the stone covered beaches or in the adjacent, dense forests of Douglas firs. Cooling comes free of charge from Mother Nature. Temperatures on the hottest days in early August reach the mid 70's. Most of the Chuckites plant small gardens, and flowers and berries were abundant by mid-summer. A few of the hamlet's dwellings are located on tiny islands of rock. The state of Alaska built a large dock in the sheltered harbor, and it would fill up with yachts and fishing trawlers seeking overnight refuge from the often, stormy Clarence Strait.

Cliff II, not to be confused with Iron Man Cliff, had been a miner, a lumberjack, a commercial fisherman, and, along with his wife Joyce, owned and operated the Meyers Chuck Lodge. When we first met, Cliff II was in his late 60's and reminded one of a rugged leprechaun. He was impressively fit and possessed a wide array of practical skills necessary for survival in a frontier community. He was quick with a laugh, a perfect host, and delightful company. Joyce fit the image of the archetypal pioneer wife. She was a substantial woman with a hearty laugh and a generous spirit. She insured that we were always well fed, although she had a misplaced fondness for casseroles.

Bruce had traveled to Meyers Chuck a few years earlier, and he arranged the Iron Men's first Alaskan fishing adventure. We flew to Ketchikan and caught a floatplane to our ultimate destination. Cliff II met us at the town dock, helped us load our gear into his aluminum skiff, and off we went to the Meyers Chuck Lodge. The lodge has a lengthy ramp to a floating dock. At low tide it lies on the rocky seabed covered with colorful starfish, kelp, and sea grape. The lodge was basically a small house with three bedrooms and two baths upstairs, and a kitchen and living area downstairs. The complex included a utility building housing the generators, a freezer for fish, and deck space overlooking the harbor. Well-attended hummingbird feeders were scattered everywhere.

Joyce awaited our arrival with chunks of heavily salted, smoked salmon and drinks. We hiked down a footpath to the home of the local postmistress to acquire fishing licenses, and then it was time to dine. Joyce's typical fare included large servings of meat loaf, green beans, mashed potatoes and gravy, homemade bread, and fruit cobbler, sort of an Alaskan version of Cracker Barrel on steroids. Although it stays partially light until well after midnight, the generators were shut off, and we were in bed by 9:00 pm.

We arose at 5 am, and Joyce would prepare a Brobdingnagian breakfast with bacon, sausage, fried eggs, juice, potatoes, and pancakes. We wondered how Cliff II maintained his svelte figure.

Cliff's fishing boat was an aging 36' Chris Craft fiberglass cabin cruiser with twin Chrysler 240 hp engines. The cabin had a small propane fueled iron stove serving the dual purpose of heating the cabin and cooking our seaborne meals. We would cruise out of the Chuck into the Clarence Strait with three lines in the water set to depths ranging from 75' – 150'. When a fish took the bait, the line would snap off the downrigger, one of us would grab the rod out of the holder, pull hard to set the hook, and reel in the fish. The first morning out, we brought in about 20 Silver (Coho) salmon ranging in size from 12 – 25 lbs. We'd reel the fish in close to the boat and bring it on board with a net. Cliff II would club it in the head with a weighted, short handled baseball bat, and then it would go into the hold.

One morning while motoring out of the Chuck, we were accompanied by a pod of whales cruising within 100 yards of our boat. Eagles were as common as robins. Sightings of sea lions, whales, various sea birds, bears, and other assorted critters added to the wonderment of Alaska. Oftentimes while fishing about 1-2 miles offshore, we would release a freshly caught fish that was too small or out of season. An eagle perched atop a large Douglas fir would eye the disoriented prize, fly to the spot, circle, head into the wind with its flaps down, snatch the 10-20 lb meal in its talons, and fly back to its perch.

130 Lb Halibut

After a morning of trolling for salmon, we would motor to one of Cliff's secret halibut spots, an underwater plateau about 200' in depth a few miles off shore. We would bait our hooks with fresh herring, attach a five lb weight and start bobbing on the ocean floor in the hopes of landing a large halibut. Halibut are shaped like a flounder with camouflage coloring on one side of their flat bodies and white on the other. At birth they have an eye on each side of the head, but upon reaching adulthood one eye migrates to join its companion on the gray-black side of the head, resulting in one goofy-assed looking fish. They can grow to several hundred pounds in size.

It was my good fortune to be on the other end of the hook when a large halibut took the bait. Cliff II quickly realized I had a big fish on the line and helped me strap a cod-piece device around my waist in which to set the base of the pole freeing both arms for pulling. The big "but" was running away from the boat, and I let it go until I felt a release in the tension on the line and would then reel vigorously. After a while the fish appeared to tire, and it could occasionally be seen near the surface of the water. Cliff II went out on the swimming platform off the stern with a harpoon in his hand. When the fish got within 10', he threw the harpoon with the force of an old whaler causing it to again retreat a few hundred feet, but now dragging a 3' diameter red float attached to the imbedded harpoon.

After a few more minutes of fighting, the fish tired, and I once again reeled it in. As the exhausted creature neared the boat, Cliff II took his .22-caliber Luger pistol and fired three rounds into its head. This inspired the giant flatfish to race off against the strain of the line, the harpoon, and the red float. Once again I reeled the fish close to the boat, this time bereft of its fighting spirit. Cliff II using a large gaff hook brought it on board, clubbed it in the head, and hogtied it. It seemed excessive, but Cliff II assured us, "I don't want that butt's last thrashings to knock one of you boys out of the boat."

We returned to the Chuck around 4 pm in the afternoon and hauled our catch to Cliff II's cleaning station. After a quick shower and preparation of the first round of refreshments, we would gather to watch our captain clean the day's catch. He was a highly proficient fish cleaner, first sharpening his tools, quickly gutting the creatures and tossing their offal onto logs floating near his dock. Eagles would descend to gather their easily acquired treasures, and we would marvel in wonderment.

The Third Cliff

Cliff III introduced Bruce to Meyers Chuck on an earlier fishing trip for several business associates. After retiring, Cliff III spent his summers in Meyers Chuck and winters in New Zealand. His cabin was small, but exceptionally cozy, arguably the nicest dwelling in the village. He was most proud of his compost crapper. It was much like a throne. One ascended several steps to reach the seat that rose above the hermetically sealed device that turned crap and urine into goldfish crackers.

Cliff III held court for his guests on the deck overlooking his dock and fishing boat. He was a knowledgeable, interesting host and provided a pleasant diversion before we returned to the lodge for our evening poker fest. Coincidentally, we were situated in one of the most isolated places in the United States with a peak population of 11 people, three of whom were named Cliff. Go figure.

Life in the Hamlet

Cliff II and Joyce's place served as the only commercial enterprise in the Chuck and provided a bar open to the yachtsmen or fishermen who would tie up to the government dock. The lodge living room also served as the gathering place for local villagers. On the few days when we'd be weathered in, we'd sit around the fire, play cards, and read, and would be accompanied by Joyce and her friends' morning exercise class.

Cliff II often spoke rapturously about the lovely Amy*, who lived on an island in the middle of the Chuck. In preparation for our departure, Cliff II engaged the younger woman to assist him in assembling and labeling our fish into packages suitable for shipping. Upon first espying Amy, it was apparent that Cliff's taste in women either favored heft, or the isolative life style left a paucity of options.

Over a six-year period we became increasingly at ease in the Gardner's home and hoped they felt equally at ease with our peccadillo-ladened group. During our final trip, a potential buyer of the lodge flew in. Cliff II had his place on the market for several years but had few prospects. Sadly, for Cliff II and Joyce, no offer was forthcoming. Any hope for the Gardner's enjoying a retirement featuring a less arduous life style was dependent upon their ability to sell their modest lodge. Two years after we last traveled to the Chuck, we learned our beloved Alaskan retreat burned to the ground.

Sitka, AK

After the demise of our Meyers Chuck destination, the Iron Men experimented with several other fishing venues, all unsatisfactory alternatives, when Bruce discovered another Alaskan option.

Our captain, Robert* and his deckhand Henry*, made introductions as we set out from Sitka harbor at 6 am in late June. The lodge was chosen primarily on the basis of their 31' twin hulled fishing rigs with walk-around deck, twin 300 hp Suzuki outboards, and state-of-the-art GPS navigational and fish finding electronics. The equipment was first rate, and Robert kept his craft spotless and impressively ship shape. The weather was cloudy, spitting a little rain, and a cool 50 degrees.

Captain Robert started off abruptly, "My mission is to insure that you guys kill a ton of f'ing fish." What he didn't say, but should have, was that finding and killing fish was his only concern, customer comfort and wellbeing were not on his agenda. I never once heard Robert say, "catch fish" instead it was "kill, slay, or annihilate," and it was never "fish," it was always "f'ing fish". The six guests on Robert's boat included the four Iron Men and two Californians, Jeremy, a former army ranger, now a periodontist, and his Dad, Frank, a 70-year old weight lifter.

Robert was a big, 38-year old with a loud, booming voice, baby face, mega-type-A personality, red hair, and quick, hearty laugh. He was extraordinarily competitive and sought to out-fish any other boat in Alaska every day out. Robert's passion for fishing was readily evident, and he almost drooled when pontificating on this subject. When not working as a charter captain, Robert dives on the floor of the Gulf of Alaska at depths of 150' - 180' for sea anemones and sea cucumbers. He told us he plans to crew on one of the crab ships in northern Alaska in January.

Henry, age 23, looks like a Native American gansta rapper, but with a stentorian, radio voice. I could never reconcile his voice with his physical appearance, although he spoke infrequently. Henry was medium height but with biceps roughly the size of my torso. He could maneuver around the boat in the roughest of conditions like a gazelle. Neither Henry nor Robert could be mistaken for warm and fuzzy kind of people. Robert opened up the first day with an ersatz apology, "I might get a little gruff with you guys when I bark out orders, but it's only because I want to help you kill f'ing fish." We got a better flavor for this warning when he shouted, "Get out of my f'ing chair. No one sits in the Captain's chair but me! Har! Har!" His outbursts were followed with hearty laughter, apparently to let us know no hard feelings were attached.

Day 1

We roared northwest out of Sitka Channel towards our first fishing spot. We motored at close to full speed, 27 mph, for 30 - 40 miles. The scenery was uniformly spectacular, with snow-capped peaks rising steeply from the waterline in virtually every direction. While in the protected waters near Sitka the ride wasn't too bad. Once we ventured into the Gulf of Alaska, it was extremely rough with 12' swells. Robert likes to fish in places where no other charter or commercial boats are fishing. After an hour and a half crashing through the waves, we arrived at a spot for King Salmon. Henry had the fishing gear readied by the time we stopped, and Robert briefed us.

Here are the basics of killing King Salmon according to Robert: "Cast out a bit, then pull your sinker back in so the bait doesn't tangle on the way down. Keep your thumb on the reel as the bait is sinking because you get a lot of hits on the way down. Once at the desired depth, usually 100'-150', reel gently (reel with feel) with the tip of your rod pointed down the direction of your line. If you feel a bite then reel like a mother f'er! Once you've got a King on the line, follow it wherever it goes. Walk around the boat with it if need be and take your time." We got pretty good at choreographing the movement around the boat with a King on the line going over, under, and around the other five fishing lines in the water. One definitely knows when a King Salmon is on the line.

We caught our limit of King Salmon, one per fisherman per day, within 45 minutes. They were all in the 30 – 45 lb range. The smallest of the Kings was larger than any we caught during our previous six Alaskan fishing trips. Lamentably, three of the six guests were now seasick. Fortunately, I was not one of them. It was extremely rough and difficult to stabilize one's self on the rolling deck. We then went out to even rougher waters, about 20 miles off the coast, in search of "chicken" halibut (under 50 lbs). The three sick guys were in absolute misery, but we started catching fish in abundance. I caught three small halibut in the first ten minutes. For the next hour there wasn't a three-minute interval when someone didn't have a fish on the line, and many times when all three of us were trying to land our catch. We caught numerous lingcod (between 30-60 lbs), a mighty tasty fish, but they are now protected, so we were in catch and release mode. Lingcod are prehistoric looking creatures with a giant mouth and a long muscled body. A bowling ball would easily fit inside the open jaw of a 50 lb lingcod. We caught many undesirable, inedible, or out of season fish including skate, ratfish, dog sharks, and rockfish.

Henry and Robert were exemplary in coaching us, gaffing the fish, re-baiting our hooks, and getting us untangled when needed. Robert was meticulous in keeping the bait (herring) on the hook fresh and instructed, "If your bait doesn't look exactly like it was when we put it on, then change it out, because King will only hit on perfect, clean bait." They would bleed the fish we caught claiming it makes for tastier dining. Henry would have the decks cleared and cleaned of blood immediately after each landing. In our prior trips with Cliff II, we served as our own deckhands and were accustomed to using a net to bring the fish onboard. Instead, Henry would lean out over the gunnels and gaff the fish. It was only with the King Salmon that he would use the net. Once on board, Robert and Henry would kill the fish with a ball bat and way too much enthusiasm. By early afternoon it was obvious even to Robert that his three seasick patrons had endured enough, and we headed back to Sitka.

Robert was content when we got back, as the other charter captains reported their lack of success in catching Kings or anything. That might have been a function of the others choosing not to go out in those seas. Robert was dismissive of his competitors, "I don't share any f'ing information with f'ing anyone. They're a bunch of lazy f'ers, let them f'ing find their own f'ing fish."

Upon returning to Sitka harbor, we were greeted by a huge harbor seal with a head the size of a truck tire. It was flipping a 100 lb halibut around like a toy doll. Robert said the harbor seal once jumped up on the dock and chased him. I asked, "What happens if he catches you?"

Robert gazed down at me with pity for having deigned ask such a dumb question and said, "You f'ing die a horrible f'ing death." After day one, the three healthy guys enjoyed fishing with Robert and Henry, the three seasick sufferers did not.

We returned to our lodge for recuperation, dinner, refreshments, and poker. We had been pretty spoiled in our previous trips, having the

Meyers Chuck resort entirely to ourselves. We had become accustomed to being a self-contained unit in our travels, and we didn't warm up quickly to outsiders. In Sitka we stayed in a distinct portion of the modest lodgings, but we ate with other guests. A new group of six came in while we were dining, and one of their number approached our table, rudely intruded on our conversation and said, "Hi, I'm a doctor, I live in California." What a dick.

Day 2

Bonine offered the promise of relief to the seasickness sufferers, and we were ready to go. Once again we raced to Robert's "kill zone." Bruce asked Robert where we were headed, and he said, "Out to kill some f'ing fish." Bruce was seeking a little more precision with this query. Bruce and Robert, both hyper type A's, were not bonding well. The seas were calmer so the early morning ride wasn't as jarring. Henry showed us the tattoo he acquired the night before with a blue Chevy emblem affixed to his right bicep. There is nothing quite as satisfying as seeing a counterculture kid permanently sporting a symbol of American capitalism.

We caught our limit of Kings in an hour, all in the 30-45 lb range, and motored to different waters to catch chicken halibut and Coho Salmon (aka Silvers). After an uncharacteristic paucity of action, Robert commanded, "Let's roll and go after the monster halibuts." We set out due west 20 miles further off shore. Robert was truly a man in his element sitting in his captain's chair, one hand on the steering wheel, throttle at full speed, crashing over the swells, and telling fishing stories his adoring guests absorbed in earnest. All that was lacking were speakers blaring Wagner's "Ride of the Valkyries."

Robert let it be known that he gets more and bigger fish than any other charter captain in Sitka. When asked why, he explained, "I pay attention to the details." Then he held up a package of fishhooks and exclaimed with gusto, "These aren't any ordinary fishhooks. I only use super, f'ing, laser-sharp fish hooks going after the big buts." He spat out the explanation with such passion that it left us speechless. He uses special herring for bait that is farm-raised to be of uniform size, and electrocuted at precisely the right time so their skin tightens perfectly at the moment of their death.

When asked if he ever had any women guests on his boat. He said, "Yeah, yesterday," glaring at the previous day's seasick patrons! "Har! har!" He told about a Mormon father and son combo on his boat. The Dad asked if he and Henry would take some of their fish in lieu of a tip. Robert said, "Can you f'ing believe that? What kind of f'ing moron offers f'ing fish to a fishing guide?" Robert didn't tell stories so much as he spat them out. He then told us about an old guy onboard that he was worried might fall overboard, so they put him in a survival suit. When the unfortunate fellow had to take a crap, he failed to get the survival suit totally removed, and the back of it covered the crapper whilst he was squeezing off a few pungent missiles. He then spent the rest of the day cohabitating with a suit full of crap. Robert's enthusiastic storytelling had us howling, and it took our minds off the pounding we were taking in the boat.

While motoring out to the location where the 200-400 lb. halibut supposedly reside, Jeremy, the periodontist, commented, "You know, the smaller halibut actually taste better, and once a halibut reaches about 80 lbs it becomes a female and produces eggs, so it would be okay with me if we released any big halibut we might catch."

Robert overheard this tidbit and exclaimed with vigor, "Bullshit! If we catch any big halibut, they're coming on board, and we're going to f'ing kill the f'ers and eat them!" One would never mistake Robert for a tree hugger.

Once at our destination, Henry had the appropriate gear prepared, and we were ready to fish. When going after big buts one uses a short, stout rod, heavy-duty line, a 10 lb. sinker, and about 3-5 lbs of bait. Our bait consisted of cuts of pink and silver salmon and entrails saved from yesterday's catch. One drops this concoction to the ocean floor about 430 ft deep, brings it up about 10 ft, and waits.

If you've got a halibut, it will suck on the bait, spit it out, suck, spit, repeat, repeat, and then it takes off hopefully with a hook firmly implanted in its mouth. Robert's instructions for us were to then, "Reel like a mother f'er." The only drawback to this arrangement is that when you get a bite, reel it up, and find out you've got a dog shark or lingcod, you feel cheated. We caught the crap out of dog sharks at 400' depth. Robert would gaff the shark and play with it. He would take a 30 lb shark and fling it in the air off the side of the boat, then gaff it again, then fling it up and so forth, until it was suitably bloody, then he would discard it in the ocean. It reminded us of Tiger Woods bouncing a golf ball off the head of a pitching wedge. Robert declared, "I hate f'ing sharks. I bloody them up a bit, so bigger creatures will eat them."

We ended the day with a few modestly sized halibut, some yellow-eyed snapper, and a few black bass and headed back to Sitka. At the end of the day we enjoyed the company of a large albatross. It would eat any bait that floated to the surface, take off, fly around, and return to watch us fish. It was a treat to watch the goony bird take off by running on the water with its wings elevated, then glide a few feet above the sea for several minutes before landing and starting over again. Surely, a similar sight served as inspiration to Samuel Coleridge in creating the *Rime of the Ancient Mariner*.

Day 3

For a change of pace we headed southwest out of Sitka and traveled the obligatory hour and a half to the fishing zone. Within the first hour I landed a 60+ lb King Salmon, truly a trophy fish, and quite a thrill. Robert provided superb coaching during the time it took to bring it in. He said it was the biggest King he had seen yet this season.

After catching our limit of Kings, we again headed to a location in search of the giant halibut but were again unsuccessful. We kept coming up with sharks, and it is tiresome hauling anything up from 400'. Robert said, "This isn't working." So off we went to a new spot. Robert was never niggardly with fuel, bait, or effort.

Our travels took us past Cape Edgecumbe, about 30 miles due west of Sitka and the western most point of land reaching into the Pacific Ocean from SE Alaska to South America. According to the owner of the resort, Cape Edgecumbe is the reason Sitka is the best place on earth for King Salmon as all salmon traveling north or south in the Pacific must eventually pass this Cape. It is home to confused waters, as Robert called them. Again, our energies were primarily focused on trying to avoid broken vertebrae whilst crashing about in the rough water. Henry would occasionally nap while standing during these interludes, an amazing feat in itself.

Offshore of the Cape we anchored and set out fishing for small halibut and hit the jackpot. We quickly got our limit and were bringing in an assortment of shark, lingcod, Silvers, red snapper, and rockfish. We also started catching more large Kings, but regretfully we were in catch and release mode. Robert called Henry's Dad, a commercial fisherman, to inform him of his find of Kings. On the radio, however, he spoke in code. Usually, when another charter captain would call Robert to inquire about fish locations, Robert would say on air, "Not much happening here," then off air he would say, "Stupid f'ers, they think I'm going to tell them where the f'ing fish are?" The intensity of Robert's cursing made my drill sergeant sound like the virtuous maiden in a Zane Grey story.

We enjoyed a close-up view of a humpback whale sounding 40 yards off the stern of the boat. We had seen whale spouts on several occasions off in the distance, but this was the first time we were as near to one. Robert said they often see a lot of killer whales, but alas we didn't.

On the way back in to port, Robert informed us that we would have Franklin* as our captain the next day. No one was heartbroken. The resort owner runs three similar boats, each accommodates six fishermen. He described Robert as all business. In contrast, Franklin was a normal human being who treats guests like guests and helps you catch some fish.

Day 4

We arrived at the dock at 6 am, bypassed Robert's boat and went aboard Franklin's rig. The boat was the same, but the differences were noticeable. Cleaning supplies and fishing tackle littered the cabin floor,

Alan and the 65 lb salmon

the vessel wasn't spotless, and the gear wasn't ready for fishing. Greg introduced himself and Troy*, his college-aged deck hand. We then embarked on a mellow day.

Franklin followed the herd and took us to a location shared with ten other charter boats, so we had plenty of company. Alan caught a trophy 65+ lb. King after a lengthy battle, the highlight of which was when the giant jumped vertically out of the water no more than 5 feet away from the boat. We quickly caught our limit and moved on to a spot for small halibut. We caught a few Silver and lingcod, but few "buts." With Robert if we had a 15-minute lull, we motored to a new locale. With Franklin, it was, "Maybe it'll get better." By day's end when it was time to head in the seas had gotten quite rough with swells taller than our boat with a storm heading our way. Rather than crash full speed through them, Franklin took the swells at a 45-degree angle at about 15 mph making for a much more comfortable, less back breaking, but slower, trip.

We later concluded that Sitka offered a superior fishing experience, but it didn't have the same magic as Meyers Chuck. At MC we were the only guests, the isolation of the place was more charming, and most importantly the MC hospitality was unsurpassed as they made us feel special and part of their family. With Robert we felt like unsuspecting members of the crew on *The Deadliest Catch*.

The Iron Men will gather till the last two no longer stand.

FROM LEFT TOP: Charlie, Sally, Helen
FROM LEFT BELOW: author, Bill
1948

CHAPTER 9

Bowling Green
1945 – 1953

Like many returning World War II veterans, my Dad bought a new Bell & Howell movie camera to record the activities of his family in living color. One summer evening Mom, pregnant with our soon-to-be sister, Sally, was out for the evening at an Eastern Star meeting, taking a breather from the care of two little boys. Dad decided it would be a perfect time to capture some family memories. I was 3 and Bill was 4, and the scene was our tiny living room. Dad placed his camera on a tripod along with a set of floodlights that, when illuminated, would have caused the town's streetlights to dim had our little hamlet possessed such civic beacons.

Bill and I would crawl onto the back of the couch, bounce onto the seat like it was a trampoline, jump to the floor, roll around, giggle, and do it over again. Dad enjoyed tinkering with his new camera, and Bill and I enjoyed being the stars of our home movie. On my last trip, I lost my balance, fell back through the closed living room picture window, and landed in a bush in the front yard amidst the broken glass. The good news was that Dad got it on film, and I was unscathed. The bad news was that Dad had a whole lot of explaining to do when Mom came home that evening.

I consider myself lucky to have grown up in Bowling Green, MO, a town of 2,800. Dad was the band director at the high school and the music teacher for all grades and known to several generations of band members as Prof Wells. He started teaching before the war and resumed his position upon returning after four years of active service. We lived a few blocks from the high school, whose activities dominated our social calendar.

Bill and I would shoot baskets in our underwear, to more closely resemble the uniform worn by the Bowling Green Bobcats, using a coat hanger hung over a closet door as an indoor hoop and fight over which local high school basketball player we would call ourselves. The biggest star at the time was Cotton Fitzsimmons, who later went on to fame as an NBA coach. Bill always prevailed and got to be Cotton.

At the end of the school year one of Dad's duties was to drive a school bus somewhere out in the country to store it for the summer. Dad would drive, and Bill and I would ride along with the entire bus serving as our playground. We thought then, as we continue to this day, that our Dad must be the most important man in the whole wide world.

Before he married, Dad led a professional 12-piece swing combo, and traveled throughout the Midwest. He had perfect pitch and could play virtually every instrument well, but the clarinet was his specialty. He could listen once to a complex musical piece and write the music for each part in the arrangement. He could turn notes, bars, and treble clefs into music with the ease of Stephen King turning words into stories.

While he was a talented man, he was the antithesis of an outdoorsman. He often felt a need to compensate for this, and, for some unexplainable reason, he decided it would be a good idea to take his 6 and 7-year old sons on a hike to St. Clement, MO. When presented with the prospect of a grand adventure with Dad, I'm sure Bill and I said, "Gee Dad that sounds great!" So one summer morning Dad, Bill, and I trekked off on the 5-mile journey to the neighboring town. We walked about half way to our destination, stopped at a cemetery, and called it a day. We were tired, thirsty, and hungry. Somehow, Mom found us and pulled up in the old family sedan to retrieve us.

Bill

My brother Bill has always been one of my biggest heroes. He is one of the kindest human beings ever to grace the planet earth. Bluebirds land on his shoulder and tweet, "Hey Bill, hope you're having a great day." Thus, it was somewhat out of character that he spent his formative years trying first to kill me and then relenting and saving me.

One of our chores was to take empty milk bottles to the corner grocery store and return with milk. Bill pulled me in a wagon along with our cargo as we undertook this important mission. On one such trip he turned the corner too sharply upending me amidst a pile of broken glass, severing an artery in my left wrist. He tossed me back into the wagon, hauled me back to our house at a dead run where Mom somehow staunched the gushing stream of blood and rushed me to the Pike County Hospital where they patched me up.

One afternoon after a heavy rain, Bill and I were walking to the same corner store jumping into every rain puddle in our path testing our rubber galoshes. Bill pointed out a large, promising body of dark water, suggesting it would be a good one for me. I jumped in with both feet, anticipating the splash from a shallow pool, and instead plunged into storm water over my head. Bill pulled me out, attempted to clean me up, and we resumed our play.

My maternal grandparents lived in a small, two-story farmhouse in West Plains, MO. It had a wraparound front porch where we spent many pleasant evenings playing checkers and card games with my Grandfather and snuggling with my Grandmother on their cozy porch swing. They had a chicken house in their backyard, and it was a treat for Bill and me to collect eggs for the morning's breakfast, except for the times when a black snake would compete for the tasty victuals. Most notably, the house had a gravity feed heating system. One Thanksgiving evening Bill laid a trap for me by removing the floor grate in the upstairs bathroom, placing a rug over the opening, and beckoning me into his snare. Thus beckoned, I stepped on the rug and fell through the ceiling and showered my parents, grandparents, aunts and uncles assembled in the dining room below with plaster and debris. I caught myself with my elbows, so only my legs and torso dangled through the ceiling, but it was a disturbance sufficient to attract everyone's attention. My grandfather was a kind, but stern, man, and he wasn't pleased. I was not privy to the subsequent adult conversations, but I'm sure it didn't consist of Grandpa saying, "Hey, Charlie, bring the kids over any time."

We moved to a nicer house in Bowling Green when I was five years old. I used to think of the former house as a palace, perfect in every way.

Later in adulthood I had occasion to visit the old homestead and observed that it was on a dirt road, about the size of a single car garage, and would more commonly be described as a shack. The new house was on a paved road and afforded Bill and me a nearby lot where we could play baseball.

Our new home was close to the county fairgrounds. During the county fair time, Bill and I would sell popcorn to earn money that we would promptly spend on candy and amusement rides at the fair. One such evening, after we collected our earnings, Bill suggested I ride on the Ferris wheel. I said, "That thing looks pretty rickety to me." Bill assured me it was safe. While waiting to board, one of the empty cars above crashed to the ground in front of us signaling it was time to move on to other fun-seeking opportunities.

In an early display of entrepreneurialism and idiocy, I charged kids a nickel apiece to throw a rock at the storm windows stored in our one car, detached garage. My cost accounting skills left a lot to be desired, but I was able to earn a few nickels. An equally mischievous neighbor girl, Tally Lee, and I went into her basement and opened all the cans and Mason jars of stored vegetables and jams to see what was inside. These costly misdeeds did not endear me to my parents nor to Tally Lee's, particularly to her Dad. Claude was the Warren Buffet of Bowling Green and owned the local Dodge dealership and the Moon Wink's Café among other enterprises. He was older than my parents, almost grandparent like. Since Tally Lee was his only child, he treated me like a son, and his expressions of disapproval made an immediate, but not lasting, impact.

One day while ambling around town, I thought it would be a good idea to moon a few passing cars. I quickly tired of this little exhibition and moved on to other tasks before heading home kicking stones and such, oblivious to the impending doom, as news of my deeds traveled faster than I. Mom rarely used corporal punishment, but she would give the "Look" that caused far greater pain than a mere swat. Once deployed, the power of the "Look" would last for days before temptation would once again lead me astray.

Mom always had an aversion to getting into any body of water unsuitable for wading. She said it was because her Dad tried to teach her to swim by throwing her into a lake. I often thought that this might not have been a teaching occasion but refrained from voicing that sentiment. In a similar vein, it wasn't until adulthood that it occurred to me Bill's role in continually placing me in harm's way might not have been random. It is quite plausible he was only doing Mom's bidding. But I was too cute to kill.

Helen and Charlie

My mother, Helen Elaine Wells, was a pretty woman. She was tall, 5'8", thin, sported striking auburn hair, and carried herself with a level of elegance that belied our modest circumstances. She was never catty, never gossiped, rarely got upset, and was a genuinely nice person. Her oldest son took after her in that regard.

She was the oldest of five children, born and raised in Redford, MO, a tiny burg in southeast Missouri that no longer exists, even as a spot on the road. Her Dad had been a WWI doughboy who later became a teacher/principal working his way up from one-room schoolhouses to become the high school principal in West Plains, MO. Mom and her siblings picked cotton during each harvest season to help bolster the family coffers. She graduated from Central Methodist College in Fayette, MO in 1937 at the age of 17. This accomplishment was a function of both her intellect and the harsh realities of the depression. By age 18 she was teaching high school in a small town in mid-Missouri to classrooms filled by students, many older than she was.

With four younger siblings still at home, her Dad welcomed the prospect of having his oldest daughter helping support the family during the depths of the depression. Mom had other ideas, as she had met the dapper Charlie, six years her senior, and the leader of the Charlie Armstead swing band. Dad was a minor celebrity in the world of mid-Missouri music in the 1930's and also attended Central Methodist. In addition to being an accomplished musician, Charlie raced speedboats on the Mississippi River, flew a bi-plane, wore zoot suits, and, most egregiously, called fellow musicians "cool cats." It took more than a few years, and a few grandchildren, before Mom's Dad warmed up to

Charlie, but in time he did. Mom was the quiet, cerebral partner in the duo, and Dad was the chatty peacock. Years later my marriage would replicate this theme.

Travels Around Town

Bill and I traveled extensively in and around Bowling Green. We would chase one another through clotheslines laden with clean smelling laundry and play hide and seek in the cornfields surrounding the town. We'd stop at gas stations and collect road maps and gather railroad timetables from the tiny train station in town. We once took the eleven-mile train trip to the nearby Mississippi river town of Louisiana, MO, so we were vaguely aware of a world outside our little village.

We occasionally circumnavigated the highway running around town with our little red wagon collecting returnable pop and beer bottles for spending money. In preparation for later life, we also collected beer cans, most memorably Griesedick Brothers. Unbelievably, it was pronounced exactly the way one might think. We'd use our hard earned currency injudiciously purchasing tasty treats from the bakery or ice cream store on the town square. In 1950 one could go to the State Theatre, see a double feature, a serial cliffhanger, and a cartoon for 14 cents and then purchase a banana split at the Princess Ice Cream Parlor for a dime.

As everyone knows who has ever been on or coached a little league baseball team, the most inept kid is banished to right field, offering fewer opportunities to screw up. One could argue with this logic, as even good 7-8 year old ballplayers have difficulty pulling the ball, but that was the way it was and may always be, as convention is a powerful force. So on the few occasions I was actually in the game, I found myself contemplating life's mysteries in right field. Bill could be found on the pitcher's mound or at shortstop. Games were played on a field near the county fairgrounds, and cornfields defined the perimeter of the outfield, typically in full flower by mid summer.

One evening I was standing in right field, my parents were dutifully sitting in the stands, Bill was pitching, and the game was barely illuminated by a handful of 40 watt bulbs on poles in the outfield. I was certain no one was paying any attention to me, it was too dark for anyone to see into the outfield, and I needed to pee. I meandered into the cornfield, thought I was shielded from view, and took care of business. Apparently my absence was noted. One of my Dad's many fine qualities was that he had a pleasing speaking voice. People often said he sounded like the famous crooner Bing Crosby. On this particular evening Dad's ordinarily mellifluous offerings came out as a shriek along the lines of, "Jesus Christ Chuck! What on earth were you thinking?"

One day while wandering into the countryside surrounding BG, Bill and I encountered a group of older boys who were catching snakes. They told us that one of the snakes in their possession was a Blue Racer that could travel faster than any boy, and, if bitten, suffering and death would quickly follow. We made a hasty retreat unwilling to test the veracity of their claim.

My school was an old two story brick building with a long metal tube suspended from the back of the second floor that served as the fire escape. We would climb in it and slide down while others would beat on it with sticks. The playground was made of tarred gravel, but one could occasionally find specks of a gold colored rock that we surmised was the real deal, and we'd pretend to be gold miners, as we'd scour the gravel in search of treasure.

An old man lived near us who made toys for neighborhood kids in his woodworking shop. My favorite was a pine replica of the WWII M-1 Garand rifle. It was intricately crafted, and I don't remember ever having a more wonderful toy. A bully once took the rifle away from me, but he returned it after I hit him in the head with a brick.

An old lady lived down the street from us, and she would occasionally invite us into her house for sorghum candy. It was a little creepy to follow her into her abode, because it was dark and dank smelling. She always wore a black dress, and her white hair was tied in a bun. She looked like the witch pictured in the Hansel & Gretel storybook, and we were frightened that she would shovel us into her stove. But the smell and anticipated taste of that warm, sticky sorghum candy would overpower any reservations, an early lesson in life's unending contest between fear and greed. She would produce long strands of the sugary delicacy, lay it out on waxed paper, then slice it into small segments, and place it in our outstretched greedy, little hands.

Bless His Little Heart

As one might expect in a town as small as Bowling Green, everyone knew everyone else. This seemed perfectly normal to an 8-year old, but may have been a bit stifling to the adults. This level of familiarity contributed to a common language used in the community. When confronted with a child's actions, either sweet or mischievous, every adult woman in town would say, "Well, bless his little heart." This always struck me as a bit affected, as often what they undoubtedly meant was, "I'm tired of that little shit's antics." Whatever the intent, the phrase is now imbedded within my psyche, and I find myself uttering this inane phrase with the same level of insincerity as my forbearers.

Minnie Pearl

Marge and Vivian Williams were our next-door neighbors, close friends of my parents, and surrogate parents. Marge operated a beauty shop in the basement of her home, and Viv was the county tax collector. Marge was a small, pretty woman with a raspy, cigarette strained voice. Even though they had a high school age daughter, Suzy, they still doted on us. Viv partnered with my Dad to buy the vacant lot between our two houses, so Bill and I could use it as our baseball field.

Marge attended Belmont College in Nashville, TN, and her roommate was none other than Sarah Ophelia Colley, who would later find fame and fortune as Minnie Pearl. In 1953 Minnie Pearl was about as big a celebrity as any of us could imagine. She was a comedienne who appeared on the *Grand Ole Opry* and later on *Hee Haw*. Her signature line was a big "How Deeeeee!" and she wore a store bought straw hat with the $1.98 price tag still attached. Minnie and her husband flew to Bowling Green on their private plane to appear at the Pike County fair and then later came to Marge and Viv's house for a visit. An appearance by the newly coronated Queen Elizabeth might have been a bigger deal, but not by much. We were among those honored to meet Marge's guest, who turned out to be a pleasant lady expressing a sincere interest in our hum-drum, provincial lives.

Telephones and radio

Like most small towns, Bowling Green had an all-knowing telephone operator. This was before rotary dial phones, so to make a call one picked up the handset, waited a few seconds, and the operator would come on the line and the conversation would go like this:

Chuck: "Hello, Gladys. I'd like to speak to Bonham Ray, please."

Operator: "He's not home now, but I just saw him and his Mom walk past the drug store. If I see them again, I'll tell them you called. Why don't you try later today?"

Chuck: "Thank you Ma'am. I will. Have a nice day."

Cell phones can't begin to replace that kind of intel.

While we didn't have television, we did have a big radio, about the size of an armoire. On Sunday evening the family unit, like millions of others around America, would gather, sit around the radio, and listen to our favorite shows: *Our Miss Brooks*, *Jack Benny*, and *The Lone Ranger.*

Earl* and Priscilla*

Earl* ran the only funeral home in town, Priscilla* taught first grade and was my teacher, and they were close friends of my parents. They didn't have children so Bill, Sally, and I were the beneficiaries of their many kindnesses. They were among the first people in town to own a television, and we were astounded at our ability to watch the Brooklyn Dodgers play baseball on this amazing device. Their living quarters were situated above the mortuary, so exploring was fairly harrowing and exciting. Long drapes were always closed, keeping the downstairs rooms perpetually dark. We often explored a sterile, tiled room with a porcelain table that we presumed was where they snipped the toes off of dead people to drain their blood. Earl was a big, jolly man who lived large. He wore flashy Hawaiian shirts, was loud and boisterous, and always drove the fanciest car in town.

After we moved from Bowling Green to Prairie Village, KS, Earl came through town on a few occasions. When I was 10, I traveled with him back to the old hometown. I was most impressed by his new black and pink 1955 Ford with power windows and by the steak dinner he purchased for me in a restaurant, a rare treat. I later learned that Earl and Priscilla divorced. Mom remained close friends with Priscilla until her death.

It was only after my Mom's death in 2006 that I heard a different slant on Earl. I stopped through Bowling Green to express my condolences to a childhood friend, whose mother had recently passed. We started playing the game, "Whatever happened to so and so?" when she said, "You know the real story about Earl, don't you?" I pleaded ignorance, and she went on to tell me the following account:

"In the mid 1950's, shortly after you (the Wells' family) moved from Bowling Green, a murder occurred. An elderly Negro man's body was found stuffed in a well on a farm owned by Earl. No one was ever charged with the killing, but my Dad swore to his dying day that everyone in town knew exactly what happened. Allegedly, the man unwittingly walked upon a scene with Earl engaged in a homosexual act. Earl killed the man rather than risking having his sexual predilections become known. He later left town, and no one in town heard from him again. Priscilla took great pains the remainder of her life to prevent having her name associated with her former husband."

Unfortunately, I heard this story after the death of my parents, precluding my ability to make further inquiries.

Race

Bowling Green is the county seat of Pike County, a slaveholding county prior to the Civil War. Many residents often referred to the region as "Little Dixie." While some people don't think of Missouri as a southern state, Bowling Green was a distinctly southern town, and I've often been mocked for my semi-southern speech patterns. However, we weren't totally in keeping with local traditions as we were one of the few families in town limited to one first name. Bill, Chuck, and Sally stood out in contrast to Joe Paul, Lee Philip, Carol Earl, Billy Beau, and Skip-to-ma Lou.

As a child I was completely and naively unaware of the presence of the significant Negro population in Bowling Green. Our family employed a Negro cleaning lady/laundress, which is pretty remarkable considering we were a family of five living on a teacher's salary. Other than Alvessa, who came to our house once a week, black people were virtually invisible to me. Black children attended separate schools and lived in separate neighborhoods. At age eight, I couldn't begin to tell you where they were located, even in a town as small at BG. The races lived in two separate worlds. It wasn't as though we lived in a ritzy part of town. For starters no ritzy part of town existed. Mom continued to stay in touch with Alvessa and her family for many years, and I later learned that all three of her children graduated from college and went on to successful professional careers.

Bowling Green, like many small towns throughout America, was part Mayberry, part *To Kill a Mockingbird*, and part *Ozzie and Harriett*. But in the eyes of two little boys in 1952, it was nothing less than the center of the known universe and the most perfect place in the world.

Ben age 10

CHAPTER 10

Baseball

My brother Bill and I hail from a long line of baseball fans. Harry Caray brought virtually every Cardinal game on the radio to our great grandmother, Sarah Jane Harrison, in West Plains, MO, until her passing at age 96 in 1963. Her daughter, Mayme Welsh, was also a diehard Redbird fan and listened nightly to the broadcasts until her death at age 99 in 1993. She was blind during her last years, her radio was her constant companion, and the highlight of her day was the Cardinal broadcast. One day she insisted that my aunt take her radio and sell it at the yard sale she was having. Mayme died two days later.

Growing up in Bowling Green, MO I, too, became a Cardinal fan. Each summer Dad would take us to Sportsman's Park to see the Cardinals and their stars of the eras: Stan "the Man" Musial, Red Schoendist, Enos Slaughter, Ken Boyer, the Dean brothers, and other boyhood idols. We also attended St. Louis Browns games, and they shared the stadium with the more popular Cardinals. The hapless Brown's only claim to fame occurred in 1944 when they lost the World Series to their crosstown rivals in six games, the last World Series contest played entirely in one stadium. Should anyone question where I was in the family pecking order, Bill received a Cardinal ball cap for Christmas, and I received one from the soon-to-be-defunct Browns.

After we moved to Prairie Village, we continued to follow the Cardinals through their extensive radio network. With the A's arrival in Kansas City in 1955 our loyalties quickly shifted to our new hometown team. By the time we were 11 and 12, Bill and I would catch multiple bus rides to Municipal Stadium to root for the home team.

We were fortunate to have an abundance of boys our age in our immediate neighborhood sharing our passion for baseball. Each summer we organized a Whiffle ball league of four teams, three boys each. Our games were played every morning in the Henry's small backyard. Any ball that went over the Allen's* fence was lost, as he was an asshole and wouldn't let us go into his yard to retrieve balls. A ball over the Shaw's fence was a homerun, and any ball that hit the Henry's house was a foul ball. Somehow, we had it figured out and kept statistics and daily standings.

A boy a bit younger than the youngest in our league started hanging around and asked if he could play. We told him he couldn't, as he was too little. Cheated from the chance to achieve Whiffle ball glory, the lad, Tom Watson, proved resilient and later found fame and fortune as a hall of fame golfer.

We had zero parental involvement in our games, with one notable exception. A fight broke out among two of the older boys, Steve and Doug. Mrs. Henry must have seen or heard enough to alert her to the disturbance and came running out of her house with a golf club in hand. I'm not sure how she made her club selection, but I believe she chose a driver for the occasion. Her son Steve was the offender, and Mrs. Henry chased her wayward offspring around the neighborhood, club in hand. I don't think she ever caught him, but the fight was over and the game resumed.

Mornings were reserved for Whiffle ball, but early afternoons were devoted to "tennis baseball." We set boundaries in the asphalt parking lot of Porter grade school located across the street from our home. The advantage of this variation of the game was that we could throw a tennis ball about as fast as a baseball, it was relatively easy to throw curveballs, and we could play with a catcher behind the batter without a mask. We surmised that this would help develop our batting skills when we played "real" baseball.

We all took these games seriously, but none more so than Mike Curley. Mike was a big kid who lived several blocks away and was a regular in our games. Our basic summer outfit during the era consisted of an unadorned white tee shirt, blue jeans, and high top Converse sneakers. I don't believe shorts had yet been invented. One hot, summer afternoon we were playing on the asphalt parking lot when Mike hit a fair ball sufficiently deep for a single, with a chance to stretch it into a double. Mike went for it, the throw was on time, and he slid into the unused glove that served as second base. He actually slid on burning hot asphalt to gain an extra base in an inconsequential tennis baseball game. He instantly gained the life long admiration of all who witnessed this noble deed paying only the small price of leaving several square feet of skin on the pavement along with a six foot wet spot marking the trail of his slide.

One summer afternoon, Bill and I were among the tiny crowd watching the hapless A's play the equally hapless Red Sox. Ted Williams was still playing and Bill snagged a foul ball lined off the bat of the future hall of famer. In his excitement Bill bumped an old lady in his pursuit of the ball, making it all the more notable a treasure. Bill cherished that souvenir until it disappeared, a casualty of one of Mom's cleaning frenzies.

One of the many wonderful things about growing up in a major league city in the 1950's was that baseball players were semi-normal people and weren't yet segregated from common folk by uncommon wealth. Many of the players worked off-season jobs to make ends meet and frequently came into contact with regular citizens. Several of the Kansas City A's lived in Prairie Village.

On Halloween it was an extra thrill to plan our "trick'r treating" itinerary to include the nearby homes of Elmer Valo or Hank Bauer. But our favorite was the famed Harry Chiti, a weak hitting catcher who played for the A's from 1958 – 1960. He would answer the door of his home and hand out candy to his adoring fans. Harry later achieved fame, or at least notoriety, when in 1962 he was acquired by the expansion New York Mets from the Cleveland Indians for a "player to be named later." However, he was sent back to the Indians after 15 games as the "player to be named later" and thus became the first and only player ever to be traded for himself. I'm not certain if Harry was later responsible for writing the song "I am My Own Grandpa," but it's possible. Our tenuous claim to fame was to have once lived within a few blocks of Mr. Chiti.

My lackluster career in organized baseball began with a blow to the head. Bill started playing in little league a year before I did, and I was able to latch on to the highly coveted batboy assignment for his team. My season was shortened when I stood too close to a batter taking practice swings in the on deck circle and received a direct hit to an unprotected head. My parents oft explained away much of my subsequent behavior as a consequence of this beaning.

Due to my diminutive stature, my only asset was a small strike zone. I was the little league version of Eddie Gaedel, the midget Bill Veeck introduced to major league baseball. During my final season, I walked five times in eight at bats. The coach would occasionally put me in the game as a pinch hitter with instructions to stand still as a stone and to not remotely consider swinging. His intentions couldn't have been more obvious had he sent me to the plate without a bat. But his actions were understandable, as my only hit of the season occurred when I came to bat with the coach's son on third base. I missed the sign for a suicide squeeze bunt, instead swung away, lined a double down the left field line, and narrowly avoided decapitating the oncoming runner sliding into home. This did not endear me to the coach and was an ignominious end to my baseball career.

For two summers in high school, Bill and I coached younger boys in a league called Midget K. Kids who failed to make one of the competitive teams had the option of signing up for Midget K. We had the 8-9 year olds on Monday, Wednesday, and Friday and the 10-11 year olds on Tuesday, Thursday, and Saturday mornings. We were paid $30 per week, supervised a bunch of kids eager to learn baseball, and played penny poker with the other coaches during rainouts, a pretty sweet deal.

My teams were the Tigers (little kids) and the Dodgers (older kids). We spent half of the morning throwing batting practice, hitting grounders or fly balls, and teaching fundamentals. Then we would play games. A few of the kids were decent and perhaps had been unfairly cut in their tryouts. Most were dismal athletes but still enjoyed their baseball mornings. The coach of the team in the field would umpire by standing behind the pitcher to call balls and strikes and also to call plays at the bases, foul balls, and anything that came up. We adopted a generous strike zone in order to occasionally get the ball in play. With little coaching each of the boys quickly mastered the art of looking quizzically at their empty glove after a ground ball rolled between their legs.

The only drawback to this otherwise perfect job was interaction with the moms. Some of the sweetest little guys bore the burden of the most odious mothers. We were effective at controlling bad behavior from the boys but were not prepared for the meddlesome moms. Many would attend every game, complain that their little darling wasn't getting sufficient playing time, should be pitching or playing shortstop, and curse the coach/umpire for bad calls. Some were in complete denial that they may have borne unto this world a child with little athletic promise. We considered the summer a great success if each kid had fun, got to roll around in the dirt, and ended the season a little better than they were before.

My lack of talent in no way diminished my love of the game. If anything, my inability to hit an elusive curve or a high hard fastball only made me appreciate the skill levels of those who could. Arguably the best hitter ever, Ted Williams, once said that the most difficult skill in all of sports is hitting a baseball. Coincidentally, as possibly the worst batsman ever, I came to the same conclusion.

And so it was that my son, Ben, became a baseball fan. He loved playing and watching baseball. When he was ten he told his Mom that his idea of heaven would be, "Being at bat all the time." Ben wrote an essay for a fifth grade assignment signaling a glimpse of his feeling for the national pastime:

A Baseball
By Ben Wells (age 10)

A baseball, one of the better things in life.
Such a simple object, no moving parts, and yet,
You can play with it for hours and then come home and rest,
As you rub the soft leather on your cheek.

The evenly sewed stitches shining a bright red.
A long twisty line traveling on and on, but never crossing over.
You can slowly run your fingers across the stitches like
*   a fine massage.*
The two curvy ovals of leather break apart and you can see
*   string wrapped around a sphere.*

If you unwrap the string you find green yarn wrapped
*   around another sphere.*
The yarn is flat and pushed down from the tight leather packaging.
More layers of string and yarn follow until you get to a
*   little rubber ball.*
That's it, some leather, string, yarn, and a little rubber ball.

Baseball Odyssey

The idea originated while attending a Boston Red Sox game in Fenway Park in June 1989. Ben suggested, "Wouldn't it be fun to go to all of the major league ball parks?" The answer was obvious, and so we set out on a father son adventure that lasted the next six summers, attaining our goal in Minneapolis at the Twins' last home game of the 1995 season.

It was an inauspicious start. The day after we watched the Toronto Blue Jays come back from an eleven run deficit to beat the hometown Red Sox, Ben 8, Lucy 13, Judy, and I were posing as tourists in downtown Boston. We entered the Government Center subway station intending to return to Harvard Square. A train was at the ready as we descended the stairs to a boarding platform. Ben sped ahead and hopped aboard. Unfortunately, he was faster than the rest of us, and the doors closed between us. His normal boyhood bravado faded quickly upon grasping the situation, and his eyes expanded in fright. I was walking, then running along with the train in an unsuccessful attempt to pry the doors open. When it became apparent that I wasn't going to get onboard, I attempted to communicate a plan to reunite. I yelled, "Ben, get off at the next station and stay put until I catch the next train and get you!" Whether this message was understood was unclear. The train entered the dark tunnel, and Ben was gone.

Judy was beyond apoplectic at this moment, as was I. Our imaginations were running at full speed conjuring ghastly outcomes. For any male who has ever been married it goes without saying, I was at fault. While a reasonably precocious child, Ben did not know the contact information of the friends with whom we were staying in nearby Weston, MA. This occurred before the ubiquity of cell phones, so he had no way of contacting us.

Just as I was preparing to get on the following train, a security guard approached us from behind with Ben in tow and said, "Is this your little boy?" We were overcome with relief.

After a few smothering hugs, Ben explained what happened. "Some teenagers on the train were watching after I got on and asked, 'Do you know that man?' I told them that is my Dad. They contacted the conductor, who stopped the train, backed it up, and then this lady brought me here."

It was a harrowing experience, so to compensate should such a separation occur again we gave Ben a $20 bill to put in his shoe along with a note containing essential contact information. One day later we were walking in New York City about to enter Bloomingdale's, I turned and observed Ben sitting on the sidewalk, removing his tennis shoe, taking the twenty, and giving it to a teenaged panhandler.

The Plan

Every spring I would obtain a copy of the major league baseball schedule and plot a plan that would fit Ben's little league and my work schedule. New York, Chicago, Los Angeles, and San Francisco would require two separate trips as metro areas hosting two teams rarely schedule home games at the same time. Our most efficient outing was a five day weekend that took us to Detroit, Toronto, Pittsburgh, Cincinnati, and Cleveland including a stopover at Niagara Falls and lunch in Buffalo. We made several weekend trips covering two ballparks: Philadelphia/Baltimore, Atlanta/Miami, New York (Mets)/ Montreal, Seattle/Oakland, Chicago (White Sox)/Milwaukee, Houston/Arlington, and Los Angeles (Dodgers)/San Diego. The remainder of our trips was solo affairs.

Other father/son combos joined us on several of our outings. Larry, Sr. was particularly delightful company, as he would always bring candy, a light heart, and could hum the fight song of every major and minor university in the land. He would sing, "Da, dada, dadada, da, ump pa" and then shout, "What fight song is that?" We'd guess incorrectly, and he would boisterously exclaim, "No, you fools, that's the North Dakota State Bisons!" We were easily amused.

Early on we developed a rating system that included several categories: respect for the baseball traditions, 7th inning stretch, food quality and price, babe factor, fan entertainment between innings, general ambience, etc. With the noticeable exception of Camden Yards, we preferred the classical older stadiums: Fenway Park, Tiger Stadium, Wrigley Field, and County Stadium (Milwaukee), preferring the irregularity of the more ancient structures. St. Louis, Cincinnati, Philadelphia, and Pittsburgh were the worst stadiums and were built in the 1960's to accommodate both baseball and football. The domed stadiums of the era were uniformly ghastly in terms of appearance and respect for tradition. Oddly though, it rained hard during each of the games we attended in Seattle, Houston, Montreal, and Minnesota, and it was 114 degrees in Phoenix the day we attended a Diamondback game, thus increasing our appreciation of the ungainly parks.

In terms of the babe factor, general attractiveness of the locals, Cleveland loomed large on the negative end of the scale. I had never seen such a heavy concentration of unattractive people, all smokers. In contrast, nearby Cincinnati rated highly. Arlington, TX ran away with first place with honorable mentions going to Kansas City, LA, and Colorado.

Milwaukee received our highest rating for food choices followed closely by Camden Yards. Toronto stood out as the worst, with McDonald's franchises dominating the food offerings in the stadium, serving possibly the worst chilidog ever concocted in North America. Cincinnati had the cheapest food. Houston and Arlington featured quality BBQ. Sadly, the regional differences in the U.S. were becoming more and more homogenized by the early 90's, so the food distinctions weren't as great as we would have preferred.

Ben was greatly offended by the respect for baseball tradition at Busch Stadium in St. Louis, because they played the Budweiser theme song during the 7th inning stretch rather than "Take Me Out to the Ball Game." Much to my chagrin, the game at the home of my formerly beloved Cardinals had transmogrified into a nine-inning beer commercial.

Camden Yards was the most impressive of all the stadiums. It was beautiful, fan friendly, respectful of baseball traditions, and well done in every way. The week before Ben and I were to journey to Baltimore, I was meeting with a new business acquaintance and mentioned the upcoming trip. He said, "Every game is sold out well in advance. How do you plan on getting tickets?" I said we'd use scalpers as a last resort, but it would work out somehow. He then volunteered, "My ex-wife is dating the president of the Orioles, and I could see if she could help." And she did. Thus, we left for Baltimore with instructions to go to a certain entrance at the stadium and say we're guests of Mr. L.

First we flew into Philadelphia on Friday afternoon and caught a Phillies game. It turned out we were to see the worst and best stadiums on consecutive nights. Philadelphia's Veterans Stadium was dirty, the people were foul-tempered and unfriendly, and this was one to just check off the list. The next morning we enjoyed viewing the Liberty Bell and Independence Hall, and then we headed for Baltimore.

Camden Yards is located in a newly renovated harbor area full of interesting sites and sounds. We arrived at the assigned spot, mentioned we were guests of Mr. L, and were then greeted like royalty. It became, "Right this way gentlemen," and we were whisked away to our seats in a section of VIP suites. Waitresses took our orders for crab cakes and other regional delicacies. Ben noted that we were sitting in the same section with Anita Null, the teenaged Olympic swimmer, and the Oriole Hall of Famer, Frank Robinson. The ex-wife came by to see if we were being well treated, and we were. In addition to being stunningly attractive, she was a most pleasant hostess. The stadium would have been magnificent from a general admission seat, but the luxury of a suite experience was an added bonus.

In late September on a Friday night, Ben and I along with Larry and his oldest son flew to Chicago to attend a White Sox game at their new stadium on Chicago's south side. It was unimaginative, ordinary, and disappointing. We were told that the owner had the chance to build the Camden Yards design but took a pass, as it was deemed too radical. They subsequently built one of the worst of the new stadiums.

We were sitting in the first row of the upper deck behind home plate. A soft foul ball was hit to a guy sitting a few seats to our right, he muffed the ball, and it fell to the seats below. We were commiserating with the guy saying something like, "Nice hands fumble fingers," when another soft foul tip was hit to the same guy, and he dropped it once again.

On Saturday morning we drove on to Milwaukee to attend a

Brewer's game. We pulled into a convenience store to acquire some healthy snacks and ask for directions to County Stadium. In the parking lot we encountered a skinny, derelict looking guy resembling Charles Manson who responded to our query with incomprehensible instructions. He was intrigued by our father-son adventure and, in a twitching manner reminiscent of a recovering druggie offered, "Hey, hey why don't you guys come over to my house and we'll have some food, and then I'll take you to the game. I live in Peewaukee just a few miles from here." I was thinking the guy could be Jeffrey Dahmer on his lunch break and declined his generous offer. Our prospective host was insistent but finally relented, "Well, if you'll just follow me, I'll show you the way to the stadium," and he did.

It was the last day of the season and was warm and sunny. We pulled into the parking lot and joined the hundreds of people tailgating. The smells of grilling brats filled the air. As we walked to the stadium, complete strangers asked us to join them for beer and brats, which we did. When we got in the stadium, people sitting behind us gave each of the boys a beer cup full of nickels so they could join in a betting game. By this time Ben and I had been to all but two stadiums, so our new friends wanted to hear about our experiences and see how County Stadium stacked up.

After the game we went to a city park, where the grass was nicer than most golf course fairways, and we played football. Later that night, we dined in a great Polish restaurant. Milwaukee rocks.

Shortly after our flight arrived, we went to the rental car counter in the Seattle airport. We were chatting with an older gentleman manning the Avis counter and mentioned we had flown in to see a Mariner's game. The guy was incredulous, "You mean you flew all the way from Kansas City to see the Mariners?" We responded affirmatively and inquired if he thought we would have any trouble getting seats. He exclaimed, "Are you kidding? Hell, they'll probably let you sit on the team bench."

It was a typical rainy evening in Seattle, so it was good that the game was indoors, but the Kingdome was a pretty grim ballpark. Sometime in the middle of the game one of the Mariners hit a home run, and they ignited a major fireworks display, which then clouded our view for the remainder of the inning. I'm certain few Seattleites were saddened when the Kingdome was blown up.

One of our fellow travelers, Frank, used to be a neighbor of John Schuerholz, who had once worked for the Kansas City Royals and had recently become the general manager for the Braves. He was gracious in arranging great seats for a nondescript Braves game.

En route to see the Florida Marlins, we traveled to the Everglades, toured an alligator farm, and took an airboat ride. The guy running the cheesy gator farm made the toothless hillbillies in the movie *Deliverance* look like Franklin Delano Roosevelt in formal attire. Gator man was telling us about his critters and bragging on his expertise. Ben couldn't take his eyes off his deformed hands and politely asked him why half of his fingers were gone. The Everglades airboat guy was equally goofy. He said, "We're not supposed to feed the gators, but I know you people want to see gators." So he threw a dead chicken in the water, and, sure enough, an abundance of the beasties appeared.

The Double Play of the Century

After Ben's junior year, I managed his team in a summer league. We had some pretty good players, mostly from Ben's high school team, but we were often short of bodies on the weeknight game times. One evening we had nine guys, but one of the boys showed up sporting an injury to his right hand from a lawn mower accident. He was a brilliant kid, a virtuoso violinist. He spoke three languages fluently, received perfect scores on his SATs, and yet nearly lost a finger to a lawn mower. He showed up and said, "Coach, I know you need bodies so where do you want me?" I put him on first base where his inability to throw wouldn't be too obvious.

Ben was pitching, and it wasn't too long before the other team observed our weak spot. Perhaps it was the claw shaped bandage? A man was on third with one out, and the batter bunted back to the pitcher. Ben looked the runner back to third, then sprinted toward first and threw for the second out. The runner dashed for home. Our injured first baseman flipped the ball back to Ben with his glove hand who turned and fired home getting the runner out for perhaps the first and only 1-3-1-2 double play in baseball history.

Goldilocks

I was meeting with a business acquaintance and mentioned my family was going to Florida for spring break and intended to catch a few spring training games in the Tampa area. He said we would be welcome to stay at his vacation home in St. Petersburg Beach for the week. We accepted his generous offer and arrived at the house just before dark on a Friday evening. Our host told us where he would leave the key, but we didn't find it, so Lucy, then 14, took Ben around the back of the house to explore. A few moments later, she opened the front door in the manner of a grand dame and took us on a tour. The house was U shaped, surrounding a beautiful infinity pool and cabana and directly faced the inland waterway. The house was exquisite, the kids put their dibs on their respective rooms, and we couldn't believe our good fortune.

The next morning I called our host. "Anver, we can't thank you enough. Your house is just perfect, the kids are having a great time and are enjoying the pool as we speak."

"What pool?"

After getting the correct directions to his house, we made the beds along with a hasty retreat, before our Goldilocks-like misadventure was discovered. Anver's house was nice, but not quite the palace we unwittingly invaded.

Postscript

Ben and I continue our odyssey as new stadiums have been constructed.

PART II

ON DUTY

CHAPTER 11

Riverton Bill

They called him Buffalo Bill in rural Nebraska, Malibu Bill in southern California, Pocono Bill in upper New York state, and, in Riverton*, he was predictably Riverton Bill*. I once told him, "Bill, you know when out of earshot, they just call you asswipe."

He'd laugh and say, "No, they really love me." And he was serious, albeit delusional.

By the mid 1980's two weakened hospitals in Riverton were embraced in a death struggle. With a recipe of three parts wisdom and five parts desperation, the boards of trustees of Fullbright* Memorial and St. Catherine* Hospitals saw fit to end their healthcare arms race and merge. Then in a brilliant and, ultimately, tragic move, the newly combined board hired Bill as their new chief executive officer.

Bill previously worked for a large for-profit chain and had a strong track record turning around troubled hospitals, making many enemies, and quickly moving on. In Riverton he inherited an entity that lost $2 million the year prior to his arrival and had recently consolidated operations at the St. Catherine's site, the least obsolete of two aging facilities built in the 1920's. He encountered two unhealthy corporate cultures, each harboring strong resentments towards their former competitor and having a distinct aversion to change. One obstacle to success of the merger, however, was the tenuous relationship with the Riverton Clinic, the largest medical group in town that just lost their power to play one weak hospital against the other. The docs were taking a "wait and see" attitude in assessing the new landscape.

Upon meeting Bill I was struck by his physical appearance and bearing. He was handsome, athletic, and fit. He had a quick wit and a pleasing but raspy voice. He could be charming when it served his purpose. We met in 1990, when he was in his early 40's. He had served as an infantry captain in Viet Nam, but he rarely spoke of his war-time experiences. Over a two-year period I spent a lot of time with Bill, but can't say I ever knew him well.

Bill filled a room with his exuberance. He was loud, commanding, and confident. When most hospital CEOs wore a suit and tie, Bill sported pastel sweaters, often draped over his shoulders in a manner parodying preppies. The norm in the trade was to maintain a low profile, but Bill sought the spotlight. He drove an expensive, purple, 7 series BMW sedan, an uncommon mode of transportation in Riverton. He stood out.

I was hired by Bill to serve as the financial adviser to the newly formed Riverton Regional Healthcare System (RRHS) as they sought access to the capital markets in order to build a replacement hospital. The organization's creditworthiness was weak by any measure. Bill's mission was to restore sustainable profitability immediately. How he did it was counter-intuitive, but brilliant.

Like any new CEO of a major Riverton institution, Bill wisely involved himself in the community. He made a big splash at a downtown Rotary luncheon one day announcing publicly, "People in this town are so stupid, it takes them two hours to watch *60 Minutes*." He was equally adept at endearing himself to the medical community.

Over the years I've promoted the "Equal Distribution of Assholes Theory." No matter how you slice up the human condition, there is roughly a similar bell curve in terms of decent folks vs. assholes: rich/poor, fat/thin, white/black, urban/rural, liberal/conservative, even lawyers. And so it is with physicians. In many respects it's understandable, and even desirable, for some physicians to be a bit arrogant.

Consider the perspective of a skilled surgeon who just had a patient expire after heroic efforts, then a few minutes later must enter an exam room to meet with another patient and his/her family and convey the air of confidence necessary to be effective. Gifted physicians can pull this off. However, some docs maintain the conceit that medical expertise translates into knowledge in all areas. Hospital administrators learn early in their careers how to deal with this phenomenon by saying, "Dr. ____ that is an interesting and insightful observation. I will keep that in mind as we deliberate further on this matter." Bill, in contrast, voiced his true sentiments and once said, "Dr. ____ you must have total shit for brains to say, much less to think, something so moronic!"

St. Catherine had a large chapel within the hospital. Bill had a casket placed in the sacristy, lined up the employees from each shift, and requested that they place their old name badge in the funereal receptacle. Then, as they passed by, Bill handed out new Riverton Regional badges. He had a flair for drama.

Bill also had a mean streak bordering on cruelty. He was intolerant of fat people and those who smoked. Be advised that there are a significant number of obese healthcare workers and smokers. To Bill they were merely objects of derision. In walking the halls of the hospital with Bill it would be common for him to approach a young, obese woman, "Hey, how's the weight program going?" He could be an insufferable asshole.

By now the observant reader might inquire, "What's so brilliant about this guy?" In Bill's first year at RRHS, the bottom line improved from − $2 million to + $2.5 million. Land was acquired, architects hired, and the planning for the new hospital was well underway. Whether by a cunningly well-crafted strategy or dumb luck, Bill accomplished what none of his predecessors had. He unified the community, the medical staff, and the hospital employees in an ardent antipathy, if not outright hatred, for their new CEO. Amazingly, the energy resulting from this animus was channeled into making the hospital better.

No one who worked near Bill escaped his occasional wrath. After a particularly disagreeable meeting with the medical executive committee, Bill challenged the chief of the medical staff to a fistfight. The physician wisely declined. I was once on the receiving end of one of Bill's tirades. We were having lunch at the Riverton Country Club with several others, and the attack erupted when I recommended bringing in a consultant specializing in physician coding. After being berated with great vigor, he attempted to soften it by saying, "Hey, you know I really love you." I didn't.

Shortly after Bill skewered me, he appeared unexpectedly in Kansas City one Saturday morning at my son's baseball practice, a lengthy drive from Riverton. His arrival came as a surprise and was more than a bit creepy. He approached me on the field and said, "Hey, I want you to know that the little scene this week at the country club was just a bit of posturing, and you shouldn't take it personally. I was actually doing you a favor by putting some public distance between us."

The new location for the hospital was selected primarily to meet the requirement that the new facility's front door be over 25 miles from St. Benedicts*, the nearest neighboring hospital. According to Medicare regulations, RRHC would qualify for status as a "sole community hospital" if, among other provisions, it met the 25 mile distance criteria. To many in the community it seemed incomprehensible why the new hospital was located on the west edge of town in a farm field, but qualifying for this provision would produce an additional $4.3 million annually in Medicare reimbursement and would mean the difference between barely surviving and prospering. Bill and I drove various routes between St. Benedicts and the new site on several occasions to measure the distance. Additionally, the distance was measured by multiple independent sources including local police, the highway patrol, and hospital staff. Various routes produced distances ranging from 25.1 to 25.3 miles.

Planning progressed well during the spring of 1991. Bill harangued the architects, the equipment planners, the financing group, and everyone involved in the project. In spite of the atmosphere of intentionally concocted conflict, the project team continued to do their jobs.

Late in the spring of 1991, Bill related an incident that occurred at a board meeting. He told the story in a casual manner, and it seemed odd but not terribly serious. Essentially, a young female anesthesiologist, a member of the Riverton Clinic, came to a board meeting and requested that medical staff privileges be granted to another anesthesiologist who wanted to join her in practicing in Riverton. She was seriously overworked, stressed out, and pleaded for help. The board rejected her request in keeping with Bill's recommendation. Their reasoning was that the candidate she was promoting was currently in prison, serving time for illegal drug activities, was due to be released soon, but did not possess a valid license to practice medicine. Bill assured the young anesthesiologist he would do everything he could do to recruit someone else to lessen her workload. She was furious at Bill for this response.

In early June, Bill organized a lavish board and medical staff meeting held in St. Louis. The newly combined board was beginning to gel, Bill was easing up on his more outrageous behavior, the medical staff was lying low, the hospital's financial condition continued to improve, and the prize of a new hospital appeared within reach. The $30 million financing was scheduled for September 1991.

Bill's wife, Sue Ellen*, was a beautiful and gentle lady. She had been a cheerleader at a Southeastern Conference University. Once while doing a back flip from the top of a six person pyramid, she slapped her thighs to signal her impending leap, a gesture missed by her catchers, then proceeded to do a double backwards somersault, landed on the hardwood flooring, and broke her back. By the time I met her she had recovered fully, given birth to a healthy young son, was running marathons, and gracefully entered Riverton society. Bill and Sue Ellen purchased a handsome antebellum home and were in the process of restoring it to its former grandeur. Bill was a completely different person in the presence of his stunning wife and son, where he played the role of loving husband and doting father.

In late August 1991 Bill took his family on a two-week vacation to Europe. Mid-way into the trip a series of events occurred that would dramatically change his life. The young female anesthesiologist died of an apparent suicide. Several prominent physicians publicly claimed that Bill was singly responsible for the young woman's death due to his earlier recommendation that a convicted felon not be admitted to the medical staff. It's possible they actually believed this canard but most likely saw this as the opening for which they had been waiting. They demanded that the board fire Bill, or their support for the new hospital would be withdrawn. Prior to learning of the board's response, a number of the physicians placed an ad in the local newspaper declaring their opposition to the replacement hospital project. After difficult deliberations the board fired Bill who was still in Europe and had yet to learn of his fate.

For those with an appreciation for the complexity of attracting $30 million in financing to an unrated, rural community hospital with a weak balance sheet and a history of poor performance, suffice it to say that these developments were not welcomed. Lenders like stability and abhor chaos. The Riverton medical community had descended into chaos.

On a Friday evening in early September, coincidently the first night of the high school football season, a community meeting was arranged at the Holiday Inn to discuss the status of the new hospital project. The board asked me to facilitate this meeting, along with the acting CEO. The room was packed with over 500 people, and most were highly agitated. Bill had been thrown under the bus, but the citizenry wanted more. Retribution was the order of the day.

We emphasized that the community needed a new facility, this turmoil would only raise the cost of capital and damage the prospects of achieving this important goal, and the community's reservoir of anger at Bill was misdirected. Bill was not present, a good thing, as his safety could well have been imperiled. Our message was universally ignored. The citizenry was enraged and wanted blood. "That man killed that poor woman by his insensitivity." "How can you possibly defend such an evil man?" "How can this board have tolerated that man for so long?" I had no knowledge of the specific agendas of the numerous critics, but the uniform chorus of anger approached mob psychology.

One bright spot during the meeting occurred when Sue Ellen stood up and defended her husband. She was emotional, but articulate, in stating that no connection existed between the anesthesiologist's death and Bill's actions. She calmly and methodically reminded people of all that had been accomplished during his tenure. She was shouted down.

After about three and one half hours with nothing accomplished, save the release of steam, the meeting ended, and the crowd dispersed. I walked out of the large ballroom into a darkened hallway near the restrooms. I was stunned to see Bill as he approached me out of the darkness. He was unshaven and disheveled with a maniacal look on his face. He said in a hostile and threatening manner, "Do you want to take a drive with me?"

I said, "No, I'm tired, I'm sad, and I just want to go home."

He said, "I think you will want to reconsider, because I can show you a route from the new site to St. Benedicts that is only 24.3 miles."

If true, Bill's revelation would mean that everything done to develop the new hospital for the past two years was for naught, and I believed I would be responsible for this error. I said, "Bill do what you will with that information, but I'm not getting in a car with you. I'm going home." I received a speeding ticket en route making a bad night worse.

Postscript

The financing for the new hospital cratered in September. The medical staff withdrew its pledge of $500,000 in support of the project, and it was never restored. All but two hospital board members resigned. Five months later Humpty Dumpty was pieced back together with an interest rate of 9.25% vs. the 6% they would have achieved without the cataclysmic events of August/September and with terms so onerous that a refinancing was required several years later.

It turned out that the 24.3 mile route to St. Benedicts that Bill mentioned was a dirt road used only for farm vehicles, thus not jeopardizing RRHS's compliance with the sole community hospital regulations.

Bill later called to tell me that a few weeks after the Holiday Inn meeting, the deceased anesthesiologist's husband, a general surgeon also practicing in the Riverton Clinic, moved to Florida with his lover, one of the non-obese nurses. The father of the deceased anesthesiologist was a retired highway patrolman. After his son-in-law abruptly left town with his new/old girlfriend, the father became suspicious about his daughter's alleged suicide. He initiated procedures to have the body exhumed and conduct a more thorough investigation of the circumstances surrounding her death. Before he succeeded in this effort, he died suddenly. According to Bill, neither of these cases was investigated further.

Bill landed a new position as the CEO of a large hospital in the Dallas

Metroplex where he lasted a few years. He would periodically call out of the blue to bring me up to date on his activities. I later heard that he and Sue Ellen divorced, and Bill opened a floor-covering store in Pittsburg, PA. The last I heard, Bill had become a missionary in Africa.

Riverton Regional Healthcare System continues to grow and prosper. It is one of the more successful regional hospitals in the country. Thus far no statues have been constructed in Bill's honor for his role in this civic achievement.

CHAPTER 12

Cochise County

It started with apples and a good ole boy attorney from north central Missouri. We met in the late 1970's, the friendship was genuine, and our business relationship was mutually beneficial. Kenny* was 15 years my senior, a successful attorney, and entrepreneur. He was sophisticated in a countrified manner and possessed a charismatic aura. In addition to maintaining a general law office, he served as financial adviser to rural hospitals and nursing homes.

He was small in stature but carried himself like a larger man. His pipe was a permanent companion, and he busied himself with it constantly whether lit or unlit. He spoke in a sincere country voice and presented himself in a self-deprecating manner that partially disguised his formidable intellect. He quickly earned the trust of rural hospital board members.

Kenny owned a twin engine Beech Baron aircraft, a luxurious alternative to the long drives that were the norm for our travels. After attending board meetings in distant locales like Elkhart, KS or Memphis, MO we would hop into the plane for the flight home and unwind as though we just finished an athletic competition. We fancied ourselves mini-masters of the universe playing poker, drinking whiskey in the Baron's spacious cabin, and flying hither and yon over the great American heartland.

Shortly after we met, Kenny won a 640-acre parcel of ground in a lawsuit. The land was located in Cochise County, AZ, in the southeast corner of the state and comprising an area roughly the size of Connecticut. Kenny's land was located midway between Willcox, AZ and the Mexican border and lay in the shadow of a mountain range dominated by the 9,800'

Chiricahua Peak. Chimney shaped spires and columns adorn the mountain's shoulders and add greatly to their majesty. The rugged terrain provided shelter to the eponymous Cochise and to his successor, the equally famed Geronimo.

The valley rests atop an aquifer yielding an agricultural cornucopia similar to the San Joaquin valley in California. Irrigated fields of chiles, roses, tomatoes, cotton, pears, pistachios, and pecans stretched for miles. Kenny probed for ideas about how best to deploy his newly acquired asset. He engaged a University of Arizona horticultural professor, and he suggested an apple orchard. Several growers, processors, and brokers were already operating in the area benefitting from the aquifer located 300' below the desert floor.

Kenny traveled to the apple growing regions of the Yakima Valley in Washington State, San Joaquin Valley in California, and New Zealand. He studied the pros and cons of differing varietals and their suitability to southeast Arizona, various methods of irrigation, growth rates, market futures, and all matters pertaining to water rights and reserves. He was a voracious reader and quickly determined whom to believe and whom not to as virtually every aspect of the business lent itself to strongly held, but differing, opinions.

We raised funds through a limited partnership to develop the orchard. Kenny served as the general partner with 51% ownership rights and put up 51% of the capital. Later, I asked Kenny's brother, a car dealer in Northwest Missouri, why he didn't invest in the deal. He responded with a slow, but thoughtful drawl, "It sure sounds a lot like farmin' to me." Kenny decided we would produce Granny Smith apples using an espalier growing system requiring hundreds of miles of steel wiring strung in three strand rows similar to methods used in vineyards. He chose a ground level irrigation system with a hose running along the base of each row of trees and a spigot serving each plant.

The financing provided funds for four years of development. With some luck, we thought it possible to have a marketable crop by the third year. Tax law at the time provided a 50% credit for the development cost of the orchard, partially covering our downside. Kenny had done his homework, and I believed the deal was going to work. Lamentably, several other investors placed their faith in me and later shared their reasoning for joining the partnership, "Chuck, you're the most conservative guy I know, so if you're in, I'm in."

Kenny rented a condo in nearby Sunizoma and put his law practice and financial advisory business on hold to devote full time to apples. He met with the various agri-business people in the valley, ordered steel for the espalier system, rubber hose for the irrigation, nursery stock, and farm equipment. He hired a general manager from one of the rose growers in the area and set up the headquarters on the orchard site. Within six months the 640-acre orchard was planted with the espalier and irrigation systems in place.

The orchard was 10 miles from the nearest paved road. At night javelinas (aka skunk pigs) roamed wild throughout the valley, and we posted an armed guard to discourage them from uprooting our newly planted trees. Manual labor was readily available.

The orchard prospered early. The staff worked diligently to train the tree branches to follow the wiring. Miles of shiny metal were transformed into long green hedges accented with apple blossoms. By the second spring, the flowers were luxuriant. By the following year the square mile of colorful flowers was breathtaking. However, spring also brought anxieties. Each apple blossom produces a flower with five carpels in the center shaped in a pattern similar that found on a pair of dice. Each carpel has the potential to become an apple, but the flower is vulnerable to frost for a 2-3 week period.

By the orchard's third year, the plants were looking fruitful and our farm manager and other orchard people in the valley thought we had a legitimate chance of producing a cash crop that fall. In late April, when the flowers were in full bloom, we had a frost warning. Kenny's decision to plant apples on such a large scale was influenced by the gentle slope of the land down the shoulder of the Chiricahuas. According to the U of A horticulturist, damaging frost tends to accumulate in the lower parts the valley reducing the risk to plants situated on the higher ground. Kenny hired a helicopter in an attempt to keep the air moving around the orchard in the early morning hours. He rented a frost cannon, an unproven concept based on the idea that the concussion of the blank shells would dissipate forming ice crystals. Neither effort worked, and our first viable crop was lost to frost.

No problem, we had another year's funding in place, and we weren't dependent on a third year crop for financial viability. We survived frost during the fourth spring, and the crop was again looking bountiful. We traveled to Sunizoma often, toured the orchard, met with brokers and other apple folks, played golf, and explored the Chiricahuas.

Then we found ourselves in the path of a steamroller later called the "Great Apple Scare." The actress, Meryl Streep, went on *The Phil Donahue Show*, the 1980's version of *Oprah*, and *CBS's 60 Minutes* to declare that the chemical Alar, used to prevent pre-rot in red apples, was "the most potent cancer-causing agent in our food supply."

Phil Donahue proclaimed, "You're killing your children if you're feeding them apples." The claims were baseless and later proven to be false, but the damage was done. Even though Alar was only used on 15% of the American apple crop and was harmless, the media induced hysteria sent the price of apples to near zero. A $10-billion industry was temporarily laid to waste by two nitwits and their media accomplices. We had a bumper crop in the fall of 1989 but couldn't give the apples away. Man plans, God laughs.

Now we had a problem. The painful, but obvious, solution was for everyone to contribute their respective share to fund another year's operation. From Kenny's perspective, he put more effort than anyone else into the deal and maintained the limited partners should provide the needed funds. He would not invest more cash but didn't want his ownership share diluted. We eventually constructed a compromise, but the seeds of the partnership's destruction had been planted.

The next year, the market for apples hadn't improved, and the cost of picking would have exceeded the value of the crop. Kenny came to the limited partners to request more money, yet he was unwilling to contribute his proportionate share. The divide could not be bridged. Just as we were producing beautiful crops of apples, the market ceased to exist. The partnership disintegrated, followed shortly by the orchard.

Bisbee

We were able to salvage some good from the time spent in southeast Arizona by developing client relationships with several Cochise County hospitals.

I was already working with the Copper Queen Community Hospital in Bisbee when Jim was hired as CEO to stabilize a troubled situation. He was young, energetic, and capable. He had been a nursing home administrator in rural, eastern Montana and was ready for a new challenge in a more hospitable environment. Jim and his wife Karen were raised on ranches in Montana and quickly fit into the unconventional world of Bisbee.

Bisbee offered a mild blend of Key West, New Orleans, and Mayberry set in a wild-west mountain town of 6,000. It offered an interesting array of amusements but also some drawbacks. Karen was a horsewoman, and they rented a house with a small acreage south of town. Mexico is nine miles south of town. Within their first month, one of their horses was bitten on the nose by a Mojave rattlesnake and died within minutes from asphyxiation. A few weeks later, Jim's pickup was taken from their driveway while they slept. He reported this to the local police who told him it was most likely stolen by Mexican bandits, and he should report it to the Naco, Mexico police. When in Mexico he noticed his truck being driven by a police official. He confronted the man, was threatened with violence, and retreated across the border. Jim and Karen then decided to move into town.

Jim and I played golf several times at the course in Naco, AZ where a hook out of bounds from the 10th tee box had international consequences, as one's ball landed in Mexico. A retirement compound was located adjacent to the golf course and was surrounded by a ten-foot high chain link fence topped with concertina wire. From a distance it looked like someone placed a concentration camp on the border, but one with shuffleboard courts, a swimming pool, and a bunch of old white people. Hundreds of expensive motor homes were parked in the compound with Michigan and Wisconsin license plates. Apparently, the owners of these $250,000+ motor coaches so enjoyed the weather and cheap golf that they were willing to imprison themselves in a 40-acre cage for the winter.

Ben and Lucy

With the apple investment in place, I decided to take our family unit on a tour of Cochise County. We flew to Tucson, rented a car, and headed south. We first stopped in Tombstone, best known as the site of the 1881 gunfight at the O.K. Corral. It was a former silver and gold mining town that now exists primarily to remind tourists of a romanticized version of the Wild West.

It was dark when we left Tombstone, driving south on highway 80, and we encountered a brightly illuminated roadblock manned by the U.S. Border Patrol. We drove slowly through the checkpoint, the guards shined their flashlights into our car and asked if we were U.S. citizens. Ben, then 8, responded, "Si, Senor" before I had a chance to speak. The kid was quick, but the guards failed to appreciate his sense of humor, we were dragged out of the car, and beaten senseless. Not really. They just glared at us.

We arrived in Bisbee and checked into the Copper Queen Hotel built in 1902, once co-owned by John Wayne, and recently restored. At one time it would have been the grand dame of old Bisbee and undoubtedly had a romantic past. When we arrived the décor was a cross between Swiss chalet and cowboy whorehouse. The rooms were small and decorated with an assortment of amateurish paintings of nudes reclining on red velveteen sofas, a subtle decorating accessory that did not go unnoticed by Ben nor by Lucy, his ever vigilant moral guardian. Old Bisbee was noteworthy not only for its 19th century architecture, but also for the mountainous terrain. There are no flat spaces in town, and the Copper Queen, like virtually every other structure, was built into a steep hill.

Retired miners provided guided tours of the old copper mine and relished reliving past glory days digging in the bowels of the earth. I suggested we go, but Lucy balked the instant she understood this meant going down an elevator hundreds of feet into a dark mine shaft. Lucy was

13 and Ben was 8. She said she would take care of Ben while Judy and I rode a train deep into the heart of Mule Mountain. Bisbee's a pretty small town, so we figured they couldn't get in too much mischief. When we rendezvoused later, I noticed Ben was now bald and inquired of Lucy,

"What happened?"

"I thought he needed a haircut so I took him to a barbershop."

"How did you pay the guy?"

"I didn't. I told him you would come by later and take care of it."

After leaving Bisbee, we headed to Douglas, AZ where my father once lived. We crossed the border checkpoint into Agua Prieta, Mexico, and Ben was full of little boy bravado, as we entered the foreign land. The town looked like a setting for a spaghetti western, and we halfway expected a serape clad Clint Eastwood to appear. Wooden walkways rose above the dirt streets. The stores were empty of merchandise, other than one featuring porcelain toilets and dead flies. The heavily armed Federales appeared menacing, it was getting dark, and Ben said, "Let's get out of here," and we made a hasty retreat to the safety and comfort of the US.

High Desert Inn

The High Desert Inn originally housed Bisbee's sheriff's office and jail. Darrell, a recent transplant from New York City, purchased and renovated the 19th century structure into a six-room bed and breakfast. I had stayed in every habitable form of lodging in town and quickly concluded Darrell's place was vastly superior to other options. I learned to call well in advance, as he filled up quickly, and the penalty for staying elsewhere was severe. Darrell had been a cook, saved his money, planned his escape from the urban east, and adopted a more laid back lifestyle in the Arizona desert.

After Phelps Dodge closed their last mining operation in 1975, Bisbee's economic activity centered on tourism, primarily serving weekend travelers from nearby Tucson. Accordingly, the Inn's restaurant was only open for dinner on Thursday through Saturday evening. Patrons walked through the original jailhouse door into a small, high ceilinged room with six tables. Natural light came through the interstices of the vertical iron bars imbedded in the stone wall at the back of the former jail cell. The décor was standard southwestern fare with photos of old cowboy scenes and dried cow skulls but also with well-chosen objects of modern art. The seating was a bit claustrophobic, but the food was exceptionally good, and Darrell was always a welcoming and gracious host.

I arrived in Bisbee mid afternoon on Friday for weekend meetings, and I checked in and was greeted warmly by Darrell. He said, "Be sure to dine with us this evening. I'm preparing something special that I think you'll enjoy." I told him I would and made a reservation.

Darrell seated me at the table in the center of the small dining area, brought a bottle of wine he had recommended, along with delicious lagniappe for which he was noted. The other tables were already occupied. Dining alone, I had ample opportunity to observe my surroundings.

On my left were two attractive young ladies, apparently lesbian lovers and very much infatuated with one another. They were reaching over their table holding hands, gazing into one another's eyes, mining facial orifices with their tongues, and all but engaging in intercourse. On my right were three young men dressed in expensive, but casual, attire that would have been suitable in the most expensive clubs in LA or NYC. Their conversation centered on the art business, and I presumed they were either art dealers or serious collectors. Three middle aged men and two women occupied the table behind me. The men wore white cowboy style shirts adorned with string ties cinched to the neck with silver and turquoise bolos. Cowboy hats were hung on the rack next to their chairs. The two women dressed as if they were going to a square dance. The material in their dresses reminded me of the tired drapes that once adorned my Grandmother's house. Their boisterous conversation was about cattle. Two gentlemen roughly my age were sitting at the table in front of me. One of them was dressed in a turtleneck sweater that didn't flatter. Though thin, he had a flabby body made even less appealing by a set of man boobs accentuated by the skintight pullover. The other was shorter and equally nerdish in appearance, but he appeared to hang on every word of his companion as he exposited on the merits of various search engines on the world-wide-web, a fairly new topic c. 1988.

I was intrigued by the motley assortment of patrons. When Darrell brought my rack of lamb, I inquired how many people in the restaurant were tourists. He took a quick look around and said, "Just you." That's Bisbee.

The Scorpion

I arrived in Bisbee late one August evening in preparation for a workday at the hospital. Unfortunately, the High Desert Inn was full, so I took my chances by staying at the Jonquil, an older motel located up one of the canyon roads. At best, it was a set piece for the next *Psycho* movie. Several small buildings surrounded the office, each containing two rooms. I checked in around midnight and had to awaken the night clerk to get my key. She pointed in the direction of the unit containing my room, slammed the door behind me, and turned out the lights before I descended the stairs. I drove to my unit, and upon entering I beheld the tiniest motel room I had ever seen. The bed consumed virtually all the floor space leaving barely enough leeway for the front door to swing open. The bathroom was roughly the size of a phone booth.

I regretted not being more prompt about making a reservation elsewhere, but it was late, nothing was to be done, and I settled in. After showering I lay in bed in my tee shirt and undershorts intending to read myself to sleep. I was more than a little startled when a scorpion roughly the size of a Schnauzer fell onto my chest. I responded, as most people would under those circumstances, with a shriek and flew out of bed. One instant I was lying in bed, the next I was standing in the tiny margin between the bed and the interior wall. I grabbed the small towel I rolled up for a back support to use as a weapon, as I searched for the scorpion. I wasn't thinking clearly, as I later determined I needed more firepower than a threadbare hand towel to deal with this monster. I pulled the sheets and covers off, looked everywhere but couldn't find the intruder. I was holding the rolled towel in my right hand poised to strike, when I noticed movement on the erstwhile weapon. I saw the scorpion crawling towards my naked hand and again did what seemed logical. I shrieked like a child facing mortal danger and threw the towel across the room.

I never found that scorpion. I called the office, but no one answered. I stayed in the room that night, but it was not restful. The next day I told the people at the hospital about my eventful evening, and they laughed and volunteered, "Had that scorpion bitten you, you would have spent a week with us as a patient."

Marvin*

Sierra Vista is a relatively large community located on the eastern edge of Cochise County and is home to Fort Huachuca, a U. S. Army base. One of the most distinguishing characteristics of the town was the perpetual smoke emanating from the nearby mountain range, a consequence of the continual forest fires ignited by illegal immigrants seeking warmth as they trekked northward from the Mexican border.

Marvin* was the CEO of the Hospital. I first met him when Jim and I traveled to Sierra Vista to discuss a joint venture between their hospitals. Marvin's secretary escorted us into his office where we were seated and offered refreshments. I had been in over 400 hospitals and had worked with a wide variety of CEO's, but little prepared me for Marvin. His office was a shrine to Emmett Kelly, the man who created the "Weary Willie" character known to clown aficionados by his signature act of cleaning up for other performers by using a broom to sweep away the pool of light from the spotlight. Dozens of paintings, photos, and memorabilia paid homage to Kelly and other famous clowns including Red Skelton. We politely inquired about his collection, and our host launched into a passionate dissertation on his love of clowns. It was mildly creepy, and this hobby seemed out of character for the gruff ex-Marine.

He was also an industrial strength hard ass when it came to negotiating. His bargaining mantra was, "I win, you lose, and, by the way, go f'_k yourself." After a reasonably futile meeting, Marvin looked out the solo window in his otherwise darkened office and saw something that prompted him to tell us the following story:

"You see my parking spot out there? For several days in a row one

of the docs on the staff decided he would park his SUV in my spot. He did it knowing it would piss me off. The third time he invaded my space, I called a couple of maintenance guys and told them to jack up the doc's vehicle, remove the wheels, hide them, and then drop it down on blocks to its original level. They did as instructed and left. Later in the afternoon when I knew the doc would be leaving, I called them to come to my office, so they could see the results of their handiwork. The doc was a pompous shit knuckle and got into the driver's seat not noticing a thing. We watched as he started the engine, shifted into reverse, put his right arm around the top of the passenger seat, looked back, and hit the accelerator. Obviously, nothing happened, so he gunned it and still nothing happened. We were rolling on the floor with laughter, as he got out to survey the situation. Once he realized what happened, he glanced at my window and flipped me the bird. I returned the favor. We didn't get along all that well."

Predictably, Marvin moved on to other opportunities shortly after this episode. I ran into him at a hospital industry meeting 20 years later and reminded him of the story. He laughed at the recollection and expounded further on the perfidiousness of the offending doc.

Origins in Cochise County

The San Pedro River lies about 10 miles west of Bisbee midway to Sierra Vista and is the only river that runs north from Mexico into the United States. It forms a riparian oasis for numerous species of birds, butterflies, and bats that use this corridor to migrate between South, Central, and North America. The San Pedro valley in springtime is a spectacularly colorful contrast to the more dominant desert terrain. It is also home to a number of small resorts that appeal to birdwatchers and nature lovers venturing from all corners of the globe. One of the hospital board members owned and operated one such bed and breakfast, which she offered as the site for the hospital's annual planning meeting. I was invited to facilitate.

The night before my departure, our family was dining with Mom. Dad had recently passed away, and we dined with Mom every Sunday night. She politely asked where my travels would take me for the coming week, and I mentioned going to a resort near Sierra Vista. She said, "You know, dear, you were conceived at Fort Huachuca while your Dad was stationed there." Most people don't relish contemplating the sex lives of their parents, but later I appreciated knowing this morsel of personal history and my limited connection to Cochise County.

CHAPTER 13

Albany John

A tall, thin, young man arrived at the Kansas City airport on a flight from Paris, France on a Saturday afternoon in May 1999 wearing a full-length black leather jacket. Apparently, he was unaware of the recent tragedy in Columbine, CO where two students wearing similar attire turned their suburban Denver high school into a killing field. Otherwise, he might have understood why he encountered such difficulty in hitching a ride to his ultimate destination, Albany, MO. After wasting several hours in the failed attempt, he negotiated a fare with a cabdriver to take him the 100 miles north. The Frenchman traveled the 5,000 miles in response to an ad offering a 1941 Dodge for sale by my friend John, CEO of the local hospital.

John lives on a small acreage east of Albany with a ¼ mile driveway leading up to the house and menagerie where he raises goats, llamas, roller pigeons, chickens, and a variety of other domesticated critters. He was expecting the young Frenchman, as they had exchanged numerous emails about the car. They tentatively agreed on a $2,000 price for the fully restored, antique vehicle subject to an on-site inspection.

The cabdriver discharged his passenger and headed back to KC. It was apparent that this strange looking young man had more than a passing interest in the old Dodge. John greeted his guest warmly, introduced him to his wife and son still living at home, and took him to his garage to see the object of his desire. The Frenchman studied the car carefully, examining every square inch of the exterior and interior. They started it up, and he listened to the motor with a knowing ear. He told John that his plan was to drive the car to Boston where he would arrange for it to be shipped to France. He then asked in his heavily accented English, "Will you guarantee that this car will make eet to Boston?"

John said, "I will guarantee you that the car will make it to the end of my driveway."

The Parisian harrumphed, "Well, if you won't guarantee the trip, I'll not pay the agreed upon price."

"Tell everyone in France hi for me," John retorted.

The Parisian's cab was gone, he was 100 miles from the airport, he had invested over $1,000 to view an old car, and he just pissed off its owner. John later took pity and arranged for someone to take him back to the airport but failed to receive a modicum of appreciation in return.

John later sold the Dodge to a dealer for $3,000, and it can still be seen occasionally driving around northwest Missouri.

Washer

Wacky stuff happens in emergency rooms all over the world. People love televised stories of the dramas that play out daily, some tragic, some heroic, and some funny. My favorite occurred in Albany. Unlike large urban hospitals, many of their rural counterparts don't have a physician on the premises 24/7. Instead a local doc is "on call" and comes in when needed. One day John received the following call from the ER nurse on duty:

Nurse: "John, you're not going to believe what we've got now. A guy from Sugarton* checked in, and he has a metal washer stuck on his erect penis. I've called Dr. Brush*, and he's on his way."

John: "Well try to find the least attractive nurse you can to work on this. We certainly don't want him to get more aroused."

Lacking the option of a male nurse, they located someone who gamely tried, unsuccessfully, to apply lubricants to remove the offending metal ring. Eventually, the doctor arrived and injected Novocaine into the man's constricted unit, providing a welcomed release of pressure, and the washer was removed. This event occurred before the advent of HIPAA, patient privacy laws, so word spread rapidly about the patient's unique condition. The man presumably appreciated the successful treatment and left without offering any explanation. Amused observers were left wondering, "WTF?"

Two hours later the odd visitor reappeared and approached the doc who was still at the hospital. He inquired, "Can I have my washer back?"

The Doc said, "Sure, but next time I'd recommend getting one a few sizes bigger." We later speculated the patient must have been confused about the intended role for a washer: preventing leakage between a nut and a screw.

Minnows

One day John and I were going fishing at a lake community north of Albany and stopped in a small bait shop in the tiny hamlet of Altamont, MO to buy minnows and snacks. We encountered an unpleasant young woman tending the store, her rudeness somehow sparked a bit of orneriness in John, and the following exchange occurred:

John: "Young lady do you have any idea who I am?"

Bait woman: "No, should I?"

John: "My name is John W. Richmond. I'm with the Bureau for the Protection of Unendangered Species, and I'm seeing things around here that I don't like one bit!"

Bait woman: "What on earth are you talking about?"

John: "Look at that bait tank over there. I can clearly see that you have adult male minnows sharing a tank with juvenile females."

Bait woman: "So what?"

John: "What do you think happens in that tank every night after you go home? Do I need to tell you of the trauma that the unwanted attention from those adult males can cause those juvenile females?"

Bait woman: "Really?"

An older man in overalls was sitting in the corner of the store about to pee in his pants, but he continued to observe quietly.

Bait woman: "I just work here, I've only been here for three weeks. You'll have to talk to the owner."

John: "Young lady, I can clearly see you are present and a party to this travesty and have done nothing to stop it, so it doesn't matter whether you're the owner of the store or not."

Bait woman, now with a hint of concern: "Is there a fine or something?"

John: "Yes, there's a fine, and you could face jail time up to 24 months! I've got a team of agents in the area that will descend upon this store within minutes of my call." He paused for a moment to let this sink in. "However, we might be able to ease up on you a bit if you would be willing to roll on the owner."

Bait woman: "Hell yes, I'll roll on that bitch! I can tell you stuff that will curl your hair. You can't believe the shit that goes down in this store!"

By now the old man in the corner was exploding with laughter, and a spark of sanity finally ignited in the young woman's noggin.

Bait woman: "You've been pulling my leg, haven't you? I can't believe I fell for that."

John: "Where did you go to high school?"

Bait woman: "Winston."

John: "That explains it."

Tornado

A tornado warning had been issued for northwest Missouri around 3:30 pm on a spring Wednesday afternoon. Such warnings indicate that a tornado had been sighted and are taken seriously by most people in the Midwest. It was one of the busiest times of the day at the hospital, as a shift change was in progress and clinic visits were in full swing. The Albany hospital is shaped like a starfish with five arms radiating from a central disc. John and his staff knew where the tornado first touched ground, its general direction, and that it was a clear and present danger to the hospital and its occupants. They started to herd everyone into the central nursing station of the hospital. Just as the last non-ambulatory patients were wheeled into the hopefully safer area, the lights went out, and the emergency system kicked on. Someone noticed that the doors to the west wing of the hospital were not yet shut, so John hustled over to close them. Just as he reached the open doorway, the tornado hit that section of the building. The nearly 80 people huddled together were horrified to see John disappear into the vortex of the storm.

John later reported that he was sucked down the hallway flying head over heels and, in an instant, was released from the storm's grip and dropped to the floor. The roof of the west wing was gone, and John was shaken but alive. He walked back into the central hub of the hospital much to the relief of his colleagues, and that is how John became known as Dorothy.

Jay

John grew up in Kansas City and was working there when he was recruited to take the position of CEO at the Albany hospital. It turned out to be a mutually beneficial match. The hospital was losing money, had no cash reserves, and was in danger of closing when John arrived. In a fairly short period of time, he began the process of restoring the organization to health.

John's efforts were noticed and appreciated, and he and his family were quickly absorbed into the community fabric. Shortly after John and Aileen moved to Albany, their third son, Jay, was born with numerous, severe handicaps, requiring round the clock care. He has never been able to speak, walk, or care for his basic needs. Shortly after his birth, the medical professionals told John and Aileen that it was rare for babies with Jay's condition to live past their third birthday. Jay could not be left unattended for even the few minutes it would take Aileen to walk down their driveway to pick up mail.

If anyone has ever doubted the proposition that God has placed angels amongst us, they need to meet Aileen. The entire community lent a hand, the older boys grew up quickly and accepted a share of the responsibility for Jay's care, but it was Aileen who remained steadfast in providing love and 24/7 care for Jay year after year. She would be quick to tell anyone offering sympathy that it was she who has been blessed in caring for this special child.

For the first eight years of Jay's life, he was unable to communicate in any fashion with those around him. One day an occupational therapist from the hospital was staying with Jay to give Aileen a brief respite. She was playing with a stringy "Koosh" ball and would put it on Jay's forehead and ask him questions requiring a binary answer. Over time she learned that Jay's mental functioning was good, but he had no way of expressing himself. Eventually, she learned that Jay had savant-like capabilities. She would place the "Koosh" ball on Jay's forehead and ask, "What is the product of 146 x 258?" In their system of communications, nodding the ball off to the right meant yes and a nod to the left meant no. The therapist then offered a series of potential answers, and, when she got to the correct one, Jay would nod the ball to the right. For a brief time, the family began a dialogue with Jay. Tragically, this newly discovered blessing was lost as Jay suffered a minor stroke during a medical procedure within a year of this discovery.

Undeterred, the remarkable love of a mother for her son continues to nurture this special young man. As of the date of this writing, the family helped Jay celebrate his 27th birthday, a testament to the power of love.

CHAPTER 14

Three Funerals

My travels once took me to Okeene, OK on a beautiful April Sunday morning to attend the capital campaign kickoff for a modernization project for their community hospital. I drove to Wichita the night before and stopped in nearby Hennessey for a sumptuous breakfast in a local café with the church crowd before motoring on to Okeene.

The city fathers closed one of the main streets in town for the noon event. By the time I arrived, people were assembling from the various church services just concluded. Kids were performing on a portable stage that had been set up for the occasion. One high school boy possessed a beautiful voice and a stage presence that would have served him well on *American Idol*. The local Rotarians were manning a food line serving BBQ brisket sandwiches, potato salad, and typical Americana fare. The official program began with a local preacher offering a prayer, followed by every politician for miles around who spoke and offered praise to the citizens of Okeene and to themselves for being so doggone helpful. A few others contributed their comments about various aspects of the project, then the hospital CEO talked about the importance of the hospital to the community and made "The ask," and that was that.

Adults milled around visiting with their friends and neighbors, kids rode their bikes and ran amidst the throngs of people or played on the swings at the nearby park. As the crowd started to thin, I sat down at a picnic table with one of the hospital board members and one of her friends. I was taking in the Norman Rockwell scene and said to my two companions, "You know, this is a nice little town."

The friend replied, "Well, the truth of the matter is that we're three funerals shy of this being a great little town.

I said, "That is the perfect country song!"

She replied, "It's all yours. All I know is come Monday morning the naysayers will be drinking coffee down at Pete's (Café) saying, 'Anybody who thinks anything good is going to happen in this sorry-assed little town is a damn fool.'"

And so on the 349 mile drive back to Kansas City that afternoon, I wrote the song the world has been waiting to hear. My only regret was that I couldn't sit down with my Dad and have him plunk out a tune on his piano.

Three Funerals Shy of Paradise

My travels took me down to Okeene O K,
A sunny little place on a bright spring day.
Lotta friendly people, make you feel right at home
Neighbors helping neighbors, the kids free to roam.

What a great little town I say to my friend,
This fella overhears us and has to weigh in.
Yea, it's a sweet little town but it ain't ALL right,
You see, we're three funerals shy of paradise.

For starters we got Bonham Ray Akin,
Goes to church on Sunday, but it sure ain't a'takin.
He's a greedy man, more than willing to lie,
Nothin' much happens less his finger's in the pie.

chorus

    Most everyone round here is pretty darn nice,
    'Cept we're three funerals shy of paradise.

    Like most small towns, one first name won't do,
    It's our plight to live with Ida Maude Ballew.
    Her life's been hard. She's quick to vent her spleen,
    There's no good deed that woman won't demean.

chorus

    Most everyone round here is pretty darn nice,
    'Cept we're still three funerals shy of paradise.

    Last but not least we got hateful old Alice,
    Ev'ry bone in her body's filled with malice,
    She ain't a goin to change, and she ain't a goin to leave,
    Hope the grim reaper will give us a reprieve.

chorus

    They're a sorry lot, like grubs in a log,
    Caus'n more grief than an egg suckin dog

    Won't be long, and things will be ALL right
    After we've had three funerals in paradise

PART III

OFF DUTY

Ben beneath the summit of Handies Peak

CHAPTER 15

Colorado 14ers

2007

Ben had a few days available after completing his summer internship with a NYC firm before returning to the University of Michigan for his last year of law school. I suggested that we scale a couple of 14,000+ ft peaks in CO. We hiked up 4,000' peaks in England, and I figured this would be no big deal, but I was delusional. The plan was to meet in Denver on Tuesday, spend a few days in Vail to acclimate to the elevation, travel to Lake City, CO on Wednesday, ascend Handies Peak on Thursday, rest on Friday, scale Gray's and Torrey's Peaks on Saturday, and fly home on Sunday.

We arrived in Denver, headed west, stayed with family in Vail, and were sent on our way on a warm, sunny Colorado morning. We drove through Leadville and Buena Vista, stopped in Salida to go river rafting and arrived in Gunnison by late afternoon. We shopped for hiking provisions, and headed the 60 miles south to Lake City, a picturesque town in the southwest corner of Colorado.

We checked into our bed and breakfast, the Old Carson Inn, situated on the gravel road leading to the trailhead for Handies Peak. The owner of the B&B was occupied with her husband disassembling an airplane that had crashed on an aborted takeoff in a nearby mountain airstrip. We walked over to the airstrip, then relaxed on their porch, read, and watched the beautiful birds and other critters flit about. It was like being in a Disney movie. We returned to town for dinner and were told the season-ending performance of the Lake City Lakettes was scheduled that evening, featuring a combination clogging / belly dancing revue. We purchased the last two seats available in Lake City's recently restored opera house. The dancers ranged in age from 20 to 60 and in ability from Barishnikov to Bluto.

Critics find it hard to say which act was best, but I'm going with the routine done to the tune "Dueling Banjos" with a teenaged girl clogging the guitar part and a fleshy belly dancer undulating the banjo retort. Three bare-chested guys with their torsos painted in red lipstick to look like a face, nipples painted to look like eyes, belly buttons the mouth, with noses painted on their stomachs were a close second. Their head and arms were stuffed in a large top hat, and their lower extremities were covered with an ersatz shirt collar around the waist, fake arms dangling therefrom. The effect was a long face and short torso on tiny legs. They waddled on the stage and "lip synced" to the tune "Bridge on the River Kwai" using their belly buttons and extending their ample girth in time with the tune. I'm a pretty well traveled guy, but this was a first for me. Even Ben was amused.

Thursday August 23, 2007

We arose at 5:45 am, enjoyed breakfast that the proprietress, the lovely Bettina, was kind to prepare at that early hour, and we were on the road to Handie's Peak. Bettina warned, "It's 12 miles to the trailhead, and the road is pretty rough, so I hope you have a good 4-wheel drive vehicle. It'll take an hour to get there."

"No problem, we rented a Dodge Durango," I thought. The first five miles were reasonably well maintained gravel roads, not unlike those one would experience driving up Pike's Peak. The remaining seven were unlike anything I had experienced. We encountered a two-mile stretch on a shelf road, one car width wide, with the mountain rising sharply up and down each edge of the road. The potholes and ruts were deep and plentiful. Had another vehicle been coming from the opposite direction, it would have been impossible to pass. I implored Ben to put on his seatbelt. He obliged, and then comforted me by observing, if we were to roll off this cliff, the seatbelt would be about as useful as one on an airplane auguring into a mountain at full throttle.

Once past the shelf, the road worsened with even deeper ruts to navigate. We scraped bottom twice, once sufficiently hard to jeopardize our oil pan. It occurred to me, no tow truck operator in the world would drive up this trail, so we may well have purchased a Dodge Durango. With the exception of two men on dirt bikes, we didn't see another vehicle during the entire trip. We continued until we could see the trailhead in the distance, but the last mile was more terrifying than the preceding eleven. We had to cross a creek with an entry point so steep our bumper scraped rocks underwater before the wheels entered the stream. I'm thinking, "How are we going to get out of this creek on our return?" We trekked on, scraped bottom twice more, and finally reached the trailhead. I told Ben, "I think the worst is over." I was wrong.

It was 8:10 am, 37 degrees, 11,000 ft. above sea level, and we started our ascent to the 14,048' peak some five miles distant. All went well until we reached Sloan Lake at 13,000'. After resting and exploring the lake, we reconnected to what we thought to be the correct path. We hiked several hundred yards and came to a steep field of boulders leading up to a saddle between two peaks. We climbed it and reached a dead end. Only skilled rock climbers could proceed from the location in which we found ourselves. I'm not that sharp at sea level, but it was clear that the altitude had taken me down a notch or two. Eventually, deducing we missed the correct trail, we slid down the rock field, bushwhacked across a boulder field working our way in the general direction of the correct trail, and recommenced our climb. Unfortunately, we ascended and descended 750' in a wasted effort. We eventually reached the correct saddle at 13,500' leading to our goal, but I was out of gas. I had completely misjudged the effort required to get to this point. Even so, one couldn't help but appreciate the majestic views that now surrounded us.

After eating a quick lunch, Ben went on, and I stayed behind. I watched him disappear over a false summit. Ten minutes later I caught a glimpse of him again as he followed the ridge to the crest. It was emotional viewing the solitary figure climbing the ridgeline. It appeared he was going in slow motion, but he had surely speeded up since he no longer had to wait on me. Once at the summit he turned around a few times, presumably taking pictures, and then disappeared.

The wind was blowing hard in the saddle, and it was cold. The only shelter from the wind required climbing down a steep escarpment to the lee side of the mountain. I was shivering, my heart was still pounding from earlier exertions, my legs were quivering, and I was in a state of high anxiety awaiting Ben's safe return. At this low point in the trip, it occurred to me it was delusional to think that it was a good idea to climb my first 14er after four weeks of moderate training, a portion of which was interrupted by a week of golf and gluttony visiting friends in Minnesota.

After a few minutes, Ben returned to my line of sight and started down. Once he reappeared over the false summit and could see me, I headed down the trail to get warm. He quickly caught up, and I gave him a big hug. I asked him what it was like at the top. "Awesome! An angel greeted me and put a wreath of white sunbeams around my head."

The trip down was uneventful. It took over four hours to reach the top but slightly under two hours to get down. My hiking poles were a lifesaver on the descent.

The confidence shattering events in the boulder field seduced me into temporarily forgetting the terror of driving from the trailhead back to Lake City. Crossing the creek on the return was more difficult than the morning crossing. The creek bed was fairly level, but the exit required ascending a steep, rocky incline. The bumper scraped the rock before the tires could gain purchase, but miraculously we got out. After three miles of harrowing travel at speeds approaching 2-3 mph, we drove over a blind rise, came down into a trough, and blew the right/front tire. Fortunately, this occurred before getting to the narrow shelf road with a semi-level spot nearby. Absent a manual, it took us 20 minutes to locate the jack and tools. The good news was the spare had air. Unfortunately, it was a micro wheel that didn't match the other three. Ben changed the tire. I was of little help, other than to annoy him with meaningless advice. We were out of water, it was hot, and I was stressed negotiating the remainder of the trail in a vehicle that was crabbing on differing sized wheels.

As we recommenced our journey, I told Ben, "I am never, ever, ever, ever going to do this again."

"Why don't you wait until tomorrow and see how you feel," Ben consoled.

I was thinking, "Maybe I'll get a lucky break and come down with flu or diarrhea, or break an arm, or something, so I would have a reasonably manly way of escaping further agony."

Over the years I have maintained a mental inventory of the ten dumbest things I've done in my life. It's been many years since I last threw one off the bus. This was one of those times. In the event you're interested, the one that had to go to make room for the 14ers misadventure goes like this: When I was in my mid-twenties I attended a party held by a senior executive of an important client. His ancient wife pestered me into guessing her age. Unwisely I did. I thought she was 60 but generously suggested 45. She shrieked and left the room in tears. I must have guessed wrong. That episode has now been replaced by the Handies Peak debacle.

We returned to Gunnison, checked into a motel, enjoyed a superb pizza (Mario's), had a near miss car wreck by inches, and went to bed.

Friday August 24, 2007

We awoke to another crystal clear, deep cobalt blue-sky Colorado morning and headed to a local tire store. We left the wounded tire, went to have a lumberjack breakfast, and returned for the news. The owner said, "Your tire is toast. I can put a patch on it that will hold air, but I wouldn't drive on it if it were me." He continued muttering, "Can you believe it? Stupid f'ers watch SUV commercials and think these damn things can handle these rutted, rocky, mountain roads with 4 ply tires." In spite of inferring I was a moron, he was a nice guy and most helpful in calling around town to find a replacement. We bought a new tire and headed to Crested Butte.

We played golf at the Crested Butte Country Club. Fortunately, the course is open to the public and had a lax dress code, as we were wearing hiking shorts and shoes. We enjoyed a splendid round of golf at 9,200'. Even I could hit the ball above average distances. Ben's highlight of the round was a 210-yard shot to the green with a 7 iron out of the sand. He made the putt for a birdie. Things were looking up.

After golf our journey took us over the Kebler and McClure Passes north to Glenwood Springs. We drove through the largest aspen grove I've ever seen, a spectacular sight, stopped in Minturn to gorge on Mexican food, and motored on to Dillon.

Early in the trip, Ben told me he was on a diet. I said, "Ben's that's crazy, you don't need to lose any weight."

"Who said anything about losing weight. I need to gain about 10 lbs." He subsequently ate like Sumo boy at every opportunity, and, being the gracious traveling companion, I matched him bite for bite.

I was feeling a little better by now, almost chipper, and blessedly had not been granted my wish for a temporary, disabling disease. We retired for the evening intent on ascending Gray's Peak the next day.

Saturday August 25, 2007

The trailhead for Gray's Peak is three miles south of I-70, just east of the Eisenhower tunnel. Unfortunately, the road was almost as bad as the one we traversed at Handies. After driving ½ mile through ruts and over boulders, it became apparent why the parking lot was full at the intersection at I-70. I was in another state of panic. I didn't want to add the extra six miles if we were to hike it, but I also didn't want to drive the Durango up the horrifying road. Ben calmed me down, and we drove on without incident.

After we walked from the car to the trailhead, I realized I left my hiking poles, and Ben went to retrieve them. Bless that boy. We also had a division of labor. Ben carried the water, three quarts per person, and I carried our sandwiches.

The elevation of the trailhead for Gray's is 11,280 and the peak is 14,270. It was another beautiful, cloudless morning, 40 degrees, and we were off at 7:30 am. The outline of our route was visible from the start. We had no problem in finding or staying on the trail, as it was like following a trail of well-conditioned ants.

Handies Peak provided a few lessons that greatly aided the Gray's experience. I resisted the urge to gaze up towards the goal, as that was dispiriting. I avoided looking down the side of the trail, as that was often scary. On our frequent rest stops, I would focus on how far we had come.

It was a weekend, we were close to Denver, and the trail was busy. Numerous father/son combos were on the trail along with many attractive young ladies. Going up was quite strenuous, so the conversations between

Ben and me pretty much consisted of, "Ben, I need to stop," or, "Ben, I'm not sure I'm up to this."

Ben would calmly reply, "You're doing fine, you can do this Dad."

When we were within a couple hundred yards of the summit, and I knew I could make it, I stopped to rest and was feeling like a manly man. Just then a young woman strolled by at a brisk pace carrying a baby in a backpack, lending perspective and humility.

The top of Gray's Peak is rounded and covered with large, loose stones. The wind was blowing hard, it was cold and beautiful, but not as majestic as Handies. Some energetic souls had constructed a rock cave at the summit to provide shelter. We huddled into it, rested, and ate lunch.

We then hiked down the opposite side of the summit towards Torrey's Peak, one mile's distance from Gray's, separated by a saddle midway. We planned to hike down to the saddle where I would find shelter and wait for Ben to ascend Torrey's, thus accomplishing the goal of three 14ers in three days. I did not have the energy to take on the additional 1,000' ascent. Once we started down the ridge towards the saddle, we quickly realized that the gale force wind was a major impediment. I wanted to get off the mountain as quickly as possible, and Ben agreed.

I could hold my hiking pole by the strap and the wind would blow it nearly horizontal. Worse, it blew my nasal emesis all over my sunglasses where it quickly froze. Snot a pretty image I know. I was thinking, "Why on earth would anyone do this for recreation?"

It was a 10-mile round trip from our car to the peak and took 3 ½ hours to ascend and two hours down. We reached our car, slowly inched down the Road from Hell II, and headed for Idaho Springs where we savored a celebratory pizza at Beau Joe's. We feasted on a three-pound mountain meat pie, headed to Denver, took in a movie, and called it a day.

We drove an 850-mile circuit through Colorado, enjoyed spectacular scenery, had a few laughs, and partially accomplished our intended goals. The unpleasant aspects of trudging up steep mountains at high altitude quickly faded from my memory. I've now returned to my delusional state, where it seemed like great fun.

Judy and Ben climbing Great Wall

CHAPTER 16

China
2002

Ben took Mandarin his freshman year in college, and it clicked. He was fortunate to have a gift for languages, and he subsequently declared a major in the official language of China along with a minor in Japanese and business. His sophomore year he was invited to participate in a summer program in Hong Kong, and he spent the second semester of his junior year attending Beijing University. We joined Ben his last few weeks in Beijing, then traveled with him to Chongqing, Yichang, and finally Shanghai where he would start his summer job with a Chinese internet company.

Prior to our travels, Ben rented a movie we watched together, Yasujiro Ozu's 1953 masterpiece *Tokyo Story*. I was to later learn that the film is frequently listed among critics' choices of the top 100 ever made. The plot centers on an elderly couple's visit from their rural home in Onomichi to see their three adult children living in Tokyo. The couple's offspring could barely disguise their annoyance with their doltish parents for intruding on their busy lives. And so it was with life imitating art, or perhaps the other way around, that we traveled to Asia to meet Ben.

Day 0

We're in the Seoul airport, and I am sitting in the Asiana Lounge awaiting our connecting flight to Beijing. The 12-hour flight from Los Angeles to Korea was pleasant, they fed us exquisitely, and the time passed quickly. The hors d'oeuvres included lobster tail, duck breast and chateaubriand. We will fly out in the daylight, so we should get a better view of Korea and parts of China. We missed Judy's birthday (5/22) through the time changes. We left LA before midnight on 5/21 and arrived in Korea at 5 am 5/23, an interesting way of skipping a birthday. It is confusing to use a keyboard with Korean characters. English letters are added as a postscript. Everything is much more sophisticated here than I imagined. I was expecting water buffaloes.

Day 1

We arrived in Beijing midday, and Ben greeted us at the airport. We caught a cab to our hotel, checked in, and then embarked on a small excursion. We visited Ben's school, met his Japanese friend, Asuka, walked several blocks, and caught a bus and subway to the Lama Buddhist temple. The subways are clean and nice, but crowded. Ben and I tower over people. Even though we are 4-5 miles from the center of the city, the levels of congestion are unlike anything I've experienced in America. Even Richard Scary couldn't imagine the vehicles that exist here, mostly human powered. Walking is mildly hazardous. Sidewalks, when they exist, are apparently not for walking. Instead, people walk in the streets, which are also swarming with cars, buses, motorcycles, and bicycles. Taxi drivers treat red lights as mere suggestions.

People are employed in all manner of odd ways. Ticket takers ride on small buses, cleaning people are everywhere, and guards stand at attention in the oddest of places. We observed several dozen men in coolie hats working feverishly on a piece of ground outside the Forbidden City roughly the size of our front yard. The people we've seen are well dressed and uncommonly attractive. I've not seen a single overweight person.

Our hotel hosts initially placed us in an unacceptable room. After complaining, and with Ben's linguistic assistance, we were put into a luxury suite, deserving of its advertised five star ranking. Our elegant lodgings cost $90 U.S. per night. Ben converses easily and quickly with the Chinese. I have no idea what he is saying, but he seems to be communicating with clarity. I haven't mastered even two words. Thank God he is with us to order food, as we've been dining in restaurants that don't cater to tourists, and they don't provide English menus.

Ben worked today so Judy and I were on our own. We had an extravagant, western style breakfast before catching a cab to the

Forbidden City. One of the items on the breakfast buffet was labeled bovine stomach parts. The hotel's dining area reminds me of the Bellagio in Las Vegas. However, looking out the window immediately below our room one can observe a drab, colorless manufacturing plant with workers streaming in on their bikes to start their day.

We started our first day with a trip to the Forbidden City. The famed tourist destination was interesting, quite crowded, and worth seeing. The best part of the journey was the cab ride through the various parts of the city, mindful of an ant farm. Before entering, we crossed a major thoroughfare with the green light in our favor. Two busses barreled down at us through their red light. I hustled out of the way. Judy, of course, wanted to stand her ground and dress them down for not obeying the traffic signals. Should she survive, I know she will have left her mark on China. Did you know that more Chinese have land-line telephones (190 million) and more cell phones (160 million) than exist in the US?

Day 2 – 4

Ben, taciturn and shy in English in America, is the garrulous, gracious, conversationalist in Mandarin. Friday night we were dining in an area Ben described as outrageously expensive (about $30 for the three of us) and referred to it as the Beijing "Times Square." Judy was taken aback when our poultry entrée arrived with the chicken's head charred and prominently displayed on the plate. After dinner, a western looking man approached our table and conversed with Ben in English and told him he had overheard Ben's conversation with the waiters, said his Mandarin was impeccable, and that it is rare for a westerner to speak Chinese so well. Judy and I beamed as we walked out of the restaurant past the cages of live snakes awaiting their turn as future delectables. We then strolled around the neighborhood, found a Starbucks, and joined tens of thousands of young people promenading.

Ben's boss's wife from his internship generously offered to provide her car and driver for the weekend. She instructed her driver to take us to a remote part of the Great Wall not readily accessible to tourists. On Saturday morning our driver picked us up in a Honda sedan, a luxurious rarity in Beijing, and we headed for the Simatai portion of the Great Wall, a three-hour drive north. Ben served as translator for the steady stream of questions I posed for the driver. Example: "What is the penalty for a driver killing a pedestrian?" That seemed a perfectly normal question since it is amazing that China still has 1.3 billion living people given the number of speeding cars in their midst.

The answer, "It depends."

Beijing lies in a coastal plain and is consistently flat. On a clear day from higher ground such as the Forbidden City, you can see the mountains in the distance to the north. Upon leaving Beijing, the terrain and the buildings change dramatically. Most of the land is terraced and has something useful growing on it. The little villages feature tidy stone buildings with interesting architectural detail, and the streams are crystal clear. The drive was both scenic and harrowing. Passing on curves and hills appears to be encouraged. We passed the 2008 Olympic Village site, which is already quite developed six years early. The roads were modern and well maintained.

Arriving at the base of an access point to the wall, we loaded up with water and embarked on a 4-5 hour hike. We walked past a gauntlet of vendors, including those offering camel rides, and then hiked up a steep trail along a river gorge to reach the lowest tower of the wall. The wall was built on a steep ridgeline. Our hike took us to 12 different towers and then we came to a point where tourists are forbidden, as the wall is crumbling and inhospitably steep.

The wall was majestic in every way and truly a marvel of human enterprise. On a more mundane level, it was a difficult hike. Some portions of the wall were so steep it was more like climbing a ladder with widely spaced rungs. The steps were irregular in size with some 30" in height. We ascended and descended 2,500' in elevation. Traveling here gives you a different perspective on the issue of personal danger. There are no bicycle helmets, people don't wear seatbelts, and there are no guardrails near precipices. OSHA inspectors would love this place.

We encountered vendors selling water and Popsicles in the highest towers. They have small refrigerators with uncovered wiring extending several miles from a power source. It was a bit incongruous to hike on a 2,000 year-old, architectural masterpiece, reach a new tower after a difficult climb, and then gaze upon a Popsicle purveyor.

At tower eight a duo of Mongolian hucksters foisted themselves on us. We bought a book from them just to get them to go away. We were exhausted when we got back to the car, and I didn't pester Ben as often for translations of the return trip.

That evening Ben took us to his favorite restaurant for Beijing duck. Each plate was adorned with a charred duck head, neatly cleaved in two. Midway through dinner, a young man, who looked like a Chinese version of John Belushi, pulled up a chair and asked if he could practice his English. He complimented Ben on his Mandarin, and then we had a nice chat. He loves the NBA, Kobe Bryant in particular, and said he understands that, "Life is very easy in the U.S." He asked if I knew Chairman Mao. In Mandarin, Ben politely explained the difference between, "to know" and "to know of." I can't believe this is my kid.

On Sunday we caught a cab to the Dirt Market, a giant flea market where they sell Chinese crap. I bought a few posters of old cigarette ads featuring partially clad beauties to serve as barn wall adornments. When we rendezvoused later, Judy's bags were full of Lord knows what. One doesn't see many children here, presumably a function of the one child policy. However, when you do see little ones, they are the recipients of industrial strength doting.

After the Dirt Market, Ben's boss's wife, Mrs. Pan, picked us up to take us on a personal tour of Beijing. She drove us to the Hon Chou district where foreigners come to buy pearls. Judy picked out the kind of pearls she wanted, and then Mrs. Pan took over the negotiations. Then she took us to the Temple of Heaven.

Mrs. Pan presented us with an expensive gift and insisted that she take us to dinner. Ben explained that in China when someone offers to take you to dinner that means they will also order for you. Ben told us that when once a guest at dinner he was asked if he liked seafood. He said he did not. When the dinner was served it included fish and assorted slimy stuff. In response to his bemused look, his hostess explained that the entrees were from rivers and lakes, not the sea.

We dined at a hot pot restaurant where platters of raw food are brought to the table, and the diner cooks it in a pot of steaming water situated atop a charcoal fired heater. We had lamb, beef, chicken and a few mysterious items. I selected a piece of white meat from one of the platters that I thought might be a scallop. I cooked the white, dense meat in the hot pot, removed it, and attempted to take a bite. Unfortunately, the morsel had the texture of a snow tire. I couldn't get it down but was being closely observed by Mrs. Pan, making a napkin dump difficult. Eventually, my gastric juices prevailed, and I was able to swallow the vile chunk. After as polite a query as I could muster, I was informed that I had just consumed a segment of bovine palate.

As Mrs. Pan spoke little English, and we spoke even less Mandarin, Ben served as our interpreter. Mrs. Pan continually coached Ben in language refinements. The wait staff from the restaurant gathered around our table, I think, in part, to listen to the Mandarin speaking western boy. Westerners are fairly common in tourist spots but not in the places that Ben and Mrs. Pan have taken us.

Ben shared a story about an earlier adventure, where a group of his schoolmates went to a rural community about 100 miles south of Beijing. The locals had little exposure to westerners, so several thousand people appeared to watch the foreigners play basketball and afterwards asked for autographs.

Mrs. Pan's hospitality was exceptional. After dinner her driver dropped us at our hotel, and she arranged for a masseuse to come to our room. When we offered to take her to dinner at another time during our stay she insisted, "No, we could take her to dinner when she comes to America." Mrs. Pan's parents are both physicians, so we chatted about the Chinese health care system. China's health care system is pure cash and carry, accounting in part for the high savings rates of their citizens.

The masseuse arrived, but it was not a good experience. Fortunately, Ben was there to help communicate and to lessen the unpleasantness of the deep muscle probing. The highlight of each day is watching Ben converse with cab drivers, merchants, waitress, and everyone in a light hearted, pleasant manner.

Ben returned to school today so we were on our own. We rented bikes at Beihai Park and then traveled to the silk district. In trying to find an internet café, I got lost. While meandering around the halls of a nondescript office building, I was intrigued that virtually every office appears to be a computer technology company. Someone took pity on me, and directed me to my desired destination. Tidbits for the day: Bei in Chinese means north and jing means capital. Nan means south. The Chinese characters are the same for Mandarin as they are for Cantonese. The differences lie in the pronunciation and sequencing of words.

Day 5 – 6

I'm really struggling with the language. I have often used the phrase "tshe tshe" which means "thank you," and the looks I get would make you think I stabbed someone's cat. Ben explained that tone is as important as the choice of word when conveying meaning. For example, the word "ma" has multiple meanings depending on the tone used. It can mean mother, horse, forbidden, or "you are a worthless piece of shit."

Beijing is relatively compact, about ten miles square, and significantly more densely populated than New York City, though cleaner. There are no skyscrapers but thousands of buildings 15 to 30 stories tall. There are hundreds of building cranes everywhere, yet you don't often see them operating. Most of the buildings appear to be apartments or offices. Within the city there is little industrial activity, which we're told is located in the surrounding areas.

One sees few older people. Almost everyone is under 40. According to Ben, Beijing is an expensive city by Chinese standards, and only those who have marketable skills in the new China can survive, or are welcome, here. They have an interesting euphemism called "flexible employment" to refer to those who work outside of the state owned enterprises and includes the entrepreneurs and people working for small, private businesses.

The English language newspaper, "The China World", is fascinating. Many of the articles are written in the form of editorial tutorials explaining how capital markets work, the importance of participating in the world economy, and explaining why necessary reforms are underway. Numerous articles cover Taiwan, always referred to as a wayward province. Even the sports reporting comes in pedagogical style, "The nation's pride rests on the Chinese World Cup performance."

Air pollution is ghastly, and one feels dirty just walking around. We went to the Beijing zoo located within walking distance from our hotel, as we sought to avoid cab rides for a few days taking a breather from the associated trauma. We viewed a few caged Pandas eating bamboo. For those interested in seeing molting animals missing big chunks of fur, make sure to include the Beijing zoo in your travel plans.

We found a Carrefour store near the zoo, a French version of Wal-Mart. The prices you pay in such "modern stores" are marked on the merchandise, quite distinct from typical Chinese department stores where bargaining is an essential part of the transaction, and the actual purchase price will typically be about 1/6 of the starting point. Imagine the most crowded Wal-Mart you have ever experienced, quadruple the number of shoppers, halve the size of the aisles, and you've got the picture.

A goodly portion of the Gobi desert descended on Beijing today. We are on the 16th floor of our hotel, and most of the landmarks we have come to recognize are now invisible. Most of the population dons surgical masks to avoid inhaling the particulates. Twelve hours after the storm abated, the streets were clean. An army of cleaning people descended on the city, mostly women, with brooms resembling something out of a Hans Christian Anderson fairy tale.

We caught a cab to the Summer Palace, which is in the northwest quadrant of the city. A 30-minute cab ride typically costs about $3-$5. The Summer Palace was built around a large lake and features beautiful temples, gardens, an opera stage, and an elaborate marble boat. In the late 19th century it served as a summer retreat for the Empress Dowager, who unwisely spent 30 million taels of silver building the ornamental boat at the expense of the Chinese navy, leaving the nation ill prepared for the Anglo-French invasion of 1860, aka the Opium War. Every English language sign in the park refers to that humiliating incursion when many national treasures were burned and looted by the heathen westerners and again in 1900 by the Eight Powers during the Boxer Rebellion. While hiking around the park a pretty, young Chinese woman asked us to take her picture. I took her camera and readied the shot, but then she exclaimed, "No. No. You misunderstand. I want you and her, pointing to Judy, to be in the picture with me."

We got lost on our return to the hotel. We typically carry a business card from our hotel to hand to the cab driver, since we have no other way of communicating. Unfortunately, I didn't notice that the card had some extraneous writing on it, which the driver read as our intended destination. Fortunately, we had a compass, and when we realized we were going to the east side of town not the west, we pulled out a map and pointed where we wanted to go. We still haven't witnessed any pedestrian deaths but did note in today's paper that they average 19 per day in Hangzou, resulting in the loss of $72,000 USD GDP.

Ben picked us up at 6 pm, and we caught a cab to the eastern edge of the city to attend the Chinese acrobatics show. One guy balanced on five rolling cylinders and spun around. Small girls would sit in a barrel about 15 inches in diameter and about 9 feet long and then slide through butt first with their toes and hands touching. We marveled at the "14 people on the bicycle trick," but you can see that on the streets as well. Afterwards, Ben took us to an Italian restaurant where we had Chianti, pizza, and penne pasta. It was tasty but, by far, the most expensive meal we have eaten in China, $40 for the three of us. Ben said he treated a few Chinese friends to dinner at this restaurant, and, while polite, they meekly expressed their displeasure.

I'm the only westerner in the computer cafe today, and it is interesting to just look and listen. It is full of young people and louder than life in a pinball machine. It reminds me of the chaotic crowd scenes in Viet Nam in the movie *Deer Hunter*. I am invisible.

It is quite common to see young men walking around arm in arm, holding hands. I asked Ben to explain, as I thought homosexuality (wong ho in Chinese) would be treated harshly in a highly regimented state. After likening me to an ignorant goober, Ben explained that it is more likely that these young men would be the equivalent of a US country bumpkin bringing the mores of rural China to hip Beijing. Akin to Judy and me skipping hand in hand down Fifth Avenue in New York City wearing Dekalb Corn ball-caps.

We have had several misadventures in cabs going to unintended places. The mistake may have resulted in an extra $1-$2 in cab fares, and the cab driver would almost always discount the meter rate to adjust for the extra distance. The American style fast food restaurants are much nicer here than they are in the U.S. The workers are well dressed and beam with pride at their jobs, and the restaurants are immaculate. The power of American brands is quite amazing, as you see Coke and Pepsi containers in the hands of the least prosperous citizens.

Ben had an interview with an official at the largest State Owned Bank (SOB) related to the paper he is writing as part of his internship. SOB is really the English acronym that they use. He asked the official about their strategies for reducing the high percentage of non-performing loans (now 40%), their attitudes towards undertaking non-traditional banking services such as insurance and investment banking, and their 5-10 year vision for adapting to the World Trade Organization agreements. These questions would be reasonably difficult to discuss and interpret in English, much less in Mandarin. We have yet to meet anyone who speaks English well, even in places that deal with foreigners on a regular basis.

I'm starting to figure out some of the traffic rules. When passing around a curve on a two-lane road and another car is approaching, the two lanes magically become three. This same rule applies when passing on the right onto a sidewalk when pedestrians and bicyclists give way. When driving on a multilane thoroughfare, up to 4-6 lanes each way, if one car's bumper gets one meter in front of the car on either side, they have the right, if not the outright duty, to pull in front of that vehicle. The speed of the vehicles is not a factor. There are four major belt highways encircling Beijing, and we have been on each of them, although not intentionally. At times while our cab may be speeding along, I've noticed that the driver of the vehicle to my right is often closer than is Judy sitting on my left. The cabs are tiny, smaller than a Mini Cooper one might see in the states.

We took a cab to the main shopping district in Beijing called Wangfujing. The buildings are modern and attractive, and there are tens of thousands of people evident in a single glance. The stores are full of expensive luxury items. More interesting were the hutongs, alleyways full of shops and living quarters that are situated immediately behind the fancy buildings. This place has a Potemkin village quality to it. The food vendors sell unimaginable treats. One can buy fried scorpions on a stick, giant boiled grasshoppers, and fat worm pupae kabobs. While I admired these visual treats, I couldn't bring myself to sample them. An English speaking Chinese man engaged us in conversation, and said he used to be a visiting art professor in Minneapolis. "Very, very cold," said he.

Women use parasols to protect their skin from the sun to remain light skinned. While people smoke and spit a lot, they don't chew gum. Pleasantly, the sidewalks and subways are not glommed up with the sticky residue. We had a nice dinner with Ben last night, but he had schoolwork to finish, so we didn't tarry.

Day 7 – 9

There are 1.1 million privately owned cars in Beijing and 2.8 million people with driver's licenses accounting for a large number that aspire to drive one day. In 1980 so few cars were in evidence that those who possessed the skills required to drive a car were held in higher esteem than physicians. Yesterday, we saw a traffic jam, fortunately going the other way, on the second ring road that had five lanes of cars completely stopped for several miles. It makes LA freeways look like a country lane.

Judy and I spent the day at Beihai Park, a lovely oasis near the Forbidden City. We viewed an opera being performed on a marble pavilion on the shore of the lake. The performers were theatrical and switched back and forth between Italian and Chinese. While Judy examined the gardens, I sat on a park bench reading and people watching. Judy has taken a picture of every plant type in Beijing, and she can often be heard in the distance exclaiming, "They most certainly would not trim a tree like that in Kansas!"

We have found American style fast food restaurants to be the best source of immaculately clean, western style restrooms. Public restrooms in Chinese parks can be a wee bit nasty, merely foul smelling holes over which one squats.

Last night we took Ben, Asuka, and four of their classmates to dinner. We went to a Japanese restaurant in the northern part of the city that Asuka recommended as it reminds her of her hometown, Tokyo. Our dinner companions included girls from Japan, Taiwan, Beijing, and two Americans. I sat next to Shen Liu who is from Beijing but lives in the dorm. Many of the foreign students have Chinese roommates, who receive their lodging in exchange for enhancing the language learning experience. I asked Shen Liu if most Beijingers had ever been to the Great Wall. She said most had not, but she had been twice. Once to the Badalind area that is crowded with foreign tourists and once to a more isolated spot. She added, "The Wall is very important to Chinese people, and it is important to touch it and to use your imagination to better understand the lives of our ancestors."

I asked her if the fried scorpions were on sale just to freak out the tourists. She said, "No, it is believed that it is healthful to eat them. Many Chinese think the more loathsome and poisonous the creature, the more healthful it is to eat."

Our dinner consisted of a sushi dishes and other Japanese delicacies accompanied by ample wine, hot sake, and beer. Shen Liu is studying to be a sanitation engineer, a career choice made for her by the state. Ben later explained that it is extremely competitive to get into a university in China, and admissions are based on examinations. Those who score the highest can choose their field of study, those who don't have it chosen for them. Shen Liu's work life direction was thus chosen by the state on the basis of a series of examinations. Those who score extremely well are allowed to study abroad, and of that select group, those at the top are allowed to study in America.

After dinner, Ben shared his world travel theory with us: In the US, even if you haven't personally traveled outside the country, it is likely that you know someone who has, thus increasing your understanding of the world. In China, it is almost impossible for common citizens to travel abroad, and it is unlikely that they have ever encountered anyone who has. This isolation results in some wacky ideas about the world beyond.

Today Judy and I visited Mao's mausoleum and the Communist Revolutionary Museum at Tiananmen Square. We were entering an intersection of a busy street and observed a young Chinese woman and her small child crossing ahead of us with their heads down. Judy's atavistic warning shriek alerted them to the speeding limo barreling towards them. They narrowly missed being killed.

Unfortunately, the mausoleum was closed, but it was still well guarded. Throughout the city one finds unarmed guards everywhere, and they are usually young, pleasant looking men standing at attention under umbrellas. Tiananmen Square is different, where the guards were armed and did not appear jovial or welcoming.

It took me about 15 minutes to buzz through the Hall of Chinese Treasures, but Judy needed more time so we set a rendezvous point. I meandered through the streets and hutongs wearing my "Don't Mess with Texas" tee shirt, khaki shorts, and North Face hiking shoes. I can't figure out how people identified me as a tourist, but somehow they did. I went back to the hutongs featuring the fried scorpions and Michelin-tire-man-shaped pupae, thinking I needed a healthy snack, but I chickened out when actually faced with eating one of the vile morsels.

Ben and Asuka joined us for dinner at the Fangshan Restaurant in Behai Park. It is purportedly the most elegant and expensive restaurant in Beijing. We drank French wine and feasted on a 20-course meal including creatures from the sea that I couldn't begin to describe. The recognizable items included duck, prawns, and venison. The restaurant overlooks a scenic lake, and we dined in a room similar to the many temples we visited. Our server was constantly present and seemed to enjoy talking with Ben. Asuka's English is excellent, so it was nice to get a chance to visit with her and to learn of her experiences growing up in Tokyo. I asked her if Tokyo was as congested as Beijing. She said it is much more crowded. She had a 1½-hour commute each way to high school via subway, bus, and walking. It was as nice a dining experience as we've had anywhere and expensive by Beijing standards, $110 for the four of us.

Judy and I headed back to the hotel, where we caught the last minutes of the World Cup match between Senegal and France in the hotel lounge. The crowd had a distinctly international flavor, reminiscent of the bar scene in the first Star Wars movie. When Senegal sealed their 1-0 victory, the crowd in the hotel bar broke out in boisterous cheers in various languages. Tomorrow we fly to Chongqing, formerly and more conveniently known as Chungking, to catch a riverboat for a journey down the Yangzte River.

Day 10 – Chongqing

We arrived safely in Chongqing, offloaded our luggage onto our riverboat and are now wandering through the center of the city killing time before our departure. Chongqing is a large city, population 6 million in the old city and 30 million in the entire region. In contrast Beijing has a population of 16 million. We were told that the Japanese bombed the city continually during WWII using the river as their navigational guide to the heavily populated target.

This is a much less prosperous place than Beijing, fewer cars, and even fewer bikes. I presume the latter being a consequence of the mountainous terrain. It was a long cab ride from the airport to the river, and it was confusing to determine where we would find our boat. The cab driver offered little comfort by suggesting we could just wait at the river's edge and sign up for a later boat trip, if our reservations weren't in order.

I have yet to see another Westerner in town, so people stare at us often and openly. A young man approached us in an alleyway and led us to a computer café. He told us he was the first person in his small village to have attended a university. He aspires to become an English teacher and return to his village. He was eager to assist Ben in finding a Chinese wife and inquired, "What temperament would best suit you?"

"Have any shrewish harridans left?" I thought to myself. Chongqing was more than a little depressing, and I was not sad to leave.

Ben did well in arranging our reservations. We have a private cabin and bath on the fourth and top deck. When checking in we noticed a plaque signed by Bill Gates thanking the staff for their hospitality. The Yangtze River is the third longest river in the world running 3,900 miles from its source on the shoulder of the Himalayas to the East China Sea. The river is fast, deep, wide, and muddy. It essentially divides north and south China on an east west line about midway. We've heard English speakers refer to it with one syllable (Yahn-gst) or using two (Yang-sea). I couldn't begin to write a phonetic version of the Chinese pronunciation. The river is navigable to ocean going vessels nearly 1,000 miles inland including our starting point in Chongqing, and we observed an abundance of large ships during our three-day voyage.

We enjoyed the river and its environs while traveling the 412 river miles from Chongqing to Yichang. The mountains rise steeply from the shore leaving virtually no banks. There are terraced farms on every square meter of space where there is soil. It is difficult to imagine a harsher terrain from which to scratch a living. We passed ancient villages every few miles with more substantive towns interspersed.

The Three Gorges Dam is currently being constructed on the Yangtze and will result in the river rising 600 feet above its current level, cheating future travelers and residents of the remarkable scenes we currently enjoy. This endeavor will displace 1.3 million people. One can easily determine where the new water line will be, as the buildings below are in the process of being torn down, and those above are under construction. Unfortunately, interesting brick and stone dwellings are being replaced by gray, poured concrete, high-rise apartments.

The East Queen is 40' wide and 200' long and accommodates 100 guests with a mix of 1/3 Japanese, 1/3 Chinese, and 1/3 westerners. We played Bingo the first evening where the numbers were called in five different languages. Judy, Ben and I account for three of the six passengers on board not part of a tour group. We have been designated the independent travelers and share meals and excursions together. Our mates include an Italian couple from Milan and Rome, both of whom are professors at the London School of Economics, she a PhD in finance from Harvard, and he a PhD in economics from MIT. Our other independent traveler is a young nurse from Houston who is traveling alone and heads to Istanbul when she leaves China.

We took a side trip to Shibaozhai, a fairly large city that is being relocated to higher ground featuring an ancient temple constructed on a rock outcropping at the edge of the river. While climbing the temple's twelve stories with our fellow tourists, I kept staring at a guy who looked familiar. It turned out that he was a classmate from HBS, class of 1969, Section D: Randy Cramer. We had a mini-reunion and caught up on mutual friends and laughed about shared memories with toasts of gam bai.

We traversed the first of the three gorges in the morning mist. The river narrows and the mountains rise even more steeply. We were fortunate it was a sunny day, but the sky was hazy. Ancient carvings adorn the canyon-like walls. Most impressive were the walkways that had been carved out of granite for the ancient boatmen to use as footpaths to haul their boats upstream. Wooden walkways are still in place for the same purpose. Sadly, these treasures will be inundated when the river becomes a lake.

The boat traffic is heavy as the river is the primary source of transport of goods and people to Chongqing. We took an excursion up a tributary with our independent group. We boarded a long, ancient, wooden boat, sitting two abreast, manned by six extremely well muscled boatmen. They rowed, pulled, and towed us upstream from the Yangzte through a narrow gorge. The color of the water in the Yangzte is a blend somewhere between chocolate milk and coffee. In contrast, the tributary became crystal clear and cool about 200 yards upstream, more a mixture of cobalt blue and emerald green. It was reminiscent of a Colorado stream, except much deeper, and one could see the colorful rocks lining the stream channel. The boatmen sang a song for us on the way downstream and asked us to sing one in return. "Row Row Row Your Boat," in three-part round was the rejoinder. The Italians had never heard it, but thought it was cute. These sites will also be lost.

We were accompanied on this side trip by one of our boat's tour guides, a stunningly beautiful girl, the lovely Vivian Wu. Ben found a newfound interest in using his language skills, and they chatted constantly and didn't offer to translate. I offered Vivian a miniature Butter Finger candy bar that she accepted, took a tiny bite, and then rewrapped and stowed it. I meant well.

At the end of our cruise we arrived at the dam site under construction. The Chinese people we met were extremely sensitive to any hint of criticism of the dam. They view this project with a strong sense of national pride. Our guide on the dam tour was a young lady from Yichang, who proudly told us how Chairman Mao swam the width of the Yangtze in 1956.

We spent the night on the boat, got up early, caught a 50-minute cab ride through Yichang, a small town of 1.2 million of which we knew nothing, and caught our flight to Shanghai. Yichang was much nicer than Chongqing and is part of the Hubei province that produces more than 40% of the nation's rice.

Upon arriving at the airport, we noticed Brahma cows grazing on the front yard, and I finally saw my first water buffalo. It was a large airport, but not busy, with fewer than 10 flights a day. Our flight was full as we boarded, and we took our cramped seats featuring less legroom than the backseat of a Corvette. People seemed to stand around the aisle chatting aimlessly or holding their baggage when the plane started to back away from the gate. Only as we were racing down the runway nearing takeoff speed did the final dallier take his seat. The flight attendants were strapped in and appeared unconcerned about the prospect of unseated passengers hurtling down the aisles.

Day 11 – 15 – Shanghai, China

The 10-mile cab ride from the Shanghai airport to our downtown hotel along an elevated highway takes one through a never-ending construction site of modern skyscrapers. Shanghai is more prosperous than Beijing, $4,500 annual income v. $3,000. The Shanghainese look different, less delicate and less attractive than the Beijingers. The cabs are Volkswagen sedans, and there are many more privately owned luxury cars on the streets. The buildings are bigger, the architecture is more interesting, largely a function of the remnants of the colonial era, and everything is much more substantial than in Beijing. Shanghai has a European feel to it, particularly the area called the Bund, which is the central business district overlooking the Huangpu River. I enjoyed Beijing more because Ben was more a more knowledgeable guide there.

This and That

Given the unimaginable congestion of Chinese people who are active walking, riding their bikes, and living in a hot climate, one might expect some unpleasant body odors. Not so! The only bad experience came at the Summer Palace in Beijing when surrounded by a group of French tourists.

Ben's major task before starting his summer job in Shanghai was to either buy a new wardrobe or find a laundry. One might think that laundry services would be readily available in China. They are not. The hotels provide laundry services, but it is more expensive than buying replacement clothes.

China has only one time zone for the entire country even though it is about the size of the U.S., so when planning your travel, leave your sundials at home. It is not recommended to drink the water out of the tap in the cities. Vendors can be found everywhere selling bottled water, although one might ponder on the origins of the contents. In any event, a bottle sells for about 2-3 Yuan ($.25-$.37).

I noted that members of Ben's school group traveled to a rural area outside of Beijing on a trip arranged by one of their teachers. Ben later informed me that she was reprimanded for taking foreigners into an area that didn't represent China's image of prosperity.

Nearly 400,000 of the brightest Chinese students are currently studying in the U.S. Only 40% will return to their homeland. Lastly, Wong Ho is not the Chinese word for homosexual, and misintonation of "ma" does not really translate, "you are a worthless piece of shit."

Upon returning to KC after travels to such busy places, I am reminded of the young man who approached us in the Beijing restaurant and volunteered, "Life is very easy in American. Yes?" He has no idea how true that is for most of us.

CHAPTER 17

Mt. Huron
2010

To commemorate turning 65, I decided to attempt another Colorado 14er. I rendezvoused with my fellow hikers, Jim (60) and Fred (70), Thursday afternoon at Scarlet's, a bar in Leadville, CO. We quaffed a few and visited with some of the athletes gathered in town for the mountain run scheduled for Saturday. The town was buzzing with activity, and lodging was scarce, as 790 people had signed up for a 100-mile race through mountainous terrain including one 13,500' pass. Last year's winner finished the run in 30 hours. The runners we encountered had bodies like gazelles and must have had hearts the size of basketballs. Needless to say, no one confused us with the contestants.

We met for dinner at Quincy's, a restaurant known for their limited menu. They serve one item only, filet mignon. The only decision a patron can make is the size of cut and how well cooked. The 6 oz filet dinner was priced at $7.95. The total bill for the four of us (Judy joined us) was $44.

Jim drove in from KC to Buena Vista the day before and then reconnoitered the site of the trailhead for Mt. Huron on his way up to Leadville. This was to turn out to be most helpful, as we had no missteps the following morning when we left Leadville at 5:00 am in pitch darkness. Jim is the most serious outdoorsman of the group. He hunts elk and pronghorn sheep with bow and arrow in Montana and Wyoming. He has quartered elk weighing 750 lbs and brought the cleaned carcasses home. He told us that he rides horseback up the mountain and has a packhorse to carry his gear and the meat from anything he might kill. He also mentioned that he does not particularly like horses, so he walks his

From left: author, Jim, Fred

horse down the mountain and astutely observed, "You can't fall off a horse you're not on." Having spent a lot of time in the wilds, he has a healthy respect for the danger of bears, so he was pleased when we got above the tree line and out of bear territory.

The trailhead was a 1 ½ hour drive south of Leadville and involved 11 miles on bad gravel roads and 3 miles on a bone jarring, boulder strewn trail, worse than the road to the Handies Peak trailhead. Fortunately, Jim has a Toyota SUV specifically designed for off road purposes including 12 ply tires, heavy suspension, and guards for the oil pan, drive-train, and other sensitive parts.

It rained heavily the night before and snowed lightly at the higher elevations, so the headlights reflected off the moist Aspen leaves as we drove along the gravel road. It was a striking scene, as the road along Clear Creek glistened. We arrived at the trailhead at 6:30 am, and observed one car already in the parking lot. Sunrise was 6:21 am, so the sun was beginning to peek over the peaks. It was chilly, 37 degrees, sunny, still, and nary a cloud in the pink, early morning sky. The weather couldn't have been more perfect. We assembled our gear, signed in on the trailhead log, and we were on our way.

Fred led, I was in the middle, and Jim walked at the rear. I've learned from previous 14ers to focus only one step at a time and then look back to see how far we've come and avoid looking up at all that lay ahead. Fred had an altimeter on his wristwatch, and Jim had a Garmin altimeter hanging around his neck. The good news was that we always knew how high we had climbed, the bad news was that we knew how much farther we had to go.

We were hiking through a north-facing bowl leading to Mt. Huron so we hiked in the shadow of the mountain for the first two thirds of the climb. As we ascended, we could look back to the north and marvel as the rising sun painted the lesser peaks a brilliant golden hue.

Early on we commented on the steepness of the trail. Whoever first laid out the path was quite niggardly with switchbacks, as it seemed we were continually heading straight up. We cleared the tree line at 11,900' and encountered a small, shallow lake surrounded by a bog. We had a few hundred yards of relatively mild ascent before we headed straight up following the trail through a steep sage-covered shoulder of the mountain. At 13,000' we entered the rock field that defined the terrain for the remainder of the journey. Small birds were busy feeding amidst the sage, but once we entered the boulder fields, the only evidence of life were a few chipmunks and mouse-like critters scurrying about.

I was the new guy on the trip. Fred had successfully climbed twelve 14ers previously, including some extreme climbs such as Long's Peak, and Jim had completed seven. I was apprehensive about being a burden to the more experienced climbers, but once in the boulder field, I felt confident I was going to make it to the top, thus relieving this concern.

One of the distinguishing characteristics amongst us was that Fred and Jim took standing rests. In contrast I would collapse on the nearest rock into a sitting position whenever our expedition leader would stop. I had trained well this summer, so my feet were in good condition, and my leg strength was adequate, but nothing in my regimen prepared me for the altitude. I wasn't exactly gasping for breath, but it was close. By 13,000' it was warming up, so I shed my outer jacket.

Both Fred and Jim commented that this was the steepest climb of the 14ers they've done. It was clearly the steepest of the three I'd ascended. At 13,500' we encountered snow on the ground. Remnants of last night's snowfall remained below the line between sun and shade making portions of the rocky trail slick. We encountered a young man who passed us earlier on his way up, once again passing us on his way down. He said in a rather flippant tone, "I've got to hustle, I'm trying to do two climbs today." Asswipe! We trudged on. It turned out that neither Fred's nor Jim's altimeters were accurate. As we neared the summit, Fred's indicated we were at 13,600' and Jim's recorded 13,800'. Being at the point of total exhaustion, I wanted to believe anything that meant the end of the pain was near. We were approaching our goal along a sharp ridge, and, when we were within 300 feet, we could make out the true summit. We reached the peak at 10:30 am, certainly not record time, but we were alive and well. We didn't exactly sprint up the mountain, but we made it.

Fred said it best when we arrived at the summit, "No amount of money can buy this feeling." After catching our breath, we started surveying the panorama. From the trailhead we could see several peaks in the distance in the general vicinity of our goal, but we weren't sure which one was Mt. Huron. Once on top, we looked down on the measly pretenders that now appeared as tiny outcroppings of rock. The higher we hiked, the greater the vistas, as we could now see new mountaintops arise over the lower level peaks. We could identify two other 14ers that are also part of the Sawatch Range, Mt. Elbert, at 14,433' the highest peak in Colorado, and Mt. Massive 14,421', both situated to the north.

After reaching the summit we rested, ate our lunch, and took photos. Someone left a topographical map with the title page, Mt. Huron 14,006' (encased in plastic under a rock), and we took pictures of ourselves holding the eponymous label. Sadly, pictures taken with an iPhone don't do justice to the steepness of the trail or the majesty of the panorama. It was exhilarating to enjoy the view, experience the sense of accomplishment, and know the unpleasantness of the climb was over. Fred and Jim recalibrated their altimeters from the top of Mt. Huron, and both found they were off by over 100'. Oddly, I got cell reception and called

Ben in his office in NYC to share a taste of the euphoria we were enjoying.

I consumed two quarts of water on the climb and had one quart left for the return trip. Every drop was needed. Jim provided me with a few Jolly Rancher candies on the climb that helped keep my mouth moist without continually drinking water. Jim and Fred both carried Camelbaks that hold a gallon of water with a drinking hose conveniently held near the mouth. While I was asking for assistance from my hiking comrades to reach for the water bottles stored on the side of my pack, they were drinking from their reservoir without need of assistance. I now understand why they recommended that I acquire such a device.

We spent an hour on the summit, then viewed some storm clouds forming below, and decided it was time to descend. The wind was mild, the sun was up, and I started to shed clothes. By the time we arrived back at the trailhead, I was wearing shorts and a tee shirt and carrying the other three layers of clothing in my pack.

The best part of descending was to encounter other climbers nearing the top. We'd offer words of encouragement, "We're only twenty minutes down from the top, you're almost there." Before heading down, I unholstered the hiking poles I had purchased several years ago during our hike across England. They are an essential tool for navigating down the slippery boulders and unsteady, rocky footing. Having four points of contact with terra firma is superior to two whilst navigating from boulder to boulder.

On the way down I noticed a robust young man hiking with three kids and carrying a 12-year old girl piggyback style. If he reached the summit in that manner, he earns my super-iron man award.

Once we got back to the small lake at 12,500', we stopped to rest and looked back at the massive pile of stones from which we descended. It was a fearsome site, and it was hard to imagine that we had ascended it hours earlier.

It should not come as a big surprise that it's much easier coming down than going up, save for the wear and tear on knees. We descended at a fairly leisurely pace, eventually returning to the trailhead. Even so, my tank was running on empty, and I was thrilled to have arrived safely. Jim had a cooler full of iced cold beer readied for consumption upon our safe arrival. Fred and Jim cooled their tired puppies in Clear Creek and I rested in the back seat of Jim's SUV and enjoyed the cold Boulevard Pale Ale.

We were almost giddy as we drove down the mountain road. I asked Jim how he selected Mt. Huron for this year's climb. He said, "It looked like one of the easier ones, but, clearly, I was mistaken. The 14ers website indicated it was only 3.5 miles from trailhead to summit, so I thought the relatively short distance would indicate an easier climb. The steepness more than offset this."

Jim asked me if I would be up for another 14er next summer. I said, "Ask me in January. I need time to forget the unpleasant parts of this endeavor."

Jim dropped me off at Leadville around 4 pm, I picked up Judy and we drove 400 miles to North Platte, NE en route to Minnesota. I was fatigued at the end of the day, but feeling pretty darn good. We drove through the Nebraska sand hills the following day, viewed a number of sand hill cranes roughly the size of battleships, and made it to Gull Lake Saturday evening.

Postscript

As of this writing our aging trio just completed a successful climb of Mt. Elbert, the highest peak in Colorado at 14,433'.

CHAPTER 18

Lucy's Wedding
2007

I t's generally a good thing for the pastor to show up for the wedding. Unfortunately, Pastor Aberdeen didn't get the word on this social convention. Days later he called to whiningly explain his absence without a hint of apology, "No one called to remind me." Lucy and Fred planned a destination wedding in Mustique. From the day she was born, Lucy has had me wrapped around her little finger. I confess to being an indulgent Dad, so following the advice given to fathers of the bride for generations, I adhered to the admonition to pay up, show up, and shut up. The musician, the photographer, and the flowers had arrived in a timely manner, the weather was perfect, and Lucy and Fred were ready to formally begin their life partnership.

Lucy

Lucy is a calm person and was undaunted by this minor setback. In many respects she reminds me of my Mom. Helen was a superb grandparent and made each of her six grandchildren feel as though they were her favorite, but she and Lucy really had a connection. Like her Grandmother, Lucy is socially graceful in a quiet, demur manner, yet skilled in moving things in her preferred direction. And she can find the humor in most situations.

When Lucy was a college sophomore, we were driving to Portland, OR to start her school year with a planned stop for family togetherness at Jackson Hole, WY. We drove through South Dakota during the Sturgis Motorcycle Rally and observed thousands of bikers traversing I-90. We stopped to see Mt. Rushmore, and, while walking from the parking lot along the promenade leading to the viewing platform, we followed a

Mount Rushmore

covey of bikers. One of the females in the group appeared to be bare-assed naked from our vantage point. She wore fishnet stockings, what appeared to be a tiny string holding a bikini top in place, and microscopic, skin colored dental floss serving as a thong. Her shapely, bare buttocks served as a mild distraction as our family unit strolled to our destination. Ever vigilant, Lucy undertook the role of moral guardian to her little brother and attempted to shield his eyes from this provocative visual assault.

Judy had long ago conceded any hope for me. In fact, she actively abetted my oafishness. While dining in an upscale Nantucket restaurant with another couple, she called my attention to the entry of a beautiful, braless lady wearing a diaphanous blouse, as fortuitously that was the fashion of the day in the mid 1980's. My back was to the entrance of the dining area when Judy whispered, "Chuck, dearest, check out the tits on that woman." Her newsworthy alert occurred at precisely the same E.F. Hutton-moment when all conversation in the noisy restaurant ceased. The unintended result was one of those socially ungraceful moments when the object of Judy's observational powers, along with everyone else in the restaurant, sent dagger-like glares in our direction. I missed the viewing but not the admonitions, but I digress.

At the end of our titillating stroll, we reached the viewing area for Mt. Rushmore. There, one could pay a quarter to get a close up view of Washington, Jefferson, Roosevelt, and Lincoln through a telescope. The bare assed biker babe bent over to look into one of the telescopes offering an even more outrageous presentation of her impressive bum. When we got back to the car I said, "Wouldn't it have been funny if someone got a picture of the biker babe with Mt. Rushmore in the background?" Lucy replied, "I got it." The girl has a finely tuned appreciation for funny. I carry that picture with me in my day planner as a ready test of people's observational powers. Few notice the presidents in the background.

Lucy - Mustique 2007

The Wedding

Lucy and Fred met their first day of high school but never dated. She transferred from a small private grade school to a large public high school and remembered Fred being one of the kindest in making her feel welcome in the daunting new environment. Fifteen years later she and Fred were both living in New York, yet got reacquainted in Kansas City, and sparks flew, leading to the day of the nuptials.

Mustique is a small, privately owned island located 13 miles south of St. Vincent's. It is 2.2 square miles and is home to 100+ luxurious villas, one exclusive resort, one small hotel, a few shops, a beautiful harbor, cricket fields, and magnificent beaches. It is ringed by the azure blue Caribbean and colorful coral reefs. We stayed at Les Jolie Eaux, a five-suite villa with well-maintained tropical gardens and an infinity pool providing a panoramic view of the sea, located on a promontory at the southern end of the island. LJE was the former property of Princess Margaret. The 10-acre parcel had been given to her by the island's developer in 1960 to increase the isle's appeal to the British aristocracy.

Other noteworthy property owners include: Mick Jagger, Shania Twain, Tommy Hilfiger, Brian Adams, and David Bowie.

Judy and I were introduced to this little piece of paradise a few years earlier while attending the renewal of wedding vows of long time friends. The service was performed by the now absent Pastor Aberdeen. During that trip we stayed in Stargroves, the Japanese styled villa owned by Mick Jagger. For some unexplainable reason, everyone in our party felt a strong need to sit on his throne.

Our small wedding party consisted of family and friends. Peter and Rasha journeyed from their home in London to join the festivities. Peter and Fred worked together as rookie investment bankers in London when they were both fresh out of college, and their friendship prospered over the years and the ocean. Peter is a big, boisterous fellow with an infectious personality. In the movie Zulu a company of British soldiers are being overwhelmed by wave after wave of attacks from Zulu warriors, and Michael Caine plays the role of an imperturbable, British master sergeant calmly instructing the troops in the midst of bullets and spears whizzing by his head. That would be Peter. His exuberance was most telling during beach volleyball games, as he would be covered head to toe in sand from diving for low balls after shouting, "MASON!" to instruct others of his intent.

Rasha, age 29, is the youngest interventional cardiologist in the UK. She is also one of a handful of women in that field in Britain. She is stunningly attractive, funny, and pleasant. She and Peter met in college although their paths to Oxford came in strikingly different circumstances; Peter's from a more conventional path vs. Rasha, the daughter of Iraqi immigrants, through the possession of uncommon abilities. Rasha is also a Dolly Parton fan, in the event one needed additional evidence of her remarkable qualities. She introduced me to a new favorite word "dodgy," as in "Pastor Aberdeen's no show created a bit of a dodgy situation."

Lucy and Fred had formally been wed in Kansas City in a civil ceremony officiated by a family friend and another Fred (Pryor), but the real deal was to occur in Mustique on Wednesday November 7, 2007. We enjoyed our normal breakfast, morning poolside swimming and reading, and lunch in the pool pavilion. Lucy and her bridesmaids ventured to the Cotton House spa for pampering. The wedding ceremony was scheduled to begin at 4:30 pm. Judy, Ben, and I wore outfits selected by Lucy. Rasha fashioned Lucy's hair in an intricate web. The rest of us cleaned up, enjoyed the setting, and awaited the appointed hour.

Stanley the photographer arrived on time. Fred the guitarist, not related to Fred IV or Fred III, arrived. This Fred had a certain Rastafarian look and a red glow in his eyes that may well have been chemically induced. Arnold, the butler in charge of the villa, and the staff were dressed formally. Hors d'oeuvres were prepared and served. The red tinted sunset was cooperative with pink puffs of clouds accenting the coral blue sea. All was ready awaiting Pastor Aberdeen.

After a bit we were pacing nervously. Lucy was calm, but anxious to get on with things. Arnold and the staff were waiting in the front gardens, and they assured me that Pastor Aberdeen was very reliable, so not to worry. Lucy intended that the wedding service coincide with sunset. The location was a marble columned, Greek pavilion located at the tip of a rocky promontory overlooking the Caribbean and part of the LJE property. The setting sun waits for no man, so we gave up on Reverend Aberdeen and went to the backup plan, Peter. Spirits soared.

With one minute's warning Peter undertook the task of marrying Lucy and Fred. Fortunately, he must have attended many Anglican weddings and listened well. Everyone gathered near the pavilion. Lucy looked stunningly beautiful, and I had the honor of escorting our first child and only daughter from the villa, past the infinity pool, and through the gardens. I gave her a kiss, handed her over to Fred, teared up, and the service began. Peter, unruffled by the circumstances, proceeded to do an exemplary job in conducting his first wedding service. His elegant British accent didn't hurt, nor did his stentorian voice, but it was the warmth of his smile and the enthusiasm that made it special. Peter was to later declare that he hoped to marry off any of Fred and Lucy's offspring. Peter finished with his Anglicized version, "Until death us do part, I pronounce you husband and wife" just as the sun set over the relentless sea.

Peter and Rasha brought six bottles of chilled champagne as a gift. At first, that seemed a bit excessive, but they were consumed within an hour after the short but sweet ceremony. Arnold served the champagne and hors d'oeuvres, Stanley took more photos, we had a father/daughter dance on the leeside porch to Fred's music, and all was good.

After exhausting the champagne, it was time to journey to the Cotton House for our dinner. Peter and Rasha gathered flowers from the ubiquitous frangipani trees and bougainvillea and distributed the petals amongst us. We formed an aisle of celebrants from the front door of the villa, through the front gardens to the driveway, and the bride and groom passed through a cascade of flowers en route to their Kawasaki Mule carriage.

Fred's siblings decorated one of the Kawasaki Mules with trailing pop cans on string and off went Mr. and Mrs. Fred Coulson. The rest of us followed in our Mules and reconvened for the wedding dinner.

The Cotton House is an elegant resort on the north end of the island. The restaurant is part of an old plantation style stone building with large, gracious wraparound porches. Our group of 12 was situated on an outside porch. The temperatures were perfect as was the dinner. We enjoyed an abundance of food and drink and offered toasts in honor of the bride and groom and those associated with the lovely event. Interestingly, Chef Frederick, the place was crawling with Freds, of the Cotton House prepared the most ludicrously tasty wedding cake I have every consumed. After eating and drinking to excess, it was time to go to the Firefly Bar. The bride and groom had other plans however.

CHAPTER 19

Fort Waverly

J udy and I purchased 160 acres located 35 miles west of our Kansas City home in 1996. The property had been neglected for nearly 40 years. What formerly had been wheat fields and pasture bracketing a network of tree-lined creeks had become overgrown with red cedar and hedge apple trees. Overgrazing contributed to eroded fields lined with veins of deep gullies. But the land had promise. It featured rolling hills, two gently flowing creeks, five groves of mature walnut trees, habitat for abundant wildlife, and the second highest elevation in Douglas County. It produces seasonal bounties of Morels, blackberries, and walnuts. The apex of the property features pleasing views of Mt. Oread, the most prominent landmark on the campus of the University of Kansas in nearby Lawrence, and of the fertile Wakarusa River valley as it flows towards its confluence with the Kaw River at Eudora.

Shortly after buying the place, we built a barn and celebrated by holding a barn dance in honor of Judy's 50th birthday. We hired a square dance caller for the occasion, and he was standing around saying to no one in particular, "Some people buy a home at the lake for recreation, and some dumb shits buy a piece of dirt in the middle of nowhere." He was either unaware or unconcerned that the object of his derision was within earshot, presumably having missed common courtesy day at square dance calling school. He redeemed himself later with one of the best callings of "Chase the rabbit, chase the squirrel, chase that pretty girl round the world," I've ever heard.

During the first few months of exploring the forests, I found the skeletons of eleven cows that apparently died from neglect, aided in their demise by the plentiful predators, primarily coyotes and bobcats. I also discovered a WWII vintage bulldozer with a cable-operated blade. It was buried in vegetation and was hidden from view if one was more than 20 yards distant. I started crawling around it only to find that the operator's seat had become the nest for a family of copperheads. I quickly departed but started cogitating how to use that particular treasure. A neighbor in the construction business introduced me to a retired dozer mechanic who used to work for him. Joe lives about one mile from our farm, and he agreed to meet me to investigate. Joe is a little older than I, typically wears Big Smith denim overalls and a John Deere ball cap, and speaks softly with a hint of an Oklahoma accent. We haggled a bit, and I ended up trading the non-operating dozer carcass to Joe for $1,500 worth of operating dozer work.

Early on Joe helped us build several ponds, clear and terrace some fields, fill in gullies, and build a low-water bridge. He also came to my rescue on the times I buried my newly acquired John Deere 5300 tractor in mud up to the axles. I'd call, he'd come, smile wryly at my predicament, then unload a piece of heavy equipment, and pull me out. Being apprenticed to Joe at a young age to learn a smidgeon of his many practical skills would have been a good thing. He could build a functioning, internal combustion engine out of a sewing kit and a chicken.

The Bridge

Joe called one afternoon and asked if I wanted to buy a bridge that was for sale. I was intrigued, as nearly 40 acres of our property was virtually inaccessible because of a creek running through a deep gully. The abandoned bridge sat on its original 1930 foundation spanning the year round, modestly deep water Cedar Creek on the west edge of Olathe, KS. It had solid oak decking 3" thick, 16' wide, and 55' long. I bought it at an auction for $1,500 a few days later and became the proud owner of a 44,000 lb steel frame bridge.

The preparation of the new site took about 3-4 days of work to clear both banks of the creek, situate and pour the footings, and build a temporary ramp into the creek. We were fortunate that the weather was mild and dry so the concrete footings cured properly and the ramp/dam didn't get washed away.

At the old site, the bridge was completely covered by vines, trees, and brush. Trees were growing through the decking and steel structure. We cleared the debris with an excavator and a little chain saw work. Next, we built a temporary ramp/dam into Cedar Creek adjacent to the old bridge. Joe placed two large diameter plastic pipes in the creek to provide an outlet for the continual water flow. Then we placed a 17' "I" beam under each end of the bridge. The beam was essential to evenly support the end of the bridge, so it wouldn't fold up on itself like the bow of a canoe, as it was lifted from the contact points.

The I-beam cradles were set under each end of the bridge and held by thick chains attached to the D-9 Caterpillar dozer on the north end of the creek and to the bucket of the excavator stationed on the south end of the creek. Joe backed his 45' tractor-trailer parallel to the bridge down the temporary ramp as close as he could to the far edge of the bridge. The two equipment operators, Ed and Robert, choreographed their movements and lifted the bridge onto the trailer. A few seconds after the bridge's weight was fully transferred to the trailer, we heard a sharp sound like a gunshot. It occurred as Joe was standing alongside the back end of the trailer. He crawled under and calmly explained, "We just blew an airbag on the trailer." Seconds later another explosion announced that another airbag blew. Joe said, "No big deal, at least we didn't blow a tire." I'm not sure exactly how one fixes a blown tire on a trailer sitting on soft dirt on a temporary dam in a creek with a 22-ton bridge on board.

They centered the bridge on the trailer, strapped it down, and Joe pulled it out of the creek onto level ground with an assist from one of his smaller dozers. Ed took the big dozer and removed the temporary dam from Cedar Creek, so it could again flow freely.

Joe drove into the main driveway of our property and then went down the eastern fence line ¼ mile to the new site. He skillfully backed his trailer onto the temporary ramp/dam built into the creek that was the mirror image of the ramp/dam we just left on Cedar Creek. We unchained the bridge from the trailer and reconnected the chains to the I-beam cradle on which the bridge still sat. By this time, the cleanup duties at the old site were complete, and the big dozer was delivered to the farm using a second trailer. Joe's team again skillfully operated in tandem to lift the trailer onto the new footings. They centered the bridge within ¼" of the marks we had placed on the new piers. Joe restored the borrowed dirt from the ramp/dam to its former home, and the job was done. All that was left was the dedication and a new lifetime of use for the old bridge.

Fort Waverly

Waverly Wells Coulson, our first grandchild, was born on January 18, 2009, and we were thrilled. Waverly's arrival reminded me of the letter we received from my cousin Bob when his first and only daughter was 2-years old. He wrote, "Sarah has now mastered the violin, speaks fluent Japanese, and solves quadratic equations for recreation between naps." It was unclear how Waverly would match this level of precociousness, but it mattered not. It was love at first sight.

Empathy has always been one of my strong suits, so I started to contemplate, "What would I want as a welcoming gift to the world if I were a newborn baby girl?" The answer was obvious: a stockade fort. I needed to flesh out the vision, so I visited the internet and discovered Fort Umpqua, a stockade fort built on the Umpqua River, a tributary of the Columbia, by the Hudson Bay Company in 1836 to serve the fur trade of the era. When I noticed that Fort Umpqua was being restored at its original location in Douglas County, OR, I knew I had the model for the fort I intended to build at our farm in Douglas County, KS: Fort Waverly.

Fort Umpqua was 90' square with walls 12' in height and with one blockhouse facing away from the River. It burned in 1851 and was abandoned in 1854 as the fur trade petered out, and settlers were transforming Oregon into a farming economy. My design called for a fort 16' x 24' with an 8' x 8' blockhouse and walls 9' in height. My intent was to use materials available on our farm to the greatest extent possible, and we possessed an abundance of 40-year old red cedars. I calculated I would need 440 logs of varying lengths and diameter. It takes a 15' tree to yield a 9' log that is roughly as thick at the top as it is at the bottom.

I headed into the dense cedar forests that comprise nearly ½ of our property, focusing on areas where the cedars grew in tight clusters resulting in straight, tall trunks. I learned that I could cut and trim 20-25 trees in the time it took to use four tanks of gasoline in my Stihl chainsaw, after which I would call it a day. The most time consuming part of the task was clearing the debris created by stripping a cedar trunk of its branches and creating piles of debris that I'd later push into an area safe for burning. With my goal in mind, I had a winter's worth of work to do with a light heart.

Periodically, I would use my Kawasaki Mule to pull a trailer to collect my harvest. I had a rough idea where I wanted to place the fort, and I built a staging area to stack the assembled logs, segregating them by their dimension and ultimate use.

I enlisted the aid of many people in this enterprise. Ben helped me when he was home in accumulating the piles of logs scattered throughout the intricate road system that lines our property. Joann, a landscape architect friend, came out to the farm with her Dad, a civil engineer, to assist me in siting the fort. I had some ideas, but she quickly convinced me that hers were superior. We eventually placed it on the highest ground available overlooking a large pond. It was perfect.

In mid-May my friend, Jim Sneed, offered a week's worth of labor. He helped me gather the logs I had prepared over the winter that were too large to lift by myself. The biggest of these were hauled to a neighbor's sawmill, about a mile distant. He cut 1 ½" dimension lumber from these logs. He also split the 8' logs that would ultimately serve as the horizontal siding of the blockhouse. One of the many benefits of this project was to work with the delightful aroma of fresh-cut cedar as a constant companion.

Jim helped me dig footings, place the support columns, mix and pour the cement around the posts, and within a week had a skeleton of Fort Waverly. The remainder of the summer I was able to pick up pieces of the task a little at a time, the trickiest being building the pyramid shaped roof over the 8' x 8' blockhouse that reached about 16' above the ground. Jim came back mid-summer to assist me in assembling the log walls of the blockhouse. Willy, the 7-year old son of a friend, assisted me in establishing the distance from the interior walkways to the top of the wall sufficient to serve as a firing platform. Little by little, I completed the front gate, a back door, stairs to the blockhouse and walkways, and lastly started applying the 9' log walls to the frame using wood screws. One of the final tasks was to trim the top of the wall and to cut a point on each post so water wouldn't collect on the cut. Lastly, I installed a flagpole using the tallest log in my inventory and raised the American flag. It was an early September afternoon when the job was complete. It was sunny, and the wind was blowing briskly. I was alone, and I experienced a feeling of near euphoria, as I honored Old Glory flying over the now completed Fort Waverly.

Waverly was nine months old when she attended the dedication of her eponymous fort at our annual October farm party. She cooed sounds something to the effect, "Thank you Papa. I am pleased with your efforts."

CHAPTER 20

Banjo Camp

The dogwoods, redbuds, and rhododendron added color to the live oak and pine forests in and around O'Leno State Park, host to the 2011 Suwannee Banjo Camp. The sign at the entrance to the park reads, "Welcome to the Real Florida," an unnecessary reminder of the many distinctions within this beautiful state.

The camp's rustic buildings were built in the 1930's by the Civilian Conservation Corps. The campus-like setting borders the banks of the Santa Fe River, a black water tributary of the Suwannee. Driving in we saw numerous signs beckoning scuba divers to explore the deep, spring-fed stream. Judy and I arrived Friday at noon, walked over a swinging footbridge to the far-side of the river, watched a few canoes float past, and listened to the serenade of dozens of banjo players plucking away.

Lucy and Fred gave me a Washburn B-9, 5-string banjo as an early Christmas gift, perhaps one of the most thoughtful and life changing items I've ever received. I was a fan of folk music in the early 60's and one of my favorite tunes was the "Ballad of Greenland Whaling" by the Chad Mitchell Trio. In that song Roger McGuinn, later the leader of the Byrds, plays an intricate and appealing banjo accompaniment. I have loved the sound of a banjo ever since but never once attempted to play or even hold a banjo until a few months ago. I have now become obsessed with trying to learn how to play this magical instrument. So with a few months of internet-assisted, self-instruction under my belt, I decided banjo camp was in order.

I was one of about 80 students awaiting our first encounter with the 14-member faculty. Classes were offered for each of the two main styles of banjo, clawhammer and bluegrass, further segregated by novice, low

intermediate, high intermediate, and advanced. Fiddle, mandolin, and bluegrass guitar sessions were also available adding some musical balance for the jam sessions. I spent my time attending the novice bluegrass track. We pulled chairs in a circle in the shade of a majestic live oak, made introductions, and, with our banjos on our knees, the instruction commenced.

Friday night we dined in the communal hall with our fellow campers. I speculated to Judy en route that we'd encounter a pretty monochromatic gathering, but the first person we met was an amiable black man from NYC. His name was Rommell, and he told us the following story. He was an Army brat, and his Dad, a WWII veteran, admired the eponymous German general, and that was how he was known, until they moved to a relatively rough neighborhood in NYC. After some teasing and a few beatings, Rommell became "Row-Mell."

After dinner a portion of the faculty performed a welcoming concert featuring multiple styles of banjo. A young woman bicycling around

Florida with a banjo as her traveling companion, serendipitously happened upon our alternate universe of banjo lovers and attended the Friday night concert. She asked one of the organizers if anyone would mind if she hula-hooped on stage with the performers. Comeliness was not one of her virtues, so, blessedly, her request was denied.

Friday night I participated in my first jam session. I was a bit intimidated, as my playing skills were at the nadir of the camp's bell curve, and I had never played with other people. But the instructor of the "slow jam bluegrass" session was welcoming and encouraging, and he knew the music and words to every song anyone suggested. The rules of etiquette are pretty logical. If you don't know the tune, play softly; and/or if the song is in the key of G, and you can't discern the chord changes by ear, you can still join in by softly playing a G chord with a simple boom-chicka roll. It was much better than Miss Arbuckle's eighth grade choir where I was instructed to stand behind the fat girl and mouth the words.

Most of the campers stayed in the park cabins, but Jude and I decided to stay in a motel in nearby Alachua, just up the road from Micanopy, a town made famous in John Anderson's classic "Seminole Wind."

One of the unexpected benefits of the camp was an introduction to banjo lore. Prior to picking up a banjo for the first time a few months ago, I couldn't readily recite the names of many famous banjoists, sadly, an oxymoron. Earl Scruggs and Bela Fleck being notable exceptions. The names of individual faculty members did not mean anything to me, but, by the end of the weekend, I learned I was in the midst of America's banjo aristocracy.

Sunday morning I was one of ten attending "35 tips for beginners" taught by Tony Trischka, a noteworthy gentleman whose resume includes playing with and instructing Bela Fleck. In the middle of his class, his cell phone rang, he apologized, read the caller ID, and said, "Forgive me for not having that turned off. If you don't mind though, I'll take this call, but when I give you the signal, I want you to pluck away."

He answered, and his side of the conversation went like this, "Hi Steve." "No I'm in the middle of teaching a banjo class in Florida." "Class, pluck away for Steve, so he'll believe me." We did as instructed.

He continued, "I'll call you back in an hour."

A class participant asked jokingly, "Who was that? Steve Martin?" Tony said, "Yes, as a matter of fact it was. He's preparing for a concert at Carnegie Hall in a few weeks, and I've been working with him." Perhaps at some future time he can tell others he was working with Chuck Wells. He was a nice guy, a gifted musician, and his instructions were most helpful.

Saturday night after dinner the faculty again provided a concert. Friday night's version was a mere warm-up for the finale. It was a remarkable and varied performance. In true show biz fashion, they left the audience begging for more.

I attended the camp to learn how to improve my skill and to identify and rectify any bad habits I picked up. In the latter category I learned I should be playing with finger picks. During the jam session, when it was my turn to play lead, no one could hear me, as naked fingers don't bring out the resonance of the instrument. This served as an auditory Godsend to the other participants but highlighted a material deficiency. The next day a fellow slow jammer came up to me at a break and gave me a set of his picks.

The second bad habit I must now abandon is practicing quietly. Previously, I would take the resonator off the back of the instrument and stuff a towel under the head to muffle the sound. I've now been instructed to practice loudly, so I will hear my mistakes more clearly, a troublesome development for neighbors and animals with keen hearing.

At one of the meals I sat next to a retired professor and asked him how long he'd been playing. He said, "45 years." I asked him a few banjo questions, and he graciously replied, "Let me get my banjo, and I will show you a few things." I enviously reflected on the aphorism about the best time to plant a tree, forty years ago; the second best, today. Or, as my good friend, Benny, is wont to say, "If not now, when?"

Waverly, our granddaughter, turns eight in six years. My banjo goal is to attain a level of competence sufficient to back up her vocals in the event she has a musical affinity. One must prepare for an uncertain future.

CHAPTER 21

Nude Nuns

$\mathbf{D}$avid Martin had a farm, e-i-e-i-o, and on that farm he had a hot tub, and that is how it all started. We met in college, were fraternity brothers, and remained close friends over the ensuing decades. During our college years, I once had the misfortune of riding with David in his 1963 Volkswagen whilst backing up a mile on I-44 at midnight in a snowstorm. Miraculously, we survived this and other misadventures to make it into adulthood. Once there, David acquired a farm near Pleasant Hill, MO, known as P-Hill to the locals. He was a first rate craftsman and, with the help of his wife, Jeanne, built a handsome A-frame house offering an abundance of amusements to entertain guests of all ages. Lucy and Ben enjoyed playing with newborn kittens courtesy of the nearby barn cats. Jeanne was a horsewoman, and she would take the tykes on rides. David taught me how to operate his bulldozer and other useful machines he had acquired. Sunday afternoon family visits to Dave and Jeanne's were always a special treat.

One fall afternoon, David hosted a 30th birthday party for his younger brother, Mark. We were among an assortment of guests, many from college days. The festivities started in mid afternoon with clowns, horseback riding, go-cart races, and various activities for the kiddies. Copious quantities of beer, BBQ, and other refreshments were consumed. As nighttime fell, those with children left or put them temporarily to bed, and David heated up his newest toy, a hot tub. One of his rules was that no swimsuits were allowed, which didn't seem to bother anyone, and the tub filled quickly with unclothed people. One of the guests was a dentist from Springfield whose date happened to be an exotic dancer, and whose form once graced the pages of Penthouse Magazine. But one didn't need to be a stripper to feel at ease amidst the other nude bathers. I reluctantly overcame my inherent shyness and joined the revelers.

The tub was situated on a deck sheltered on three sides. One older couple sat on a bench inside the house enjoying the show through a set of windows. The tub was grossly overpopulated, a source of much merriment. The water quickly became turbid, obscuring whatever was happening beneath the surface. My earliest observation was how flattering the tub scene was for one of the chubby ladies given the propensity of breasts to float. Of course, the attractive ladies needed no such buoyancy boost. A plumpish lady sitting to my left, in an inappropriate display of affection, sought to make room for newcomers by sitting on my lap. Judy was sitting opposite me in the tub, and this unchaste assault on my person put her territorial instincts on full alert. She sprang with alacrity betwixt the corpulent competitor and me, thus protecting my innocence. Bless her little heart. While enjoying the warmth of the tub, the fellowship of both friends and strangers, and the abundant titillation, I concluded, "I must have one of these."

Within a matter of weeks, we made our purchase. David and I tore out a brick patio, dug a hole, filled it with moistened sand, placed the tub in the malleable foundation, partially filled it with water, and leveled it. We then installed and wired the tub pump and heater in our basement and connected PVC pipes through the pump and heater through a window to the tub. Lastly, I built a deck surrounding the tub, connected it to our sun porch, and we were ready for business.

David's "no suits" rule seemed perfectly reasonable, so it was adopted at our household tub, and thus began a series of interesting encounters. The only exception to this voyeuristic rule was granted for my Mom and aunts who enjoyed the tub using rules of their own choosing. Psychologists opine that social interaction is fundamentally good for mental health and longevity, so our new purchase was perfect, serving as an intimate conversation pit with tits. Not only did it have the obvious comforts associated with soothing, warm jets of water, it facilitated a forum for fellows with a fondness for the female form.

Fairly quickly we learned a few lessons. Men are significantly more modest than women when confronted with the prospect of removing their clothes in front of other people. However, after a few nanoseconds of pondering, few declined an invitation to hop in the tub for wine and comradeship. The colder the weather the better, as fluffy snowflakes falling on shoulders created the optimal environment.

Several years later, it came to an end when I returned home from work and observed two men hauling the hot tub out of our backyard. In response to my puzzled gaze, one of the guys said, "Your wife gave us the tub." I checked with Judy to ascertain the veracity of this claim, and she said, "It's time." It was the end of this stage of life. The kids could no longer be counted on to be sound asleep by 9 pm, and age and gravity had inexorably taken their toll. Our skin no longer fit. In between, the tub provided more than a few pleasant memories, a few of which can be shared.

The Lady Lineperson

David and Jeanne knocked on our door at 1 am on New Year's morning, along with a couple we had met but didn't know well. They were in a festive mood and said, "How about hopping in your tub?" Earlier in the evening, we enjoyed its soothing comforts with friends from out of town who were staying with us. Our guests had retired for the evening, but, not wanting to be ungracious, I fired up the spa heater for the newcomers. Several inches of snow were on the ground, and the temperature was below zero. The tub was sheltered from the wind, but it was still quite nippy, as one left the warmth of the sunroom.

The blond lady accompanying David and Jeanne worked as a lineman for Kansas City Power and Light, a unique occupation for a female in the early 1980's. Like Jeanne, she was gorgeous and exceptionally well proportioned. After sitting in the tub for a spell, the lady lineman said, "I think it would be fun to race around the block bare-assed naked." I implored her to reconsider, as her trek offered insufficient upside to compensate for the fact that she would most likely die. Undeterred by logic, she went running off into the dark stark naked, dripping with water, and shrieking. Her husband, or boyfriend, I'm not sure which, didn't budge. As David and I contemplated how to proceed, she returned and jumped into the life restoring hot waters. It had only been 1-2 minutes, but she was scary cold, her nipples had shrunk to the size of a poor man's diamond with a point capable of cutting molybdenum, and her body was encased in a thin sheet of ice. We chastised her for this dangerous behavior, and, after a few minutes of re-warming, they dressed and left. I never saw the lady lineman again.

The Missing Bauble

The mind of a wife works in mysterious ways. One summer, after a late evening of fellowship with friends, we returned to our house for a dip in the tub. Our party included the three Iron Men and their spouses, a recently divorced friend, his two female companions, and I. Judy and the kids were out of town, and I was batching it. After enjoying the comforts of the tub, everyone moved on to Nichol's Lunch, a 24/7 diner noted for serving conspicuously greasy late night chow. Upon Judy's arrival home a few days later, she asked what I did over the weekend, and I dutifully described the evening of tubbing, along with other more mundane activities.

A few months later, the same group of friends assembled as part of a larger gathering at a Christmas party. Unbeknownst to me, Judy was circulating amongst the ladies who had been present at the summer tubbing event asking, "Oh, did you leave this particular bauble in our bathroom?" To which they responded, "No, that must belong to Jean." She appreciatively accepted the return of her bauble, and the ladies apparently confirmed my innocence of any wrongdoing.

As a clueless guy, I didn't know I was under indictment, nor did I know I had been subsequently cleared of all charges until later that evening. I was, however, both impressed and forewarned at Judy's patience in never asking about the bauble, but instead waiting six months to get independent verification of the facts of the case before pronouncing sentence.

Nude Nuns

My brother-in-law, an antique dealer in Chapel Hill, NC, was in Kansas City for a few days lecturing on porcelains at the Nelson-Atkins Art Gallery as part of the National Antique Dealer's convention being held in KC. He graciously included Judy and me at a dinner with his colleagues at the Carriage Club. Afterwards, we invited some of the group over to our house for drinks and tubbing. It was a cool, fall evening, we filled our wine glasses, I explained the house rules, and we headed for the deck. Everyone hopped in the tub except for two, reluctant, middle-aged ladies sporting girls-fast-pitch-softball haircuts and wearing unfashionable, brown shoes. I was to later learn that the two were ex-nuns, lesbian lovers and partners in an antique business. Their comfortable shoes should have been a dead giveaway, but my gaydar was not well developed at the time.

My brother-in-law tried to coax them into disrobing and joining us by saying, "Look, I don't know what you're worried about. For God's sake, you know everyone here except Chuck, who is obviously harmless, so what's the big deal?" Seemingly impressed by this compelling argument, one of the two disrobed and started to step into the tub. She was rather comely as I recall, once unencumbered by her drab, matronly garb. Her companion was aghast at this apparent betrayal of affection and affront to common decency and stormed off the deck.

Unfortunately, in her haste she failed to notice the closed sliding screen door blocking her entry back into the house. She hit that screen door at full speed and bounced off leaving an indelible imprint like those featured in a Roadrunner cartoon after Wile E. Coyote falls to earth from a precipice. The now nude nun rushed to the aid of her stunned companion, grabbed her clothes, embraced her mightily pissed off lover, and they left without so much as a, "Thanks for the lovely evening." I left the screen door unrepaired for months to serve as a reminder of this remarkable encounter.

I live for moments such as this.

Epilogue

Lucy has lived in Nepal, Portland, Chicago, and New York, but miraculously returned to within one mile of her homestead to raise a family. On April 20, 2010 Lucy gave birth to twin boys, Finn and Charlie. They came 11 weeks early but have thrived and added to the busyness occasioned by their then 15-month old sister, Waverly. A few weeks before going to press with this book, I was with Lucy helping during the rush hour of feeding, bathing, and before-bedtime-story telling of her little goslings. Fred was out of town, so Lucy and I were attending to the twins in the bathtub. Waverly thought that looked fun, hopped in, and started pouring cups of water on her brothers' heads, much to their delight. The doorbell rang, and Lucy said, "Dad, watch the kids while I go get that," leaving me in a state of mild anxiety. A few minutes later, Lucy returned with her two-month old nephew and explained, "Kristen had car trouble and asked if I could watch Clarke." She took charge, gave me my marching orders, and had the four-babies-at-bedtime situation quickly under control. She is imperturbable.

Ben spent three years living and working in China and Taiwan, attended Michigan Law School, and now practices securities law in New York City with the firm of Simpson, Thacher, and Bartlett. He lives in the Williamsburg section of Brooklyn and rides his bike to work, weather permitting. We're currently planning a trip to Iceland to go mountain hiking.

Early in our marriage, Judy and I agreed upon an equitable distribution of duties. I would make all the major decisions, and she would make the minor ones. So far, nothing major has come up. In addition to being an above average indulgent wife, she is a passionate and engaged activist desirous of making the world a better place. I merely seek to be a good dad and granddad, run my business in a competent manner, learn a few banjo tunes, and enjoy and share as many mirthful undertakings as time allows.

Sadly, a few weeks after Mardi Gras 2011, New Orleans neighbors reported that Ladder Guy died. Another performer is now using his ladder. At this time we don't know the sum paid for this valuable franchise.